CROWDING OUT LATINOS

CROWDING OUT
LATINOS

Mexican Americans in
the Public Consciousness

Marco Portales

 Temple University Press
PHILADELPHIA

Temple University Press, Philadelphia 19122
Copyright © 2000 by Temple University
All rights reserved
Published 2000
Printed in the United States of America

♾ The paper used in this publication meets the requirements of the American
National Standard for Information Sciences—Permanence of Paper for Printed
Library Materials, ANSI Z39.48–1984

Library of Congress Cataloging-in-Publication Data

Portales, Marco, 1948–
    Crowding out Latinos : Mexican Americans in the public consciousness / Marco
Portales.
        p.   cm.
    Includes bibliographic references and index.
    ISBN 1-56639-742-1 (cloth : alk. paper). — ISBN 1-56639-743-X (paper :
alk. paper)
        1. Mexican Americans—Public opinion. 2. Mexican Americans—Education.
3. Mexican Americans and mass media. 4. Hispanic Americans—Public
opinion. 5. Hispanic Americans—Education. 6. Hispanic Americans and mass
media. I. Title.
E184.M5P67 2000
305.86872073—dc21   99-23808

An earlier version of chapter 4 appeared as "Hispanics and the Media" in an anthology edited by Ishmael Reed, *MultiAmerica: Essays on Cultural Wars and Cultural Peace* (New York: Viking Penguin, 1997).

For Rita, my wonderful wife; for my son Carlos, who served four years as a proud United States Marine; and for my daughter, Marie, a recent Texas A&M graduate, all of whom dream and seek to better the lives of people wherever they are.

Also, for Latinos everywhere and for all citizens of the United States, particularly Mexican Americans. May all people be persuaded that we need to work together to create a better world, especially for the less fortunate, who require help more than blame.

Contents

Preface

The U.S. Census for the year 2000 is sure to count more than 32 million Latinos out of a total population of 273 million Americans. Although Spanish-speaking Americans comprise one out of every nine citizens, Hispanics are seldom seen speaking for and representing our country in the cultural life of the United States. *Crowding Out Latinos* undertakes to point out this strange absence and the lack of Hispanic participation in the public consciousness of American life. It also proposes to explain why Latinos do not factor more prominently as influential citizens and leaders when the demographics strongly suggest that we should.

Anyone who has ever seen a low-wage Hispanic laborer ought to know that such person is not there by choice. Employment opportunities in the United States exist in part because almost everyone is constantly looking for a better job, and a Latino earning lower wages is no exception. Regardless of what people believe, he or she aspires to a better position, better wages, and a better life. We can also be certain that such a worker will do everything possible to improve the lives of his or her sons and daughters so that they will enjoy more attractive futures.

I begin with these facts because most Americans do not think of Hispanic American citizens as much more than unskilled laborers. Rarely are we seen as a people who can contribute to the social and economic growth and development of the United States. Most citizens cannot produce an acceptable answer when they ask themselves, "Why aren't more Hispanics successful? Don't they aspire to more? What holds them back?" This book endeavors to demonstrate that we Latinos want to contribute to this great country of ours as much as the next taxpayer, but certain realities continually obstruct that desire generation after generation.

As we enter the twenty-first century, Mexican Americans and other Latinos need to diagnose our situation in the United States in order to determine the legacy we would like to leave our children. Like all people, we have our own problems, but we should not be blamed for educational and media-representational limitations that essentially have been imposed on us. We are proud of our heritage and roots, but sometimes we also tend to be embarrassed and ambivalent about our circumstances and prospects. We are a conflicted, uncertain people, for reasons that I seek to explain in the following pages. Caught in the tug of such forces, too many of our people are not inclined to do more than we are used to, largely preventing us from moving ahead. We have definitely shown ourselves and everyone else that we can eke out a living in America, that a few Hispanics can also become leaders and CEOs. But, as our population continues to grow, it should now be obvious that we need to establish ourselves more prominently within the culture of the United States. Despite our best efforts, this cannot be accomplished without support from the rest of American society. That objective will require the continued articulation of our views and visions as we face the new century.

Some readers may disagree with my assessment of our current situation, and with my evaluation of our efforts so far. This literary and psychosocial study for that reason attempts to provoke wide, constructive dialogues about issues that have been avoided and forces that traditionally have kept Hispanics where we find ourselves today. My firm hope is that this book will help improve the ways in which Chicanos and other Latinos are educated, as well as the ways in which we are depicted in the media, for changes in these arenas would improve the lives of all Americans.

About the Frontispiece

The one extant photograph, found in a brown paper sack at the bottom of a World War II Army trunk following the death of the only American-born family member, the child standing up front, and of the author's father, circa 1923, at ten years of age, posing in Sunday clothes with their mother, an aunt, and four brothers, before a wooden shack used by field workers in central Texas, in Buda, etymologically *viuda*, meaning, ironically, widow in Spanish, several months after the absent father of the family died from a heart attack in the cotton fields caused by sunstroke, five years after the family made its way north from San Luis Potosí, which they left, displaced by "los años dificiles despues de las guerras," that is, "in the difficult years after the Mexican Revolution," as my grandmother used to say, experiences that, shortly after the Border Patrol was first organized in 1924, brought them to south Texas, where the family moved and where the author was born a quarter century later and grew up in the 1950s, comfortably, thanks to the unflagging industry of the young man with the hat and tie, who began a few years even before this picture was taken to sell fresh milk to neighbors, early in the morning before school, where he reached the fifth grade, learning enough English to get by, a business that led to a little stand that a short time later included the sale of cheese, bread, and other basics staples, allowing him to help support his mother and brothers, an enterprising activity that in time permitted him to court and marry a Costa Rican woman in 1946 who had been visiting her cousin in Edinburg, where that family had been incorrectly told, likely because Spanish was spoken in the Rio Grande Valley, that the finest schools in the United States were in south Texas, and where the next year, by becoming a food merchandise partner with an older Mexican American woman, who, by contributing half of the funds for the endeavor, made it possible for the self-made entrepreneurial merchants to hire a construction crew to build a thirty-foot-high, thirty-six-foot-wide and ninety-footlong light-red brick grocery store at the corner of West Stubbs Street and Seventh Avenue in Edinburg, Texas, where the author and his younger brother later clerked as boys, although they would, of course, rather play, because, as kids, nobody ever loved to play more, believing, while they attended Sacred Heart School in Edinburg, that they were at the center of the universe, until, at the city's only public high school, they learned otherwise, and where they were raised in a two-bedroom, two-bath wooden house, with a porch, a fence, and a dog, while their parents lived happily in a Spanish-speaking world for twenty-three years, dutifully helping to provide food and shelter and clothes mainly to crop-picking Chicanos, paying their yearly federal, state, and local taxes, and contributing quietly but visibly to the neighborhood—yet without any media attention or credit, which was never sought—and, as the newspapers of the town and the television and radio newscasts of the Rio Grande Valley will confirm, to the social and cultural affairs of the more than 80 percent Mexican American community, and to the Sacred Heart and St. Joseph's Catholic Churches, in an area of several blocks that, due in large part to the indigence of the neighboring Mexican Americans, who largely made a living by picking cotton and produce from the surrounding agricultural fields and by migrating north out of the state, in the early 1960s was eventually designated an Urban Renewal site and was sold in 1970 to the City of Edinburg, following the death of his father, funds which partially allowed the author to finish studying for his English degree at the University of Texas in 1970, and to continue studying for his Ph.D. in American literature at the State University of New York at Buffalo, qualifying him, four years later, to be hired as an Americanist at the University of California at Berkeley, which no one, to be sure, ever had any good reason to mention to him before that time, but where, within two years, he progressively became disenchanted with American literary scholarship, there being virtually nothing positive written on Mexican Americans, which begins to explain why he became interested in the newly emerging ragamuffin field of Chicano literature that all of these years later has led him to write the book that the reader now holds in his or her hands.

Acknowledgments

wish to thank my colleagues in the Department of English at Texas A&M University for their unflagging support since I joined them in College Station in 1991. As a member of this highly professional team of scholars and teachers, I have also had the great pleasure of working with the English Undergraduate Program, the Race and Ethnic Studies Institute, and the Office of the President. Everyone in these and other University offices has made my efforts easier, and I want to thank each of many friends for daily making my administrative, teaching, and research activities a great joy. Aggie students in some of my classes have encouraged me to articulate my views, and I especially want to take this opportunity to thank them. Mark Posada, an Aggie graduate, served as my research assistant for part of this study, and I wish to acknowledge his help. Colleagues in the Society for the Study of the Multi-Ethnic Literature of the United States, the Texas Association of Chicanos in Higher Education, and the campus Professional Hispanic Network have stimulated my thinking and development in different ways. I desire, too, to express my appreciation to George Hochfield, Ishmael Reed, and Emory Elliott for supporting my efforts through the years. At Temple University Press, Doris Braendel has been especially helpful. My *estimada* first cousin, Lupita Perez, who taught, until recently, in the McAllen, Texas public schools for many years, found and shared with me the only photograph that her father, Tio Julio, preserved, among his U.S. Army mementos, of our fathers, grandmother, and uncles as young immigrants. Neither in conception nor execution, however, is anyone responsible for my interpretation of how Latinos are perceived and treated. God knows I have tried to see progress instead of obstacles, but all evidence finally appears to point to the fact that the realities that most Mexican Americans and other Hispanics have endured throughout the nineteenth and twentieth centuries remain firmly in place. I can only hope that the citizens of the next century offer Latinos the kind of opportunities that other Americans enjoy.

Introduction

espite efforts throughout the twentieth century, especially during the last thirty years, to improve how Mexican Americans and other Spanish-speaking people are perceived in the United States, Chicanos[1] and other Latinos are not yet seen as typical American citizens. Latinos continue to receive poor educations. The media continue to represent us in ways that have not been changed substantially by the emergence of Chicano literature or by anything else attempted by American Latinos during the last three decades. There has been no acceleration of efforts to educate and develop this potentially great national human resource, and success continues to be available only to a tiny fraction of Hispanics. Although some small improvements have occurred, the great majority of Latinos in the United States still live in separate worlds connected only tangentially to the rest of American culture. Despite the efforts of many Spanish-speaking citizens to interact more meaningfully with the rest of American society, too often the Chicano barrios and other Latino communities that exist throughout the United States remain social spaces to be avoided instead of places that can be developed and enhanced to promote a town, city, state, or region.[2]

Since Chicano literature provides an ongoing record about the presence of a resident and growing Spanish-speaking population in the United States, examining the writings of Chicano writers in light of certain widely assumed views about Hispanics is a social imperative. Essentially, the issue is one of Mexican American and Latino visibility—or, visible

1

invisibility, as it were—within the larger American environment. Studying how Chicano authors have labored to improve education and analyzing how Latinos continue to be represented in newspapers, magazines, television programs, films, and advertisements should allow readers to determine where our narratives have succeeded and where they have fallen short of the needs of Latinos and American society.[3]

By examining four Chicano books in this study, I hope to focus attention on the larger but seldom-noticed social text that adumbrates the relationships between the wider American public and the permanent Latino communities of the United States. Such relationships offer a cultural text that Chicano writers and critics have been constructing one-sidedly since the Treaty of Guadalupe Hidalgo created Mexican Americans in 1848. Since such a text can be accessed from a number of sociopolitical, economic, and historical perspectives, I do not presume to speak for all American Hispanics in the following pages. Nonetheless, I believe that education and media portrayals of Spanish-speaking Americans are the two most important socializing vehicles that, generation after generation, have continued to shape and influence that very real Hispanic world that exists, however nebulously, in the American consciousness. While Chicano literature dramatizes the impact of education and the American media on Latinos, and even though many Mexican Americans and Latinos invest considerable time and effort on our relationships to American society today, the larger American public seems to remain unengaged.

United States Latinos often feel less like Americans and more like recent immigrants or life-long foreigners in our own country. Dramatized in a variety of forms, which include anger, indifference, adjustment, and accommodation, Chicano authors have long rendered frustrating sociopolitical realities and psychological responses that have remained unheeded and unaddressed. If America's Latinos are to help advance American civilization in the twenty-first century, our Spanish-speaking citizens require better educations and the American media will have to learn how to represent Hispanics more attractively.[4] The schools and the media are singled out because these two socializing vehicles continue to be the chief means that daily shape and influence Latinos. If no extra efforts are soon made to improve how Hispanics are educated and perceived and responded to throughout American society, the future promises to be bleaker than the shameful past that made it acceptable to discriminate against Latinos.

Although a number of studies have addressed relationships between mainstream Americans and Chicanos, such efforts have not especially sought to bring the people of these two American cultures to a better understanding of each other.[5] Some Latinos want and may even state a wish to remain separate and apart, but the majority of us have shown by our lifestyes that we would rather be regarded as regular American citizens. Despite the different desires expressed by Latinos throughout the twentieth century, from those who would create a separate society to those who would deny that they have special problems within American culture, I think it is time to assert a willingness to join the great American experiment that all Americans now need to facilitate and encourage.[6] Not to embrace this challenge is to consign Latino Americans to the second-class citizenship that Ana Castillo, among other writers like Alurista, Angela de Hoyos, and Evangelina Vigil, has posited.

Mexican Americans and other Latinos are noticeably absent from the media and from the life that most people recognize as "American" for reasons that need to be seriously considered. Absence, or what might be called negative presence, more than anything else, lies at the heart of many of the problems that Chicanos and other Spanish-speaking Americans experience and endure. The almost automatic response of many mainstream Americans to such a view is that Latinos, like other citizens, ought to take more responsibility for our own lives and decisions. And, like other Americans, we do. We work, pay taxes, and have become the fastest-growing consumer group in the country. Data, however, show that the images and the representations that consistently appear in the American media about Hispanics, as well as the different kinds of primary, secondary, and higher educations readily available to Latinos and to other Americans, are the prime reasons why many United States Latinos feel estranged in our own land. Although such realities may change in three or four more generations, if persuaded that all Americans will gain when Latinos are treated as regular Americans, educators and media people could expedite that process by educating and better depicting Latinos now.[7]

Although we are often conflated and perceived as Mexican citizens or as Latino immigrants to the United States, Mexican Americans and other American-born Latinos are increasingly visible in American society. Our complex relationships among ourselves, with other Latinos, and with American society in general, however, are not known well enough by the average American to engage the type of interest that could actually improve the future of Latino youths. The media por-

trayals, educational struggles, and attitudes that Hispanics normally encounter in American life, as well as our own understandably ambiguous
responses to the postcolonial environments in which we are born, grow,
and develop, are documented by Chicano historians and authors. But
even though our narratives both describe how we currently represent
ourselves and respond to how we are seen in general throughout the
United States, such counternarratives have not received wide enough
attention and dissemination to impact the rest of American society.

The writers selected for this study, two male and two female authors,
were chosen because they usefully illuminate the psychological conflicts, the identity uncertainties, and the cultural encounters, adjustments, and resolutions that most Mexican American men and women
undergo, generation after generation. Singly and together, the books
considered here unfold a long overdue, though still one-sided or culturally insulated, dialogue with American culture.[8]

Readers familiar with Chicano novels and autobiographies can point
to other needs at this juncture in our history, but I think it is also important to address readers who may be less familiar with Chicano literature.[9] In writing for the general educated reader, I attempt to explain how the education system and the American media influence the
minds of Mexican Americans, the larger Latino population, and other
Americans. Chicano authors have written about how education and the
media coalesce to complicate and sometimes even undo the lives of
Hispanics. By discussing the extraordinary efforts made by a group of
American ethnic writers interested in capturing the voices of Latinos
to establish a discourse with mainstream America, I seek to garner for
Hispanic writers the type of attention they have not yet received. Although the accomplishments of our first generation of writers are considerable, their works are still not known outside of a small circle of
readers. As we will see in Chapter 2, my purpose is to explain some of
the problems that ethnic oppositional authors encounter in creating a
literature. If Chicano writers were to expand our horizons by incorpo-
rating more of American life in their books, they might attract a greater
readership to a literature that endeavors to render how Mexican Americans, Latinos, and other Americans actually live and dream, or how we
all might.

The media, education, and Chicano literature are three distinct fields,
each with scholars who naturally write in response to the theories in

their areas. As a student of American culture, I have chosen to examine what Chicanos have written about education and the media because I find that these two socialization disciplines together fundamentally shape and influence the postcolonial Latino consciousness in ways that have not been studied. Education and media scholars derive theories mainly by studying the hegemonic mainstream culture. When taken into account, minority populations are generally studied as separate categories possessing different distinguishing characteristics. Such studies tend to look primarily at African Americans; Latinos and other minority groups are frequently excluded, or included only by statements informing us that such populations are beyond the scope of studies that have been commissioned by this government entity, company, or corporation.

When most scholars look at Hispanics in the United States, they see a wide variety of citizens with so many differences that it is difficult to make useful generalizations. Even among American Hispanics who derive from Central America, for instance, those whose ancestors came from Guatemala are very different from Americans who derive from Costa Rica, Nicaragua, El Salvador, or Panama. Similarly, American Hispanics whose parents came from Argentina or Peru have different customs and traditions from those with families from Colombia, Venezuela, Chile, or Puerto Rico, the last of which is a commonwealth of the United States. What all Latinos in the United States have in common, though, is that no one group has a sufficiently comfortable social base to speak for all the others—including Cuban Americans, who tend to be among the more prosperous Hispanics in the United States.

Why aren't the majority of Hispanics socially and economically comfortable in the United States? Largely because American society has not been hospitable enough to Latino cultures, even though many Latinos have shown that we can maintain our cultures within American society *and* be successful Americans. I am not referring to more recent Latino immigrants, but to Spanish-speaking Latinos whose families have lived in this country for more than one generation. Whereas the education system and the media wonderfully help acclimate and facilitate the assimilation of white Americans, sometimes in less than a generation, most Latinos tend to remain a distinct group of Americans. Given that reality, the narratives and statistics gathered for this study lead to the conclusion that (1) Latinos are not helped by the quality of the education readily available to us; and (2), that the ways the media represent us tend to keep us separate and apart and do not easily confer the term "American" on Latinos.

These factors harm Latinos psychologically and make many of us feel that we are not American or American enough. The fact that we speak Spanish or ought to speak Spanish is often used to designate us as foreigners, even though many of us have learned or have failed to learn Spanish in the United States, our homeland. Some Hispanics, to be sure, may disagree with this assessment, since some of us individually feel very comfortable as Americans. But when we consider where the majority of Latinos are educationally, and the extent to which we are ignored by American society, I think most people will agree that Hispanics are not on the American cultural screen. We simply do not show up in most film, radio, newspaper, television, and internet representations of the United States at home or abroad. That means that we are largely absent from the American consciousness, and, worse, very few people who are not Latinos themselves seem to have noticed this absence.

Chicano writers and community leaders have long urged more responsible attention to how Hispanics are educated and to how the media represent us. Although different opinions exist about the progress of our people, most of the evidence indicates that the great majority of Hispanics are not yet being influenced and affected in positive ways by the socializing institutions available in American civilization. Minority students who attend primary and secondary schools that lack the proper financial and pedagogical resources, for example, are not being prepared to compete with mainstream students who attend the better-financed, pedagogically more advanced schools that year after year educate students for America's more selective colleges and universities.[10] The American media also do not promote the kind of visual and verbal imagery of Hispanics in newspapers, television, films, and advertisements that would enhance our sense of ourselves in American society.

I call attention to these realities not to prompt defensiveness, but to motivate educators and the media to improve the ways in which Spanish-speaking Americans are perceived and represented, since generation after generation of Latinos are affected and shaped by the disregard that American society has traditionally offered us. Because most of the American cultural imagery displayed here and throughout the American-influenced world excludes Hispanics, or includes us only in ancillary ways and roles, many Latinos are less receptive to symbols and messages that other Americans easily embrace. Throughout the twentieth century, our reactions to how we are treated by American society have repeatedly been expressed in one form or another. Latino responses to being excluded, as we will see in the texts analyzed in this book, have been to create worlds, which we have proceeded to fill and develop as our needs and means have allowed.

For years, the psychological realities confronting Latinos in the United States, as discussed in the following pages, have variously combined to route the relatively small percentage of Hispanics who graduate from high school to enter mainly open admissions higher education institutions and community colleges. Harvard sociologist Nathan Glazer has portrayed the two-year community college as a remedial institution, given the number of courses that students are required to take before receiving college credit; and unfortunately, there is a certain sad truth to the characterization.[11] In the April 1998 issue of *The Hispanic Outlook in Higher Education*, the U.S. Department of Education reported that two-thirds of the higher education degrees received by Hispanics were awarded by 150 community colleges in the United States. In 1997, for instance, Miami-Dade Community College in Florida awarded 22,523 associate degrees to Hispanics. Four-year colleges and universities awarded the other one-third of the higher education degrees received by Latinos, telling us that not enough Hispanics are being educated to be seen as American leaders for the next century. Though Hispanics make up more than 11 percent of the U.S. population, they account for only 0.079 percent of the students in higher education, a number so minuscule that it is statistically insignificant.[12]

The internet and other high-technology features of the 1990s have not yet touched the lives of most Mexican American and Latino youths. Although the great majority of Hispanic youth are second-, third-, and fourth-generation Americans, these youngsters continue to be less successful academically because school expectations for our children are low and they are not sufficiently encouraged or challenged to attend college. With the proper financial and pedagogical support and encouragement, they, too, could be academic achievers.

This disconcerting educational reality reveals the fact that local and national leaders and educators are not paying the kind of attention to Mexican Americans and other Latinos that they need. Indeed, when the education of Latino youngsters is brought to the attention of teachers, leaders, and legislators, the usual response is to say that everything that can be done for Spanish-speaking students is being done, and that Hispanics and African Americans cannot receive special treatment that would be denied white students. My response is that once school problems have been diagnosed correctly, very specific educational strategies are needed for different types of students. Physicians do not treat all patients similarly, and what is good for one student is not likely to help another. If Mexican Americans and other Latinos were being educated successfully in proportions equal to mainstream American students, would they not secure better employment than the positions most Latinos regularly obtain?

Chicanos can be first-generation Americans like myself or fourteenth-generation natives, if one's ancestors arrived with the first Spaniards who named San Antonio in 1691, or who established that settlement in 1718 with the expedition of Martín de Alarcón. Some Hispanics are mestizo descendants of the indigenous peoples of the central regions of the Americas, or products of the mixed marriages and unions that have continued to take place since the 1521 conquest of the Aztecs, as Arnold Toynbee, Octavio Paz, and other middle America scholars have surmised.[13] Other Latinos surprise people because they also have black, Jewish, Chinese, middle eastern, or even Anglo roots, as well as ancestral connections to German, French, Italian, British, Polish, and other national groups. Hispanics, in short, make up an enormously large mix of Americans, and according to our willingness or reluctance to express cultural ties to our different countries and to our genotypic or phenotypic features, we either blend or do not into the larger American community.

Luis Valdez, Ana Castillo, and Alurista, among other Chicano authors, have emphasized the long-obscured *raza* roots of Americans who derive from and have continued to express cultural ties to Mexico and Mesoamerica. Most working-class *raza* people do not possess the genealogical records that some European descendants do, these generally having been lost through neglect or perhaps even on purpose. Regardless, most Mexican Americans likely descend either from the various indigenous peoples that populated Mexico, the American Southwest, and middle America or from indigenous ancestors who married the Europeans who arrived after Christopher Columbus discovered the New World in 1492. The indigenous peoples to which I refer include the Olmecs (1200–400 B.C.), Teotihuacanos (A.D. 1–650), Zapotecas (500 B.C.–A.D.1000), Tajinos (A.D. 550–1100), Huastecos (A.D. 1200–1521),

Toltecas (A.D. 950–1150), Maya (1000 B.C.–A.D. 1521), Mixtecas (A.D. 900–1521) and the last and best-known settlers of Mexico's central valley, the Aztecas (A.D. 1200–1521).[14] Through the unifying concept of Aztlan, the fabled southwestern spiritual kingdom of the mestizo *raza*, today many Chicanos identify with these ancestral Mesoamericans who lived throughout Mexico and Central America.[15] In *The Labyrinth of Solitude*, Octavio Paz joined others in speculating that from such a varied mix of people, cultural and class differences developed that prevail to this day, creating both real and perceived differences that effectively serve to categorize Latino people. In referring to Americans of Mexican extraction, to offer a contemporary example, Californianos or Mexican Americans from California seem to prefer the term "Chicano," whereas Tejanos or Mexican Americans from Texas, on the whole, are more comfortable using "Mexican Americans," without the hyphen.

This is not new. Such sentiments had been expressed long before 1972, when Rodolpho "Corky" Gonzalez published his wonderfully spirited *Yo Soy Joaquin/I Am Joaquin*, and they have periodically continued to find expression in the works of Gloria Anzaldúa and Cherrie Moraga's *This Bridge Called My Back* (1981) and Ana Castillo's *Massacre of the Dreamers* (1995), the latter which is analyzed in this study. The "Aqui estamos y no nos vamos" ("We are here and we won't go") street chant, popularized during the grape and lettuce strikes led by Cesar Chavez and Dolores Huerta, for instance, once simultaneously elicited both sympathetic and antagonistic responses.[16] Along with providing Spanish-speaking field workers in the United States with the most media coverage yet garnered for indigent Mexican American laborers, such long overdue protests also obscured the existence of a growing middle and upper middle class of Chicanos and Latinos. Hispanics who have actually benefited from this media attention have been those previously positioned by the educational and economic systems to reap opportunities created by the struggles of the field workers. Neither the field workers nor middle- and upper-middle-class Latinos, however, have been portrayed responsibly by the media. Mexican American publishers and writers, who generally belong to the middle-class, have also chosen to represent Chicano literature mainly as the stories and poetry that have emerged from the poorer, working people, from *raza* members who have not traditionally been the beneficiaries of good educations. All of these class, educational, geographical, and socioeconomic issues need to be better explored and articulated, for if we are to understand Latinos, the *raza* portion of the American population clearly needs sustained attention.

Corporate sponsors and patrons who subsidize advertising and national marketing campaigns have wondered, "What do Chicano people, particularly the activists, want?" The problem is that, despite various kinds of community efforts to access and enhance the quality of public education that Latinos receive, sociopolitical and business considerations have not sufficiently moved leaders and the American media to meet the needs of Hispanics at the national, regional, or local levels. In spite of the publicity raised by more than fifty years of court cases like *Delgado v. Bastrop Independent School District* (1948), *Edgewood v. Kirby* (1984), and *Hopwood v. State of Texas* (1996), as well as the writings of Chicano authors, Latino youngsters remain underserved by all levels of public education in the United States. People generally seem to know this fact, but no national entity with sufficient influential heft and resources has stepped forward to do anything about these realities.

The forgotten education publications of George I. Sanchez (1906–1972) and the political, pedagogical saga that has embroiled bilingual education in the United States from the start provide two of the best testaments to the education gridlock that Hispanics have historically encountered.[17] Guadalupe San Miguel's *"Let All of Them Take Heed": Mexican Americans and the Campaign for Educational Equality in Texas, 1910–1981*, one of a handful of insightful scholarly efforts on the subject, carefully documents the educational neglect of Chicanos. But such works have made little impact on the education establishment. Although gains have obviously been made, particularly during the last thirty years that Chicano literature has helped to create and sustain interest on these issues, the reality is that the quality of education delivered to Latinos, like that of African Americans, remains substantially inferior to that available to most white Americans. Proof of the differences experienced by majority and minority students can be found annually in test scores, college admissions statistics, and, of course, in the types of degrees and awards conferred to students of different races and ethnic backgrounds.[18]

Despite the publication of histories such as *450 Years of Chicano History in Pictures* (1976), Rodolfo Acuña's *Occupied America: A History of Chicanos* (1981), and Ignacio Garcia's *United We Win: The Rise and Fall of La Rada Unida Party* (1989), and despite the enormously influential media outlets and communication resources available in the United

Photograph taken by Russell Lee in June 1949 of a sign posted outside a restaurant in San Antonio, Texas. Russell Lee Photograph, "We Serve Whites Only," CN 06289, The Center for American History, The University of Texas at Austin.

States, little is known about the past blatant discriminations and the more subtle current exclusionary practices that Chicanos and Latinos face.[19] Since the early 1970s, in particular, Mexican Americans, who comprise the largest group of Hispanics in the United States, have made concerted efforts to communicate their frustrations to other Americans, with limited success.[20] In the wake of the Civil Rights Act of 1964 and the media's increased interest in the plight of African Americans, Mexican Americans have gained a modicum of public attention during the last third of the century. But for all practical purposes, the challenge of undertaking the creation of a Chicano literature has occurred and continues to develop in what has to be characterized as a social vacuum.

Seldom recognized or addressed by the mainstream literary establishment, Chicano literature today remains quite unknown to the larger American reading public. Readers and *literati* tend to pay more attention to how known critics and arbiters of literary taste assess books, and since the fledgling Chicano literature has not received much notice, our literature has not been given the necessary space to develop. The best evidence of this is the fact that, outside of academe, where small coteries of writers and critics work and discuss Chicano progress, Chicano literature hardly exists.

Many mainstream Americans, to be sure, do not seem to have noticed the absence of Latinos in the cultural life of American society. As a result, whereas we might now have a healthier relationship between Chicano life, Chicano literature, and the larger American community, we instead have only a few associations and foundations on which to build a healthy discourse that should have been occurring during the last thirty years. Written almost entirely by Mexican Americans and read and reviewed principally by Latino critics, mostly in English but also in some Spanish-language publications, Chicano literature has not yet made a discernible difference in the lives of millions of book-buying Americans. Nor, it must be said, has Chicano literature made much of a difference in the actual lives of the burgeoning Latino community.

Despite some truly remarkable efforts by Latino publishers to establish presses and to disseminate the literature, Chicano writing remains relatively unrecognized by America's Spanish- and English-language readers. This is particularly true among the larger Mexican American, Puerto Rican, and Cuban American populations, which are not part of the smaller Latino reading circles who support the literature. *Aficionados* of literature, of course, know the work, but by and large, the U.S. Hispanic populations do not. Aimed at fortifying and improving our images of ourselves, at building self-esteem in our young people, and at empowering Hispanics of all ages, among other goals, Latino writing today barely subsists, receiving rarely noticed endorsements and occasionally having an out-of-print text reprinted.

From the start, Chicano authors have primarily written for Latinos as well as to inform the larger American public about the lives of Hispanics in the United States. But after nearly thirty years, the most that can be claimed are mixed results. Our writers have clearly influenced the views and thinking of small numbers of students on a few enlightened campuses in a few parts of the country and abroad. But after nearly two generations in which these writers have labored intensely to create a visible literature and to promote cultural pride among Mexican Americans and other Latinos, I suspect that most Americans, Hispanics included, would be hard pressed to name a single Chicano book, poem, and perhaps even a single author.

In light of this reality, we should not be surprised to find that middle-class, tax-paying Chicanos, who understandably are still not pleased with how the media represent us, express uncertainty about our private and public roles in American society.[21] Such responses call into question the educational promises held out to all U.S. citizens by the Constitution. As a student of literature, I have taught for many years in the universities of this country with the hope that scholars would increasingly recognize the common impulses motivating writers of Chicano and American literatures. For, as I see it, Chicano literature is one of the latest and most significant manifestations of American literature, but the field has not sufficiently engaged the interest of other Americanists, largely because they have not seen Chicano writing as our literature's newest growth area. The fault for this state of affairs lies with writers from both camps, since Chicano writings are often treated by practitioners and readers as a separate field rather than as part of the ever-changing American experience.

Among my reasons for writing this book is that I have followed developments in Chicano literature since the 1970s, when I taught and lived in Berkeley, California. What has engaged my interest in both American literature and in Mexican American writers has been a certain self-consciousness that sometimes speaks confidently and at other times blatantly searches for cultural anchors. These shifting and contrary impulses, evident both in a literature already established and in a literature undergoing continued construction, are reflected in the general uncertainty and the conflicting thoughts and emotions that mainstream Americans and Latinos periodically exhibit toward the United States, toward Mexico, and toward all things American and Mexican. The truth is that Chicano texts tend to receive the approbation of most Mexican Americans looking for cultural confirmation and authentication, while the responses of other Americans less sure about what to look for in such a literature are understandably more indefinite. Since American culture, like all other cultures, is always in flux, always in the process of becoming and changing, as Alexis de Tocqueville observed in *Democracy in America*, preparing a literary work that engages all or most Chicanos, Latinos, and other Americans is as difficult as writing the proverbial Great American Novel. The result is that Mexican Americans, Latinos, and American critics who have not been satisfied by the published lit-

erature have not articulated what they wish to see, though I suspect that
people will recognize the great text when they encounter it.

What is heartening about Chicano literature are its intense, insistent
drives, as evinced in the four books analyzed here. Analyzing how these
forces operate in works by writers of both genders illuminates some of
the contradictions and adjustments that Mexican Americans and other
Latinos must live with in the United States. Although other texts could
have been chosen for this study, I have settled on two novels, an autobiography, and a collection of essays, written by two Chicana women
and two Mexican American male writers, because these books have already achieved a certain prominence and warrant further attention.
What we learn from these texts and others is that the responses of Mexican Americans and other Latinos can be quite complex, mainly because
Latinos are a large, heterogenous population with social, religious, and
political views that cover a broad spectrum of interests and concerns.

Although social change is a central component of the kindergarten
through high school experience, and even though public, tax-supported
colleges and universities profess to serve the educational needs of all citizens, when Chicanos and other Latinos have expressed concern with
the quality of our educations, the majority of our country's educational
institutions have preferred to adopt more mainstream agendas, or simply to preserve the status quo. By choosing other priorities, administrators of educational institutions deflect or indefinitely postpone the educational improvement of Hispanic Americans and other minority
populations. Such social and political realities leave the needs of the
sizeable emerging Hispanic population relegated to public policy mak-
ers who claim to lack the resources and who do not have the political
will to address this neglect. Addressing the social and educational needs
of Latinos will benefit the quality of life for all Americans. If left unat-
tended, however, Hispanics will soon present the United States with
bigger burdens, for a less-educated citizenry without the necessary cultural resources and support cannot take care of its own business, much
less flourish, as Americans are expected to do.

The neglect of Latinos also extends to the literary world. As in almost all areas of endeavor by Mexican American and Latino artists in
the United States, most Latino literary events receive little mainstream
attention.[22] When was the last time, for instance, that the American media took notice of a Chicano novel or a Latino play?

Some university professors and media literati have argued that the quality of Chicano writing needs more improvement before it can garner mainstream attention. How can this not be the case? How can the cognoscenti of mainstream literature expect better writing when few educators have made the effort to prepare our people for access to the better schools? From the start, Americans in general and the publishing industry in particular have not been inclined to work with Chicano authors. Although there are now a handful of happy exceptions, the reality today is that even the most successful Chicano writers still struggle to place their work with recognized mainstream publishers. One has only to read interviews with Victor Villaseñor, Angela de Hoyos, Carmen Tafolla, Evangelina Vigil-Piñon, and other Latino writers to learn about the difficulties of securing interest in Hispanic works from the acquisition editors of the better-known publishing houses. Even anthology texts like Roberta Fernandez's *In Other Words: Literature by Latinas of the United States* (1994) chronicle the publication travails of Hispanics.

Because of obstacles met, U.S. Latino authors have necessarily turned to alternative publishers from the start. Since the 1970s, most of our writers have published their work with Latino publishers, magazines, newspapers, and other media. Except for an occasional work, mainstream media simply have not paid attention to Latino writing. This fact is little known outside of Chicano writing circles. Literature students studying the history of Mexican American and other American Latino literatures should not erroneously conclude that America's Hispanic writers have chosen to remain separate and apart, a charge often rationalized by or attributed to language and cultural differences. Since mainstream Americans have basically resisted bilingual efforts, despite some funding for such programs by Congress, citizens seeking to maintain two or more languages have little reason to be optimistic. The English Only movement has dramatized the fact that language differences do not sufficiently explain the publication and dissemination problems that Chicano authors have had.

Three decades of writing have amply demonstrated the diversity of styles to be found among Chicano writers. The novels of New Mexican writer Rudolfo Anaya, for example, are linguistically and attitudinally different from the stories and live-voice narratives of south Texas author Rolando Hinojosa, and both of these writers have altogether different cultural coordinates from Helena Maria Viramontes, who was shaped by her East Los Angeles environment, or Sandra Cisneros, who grew up in Chicago and now resides in San Antonio. Since most American-born Chicano writers attended schools in the United States, English is naturally enough the language of choice, and only an occasional author, like Miguel M. Mendez, who teaches at the University of Arizona, writes completely in Spanish. Such realities, coupled with the fact that representatives of America's dominant literary culture remain reluctant to establish commerce with Chicano literature, help to place the history of this ethnic literature in a clearer cultural context. Editors of the standard American literature anthologies have not included Chicano writing, and are only now gingerly beginning to follow Paul Lauter's 1990 canon-breaking edition, *The Heath Anthology of American Literature*, a volume that consciously endeavored to embrace the multiplicity of the American writing experience.

Another purpose I had in writing this book was to bring out the fact that since the Civil Rights era, Latinos in the United States have worked through many avenues to cast ourselves as an important and significant component of American society. Propelled by the desire to secure better opportunities for a people who have not been educated adequately for good employment in American society, Chicano literature has sought and promoted greater visibility. This effort has required the help of the schools at the local, state, and federal levels, as well as the support and encouragement of the media and the country's leaders. In some areas of the American economic and political landscape, such as public health, crime, education, and buying power, the increasing number of Hispanics has forced a kind of reluctant acknowledgment of our new presence. But such awareness has also been stymied by fears that the "browning of America" has started, defeating the little attention and good will that has been raised by people of all races who see and understand the social and economic need to work for a better America.

The Latino community's hope is that American society will not continue to ignore a large body of citizens whose mores and ways will affect how all Americans live and interact in the twenty-first century. Discussing how Chicano writers have developed a literature and what our stories have to say about education and the media, in particular, are necessary steps in a dialogue that should occur between Latinos and other American citizens. Writers like Anaya, Viramontes, Pat Mora, and others could have been addressed, too, since their interests in educating the young are as observable as that of the writers I have chosen. Historically, this discussion could have begun with the Hispanic writing following the 1848 Treaty of Guadalupe Hidalgo, which officially ended the American war with Mexico.[23] But the Chicano literature I am concerned with in this study focuses attention on the present-day realities of education and the media, as well as the attendant psychological issues that Latinos continually address in American society. If these two areas of endeavor do not soon function together to improve the lives of Hispanics in the United States, society will not be substantially improved for everyone. American civilization, which is based on the wonderful idea of equality for everyone, should not continue to enhance and to invest in the lives of some Americans at the expense of forgetting about other, less fortunate Americans.

Although some people may believe that Mexican American culture as presented in our Chicano narratives appears exhausted in that the literature has started to replicate itself, Chapters 2 and 11 endeavor to extend our current literary horizons. Taking a fresh look at a culture that is regarded more as an onus than as a positive contributor to American life is a difficult challenge. Such efforts, however, are rewarding, for if mainstream Americans embrace Mexican Americans and other Hispanic youths who now tend to feel either ambivalent or left out and abandoned, there is no doubt that Latinos can nourish and reinvigorate American society more than anyone expects. My sense is that the literary stock that Chicanos and other enlightened supporters have been investing in over the last three decades can pay bigger profits and dividends. But to make this investment in a people mature, the rest of America needs to keep from deflecting and rejecting the views advanced in the following pages, and to work toward understanding Latino and Mexican American realities. We cannot long continue to provide for a vastly different future the few educated Latinos that American society has managed to produce so far. Indeed, what is the point of all Latino endeavors since the Civil Rights Act of 1964 if such efforts do not successfully translate into changed policies and practices that substantially improve education and how the media represent Hispanics for all Americans?

2

Chicano Literature and Irish Literature

eaders might be struck by the seeming disparity between my introductory remarks and the title of this chapter. One of my objectives in this study is to highlight how different expectations can give birth to different realities. With this in mind, I intend to compare two postcolonial literatures that are perceived quite differently: the literature of Mexican Americans and that of the Irish. In so doing, I seek to dramatize what can be called literary scale or value, that is, achievements and prospects, given how individual writers define themselves. These two ethnic groups in part have historically defined themselves and have been seen as living in frustrated opposition to the United States and Great Britain, two hegemonic countries that, respectively, forced the Mexican inhabitants of the Southwest and the Irish people to live under the banners and governments of larger imperial influences. Tangentially, as the frontispiece and Introduction suggest, my own professional life has provided me with an opportunity to observe the development of Chicano writing. By benchmarking the Chicano literary events I have witnessed, I hope to disclose a variety of issues, concerns, relationships, and anecdotes that the emergence of Chicano literature has helped bring to light.

About thirty years ago, Chicano literature began to surface almost simultaneously in the heads and hearts of a number of Chicano activists in the Oakland-Berkeley area; Albuquerque; Denver; the Los Angeles–San Diego area; Crystal

18

City, south Texas; and other Mexican American communities throughout the country. Interest in a literature of our own was prompted by the
vacuum that many Mexican Americans began to feel in the wake of the
1965 Delano grape strikes and the marches that Cesar Chavez and the
National Farm Workers Association organized in California. Dolores
Huerta's and Chavez's eventual slogan, "Si se puede!" ("Yes we can!"),
I believe, fueled the idea that we could also have a literature, ambitious
as the undertaking appeared at the time. The opinion today about what
Chicano writers and commentators have brought forth remains divided.
Discussions of Chicano and other American literatures, for example,
still occur on separate terrains, though a few scholars have made significant advances toward bridging the two.[1] Chicano writers and critics
tend to assume the permanence and continuity of Mexican American
literature, while other *literati* are more inclined to see our literature as
a passing infatuation, which, perhaps somewhat like American Tran-
scendentalism, never quite lived up to the expectations about which
people dreamed. Critics like Alvin Kernan and Leslie Fiedler have since
predicted the demise of all literature; but literatures, like most things in
life, peak and ebb, continuing to serve civilization as the needs of authors and readers decree.

In order to understand the impetus behind the writing of Spanish-
speaking Americans, one needs to recall what it was like to study literature before the advent of Chicano literature. In 1970, when I began my
graduate training in English, following two years of undergraduate
study at Pan American University in south Texas and two years at the
University of Texas at Austin, there was not a single Chicano novel or
known poem that was readily available to the reading public. Chicano
literature did not exist as a field, so when it was time to select a subject
area for further study I chose American literature, sensing that our literature would develop as I continued to study Emerson, Thoreau,
Hawthorne, and Melville, writers whose work I thoroughly enjoyed,
despite the fact that people thought it strange for a Mexican American
to be familiar with works like "Experience," *Walden*, *The Blithedale Romance*, *Mardi*, and *Pierre*.

Following four years of graduate study at the State University of
New York at Buffalo, the University of California Berkeley, to everyone's surprise, including mine, hired me. I hope readers can imagine my
discomfort when I soon learned that I was the first Chicano ever offered
a tenure-track appointment to teach American literature in that distin-

guished English department. I have never enjoyed being an experiment, and yet that is how I knew I was seen when I first arrived and all the professors civilly sized me up. Shortly after beginning to teach at Berkeley I met Ishmael Reed, today a leading African American writer, and then a senior lecturer who had been promised tenure. Reed had just founded the Before Columbus Foundation, a circle made up primarily, though not exclusively, of ethnic writers who consciously sought to connect their writing to the indigenous peoples of the Americas. I had read Alvar Nuñez Cabeza de Vaca's *La Relación*, a book that I still teach in my course on the literature of the Southwest, so I immediately embraced the idea of doing what could be done to keep the memory of America's native inhabitants alive. Through Reed, I met Rudolfo Anaya, whom I later introduced at a public reading held in the Oakland Museum of California. In this period, I also met Octavio Romano and Herminio Rios, and by 1976, I was serving as a reader and editor for some early Chicano texts published by Rios's Editorial Justa Publications, Inc. Behind the scenes, I worked on books like Rudolfo Anaya's *Tortuga* (1979) and other lesser-known manuscripts by Chicano writers. I also became professionally active as Chicano literature grew and began to be taught more regularly in college and university curricula.

Although I have published mainly in the field of American literature since then, at the time I also started teaching Chicano literature, offering the first such course as a special topics class in Berkeley's English department. Since resources for the publication of Chicano books were scarce, and I was an assistant professor working toward tenure, I chose to translate for publication only one fine story by Miguel M. Mendez wonderfully entitled "Ambrosio Ceniza." In many ways, I saw that story as the best symbol of the Mexican farm worker who, lured by the promise of America, crosses the border to work in southern Arizona only to learn that the food of the gods, suggested by his first name, turns to ashes, as his Mexican surname has it, in the United States. I had seen similar instances of disillusionment with America throughout my childhood. When my father owned a grocery store, we used to take the groceries out to the *braceros*, that is, the field workers legally allowed in from Mexico during the Eisenhower years. Mendez's story partially captures some of the background for many incidents and events that I experienced more fully and could talk about at some length.

When my own work did not satisfy that difficult-to-please faculty four years later, I was fortunate to receive an offer to return to Texas to teach upper-level students at the five-year-old University of Houston at Clear Lake, located next to the NASA Johnson Space Center near the Gulf of Mexico. From this position I worked to stay in touch with Chicano authors and publishers. Among other activities, I channeled Chicano writers into print, including Leonel Garcia, a Texas A&M graduate and neighbor, who has since published a number of novels that have won several literary awards. These activities and my membership in the society for the study of the Multi-Ethnic Literature of the United States (MELUS), which was founded in 1973 at the University of Southern California, provided me with ongoing opportunities to watch developments in Chicano literature and a number of related literary fields. In those years, a number of Chicano journals and publishing outlets appeared and continued producing issues while support and resources endured. The leading journals that provided stability and continuity to the field of Chicano literature were *El Grito*, published in Berkeley by Quinto Sol Publications, and *Revista Chicano-Riqueña*, which was initially edited in Gary, Indiana, by Nicolás Kanellos and Luis Dávila at Indiana University Northwest. There was also a host of other publications, including *De Colores*, published by Jose Armas in Albuquerque, as well as *Aztlan, Mango, Metas, Puerto del Sol, Third Woman, The Rican, Explorations in Ethnic Studies*, and *MELUS*, among the ones that were most instrumental in shaping Chicano literature.

Virginia Woolf pointed out in her great little book, *A Room of One's Own*, that literatures are formed slowly over a number of generations, and Chicano literature is no exception. Its future depends entirely upon a variety of factors and support that I discuss in the following pages.

The late 1960s and early 1970s were heady days for many Mexican Americans like myself. Many of us in the educational pipelines were filled with the hope of improving the world for our people. If we look today at the shelves of books published during that period, we find stodgy products that mask the rather high-minded effervescence that was widely felt among Mexican Americans working on many fronts to create a new literature. The idea was to publish narratives that would allow Chicanos—a voiceless, postcolonial, oppressed people, who had not been educated like other Americans—to awaken to a desire to transform our world through the power of the written word.

Since the northern territories of Mexico were annexed to the United States in February 1848 by the Treaty of Guadalupe Hidalgo, following President James Polk's 1846 war with Mexico, Mexican Americans have been part of the American population. Although the relationship between these peoples had been problematic from the start, over the years Mexicans, Mexican Americans, and Americans learned to settle differences in a variety of ways, both in and out of the courts. Following President Lyndon Johnson's Civil Rights Act of 1964, a central, unarticulated goal of the second college generation of Chicanos after World War II was to create what Mexican Americans, Puerto Ricans, and Cuban Americans, the three largest groups of Latinos in the United States, needed in all areas of cultural life. Aside from issues of equality and recognition, we were essentially after what intellectuals often long for, a paradigm shift. We needed a literature that would capture and mirror our efforts, that would show the world something—almost anything, at that point—that Mexican Americans and other Latinos could properly point to and say: This is what the Hispanic experience is about in America.

For the first time, a like-minded generation of Mexican Americans had begun to recognize that ours was a subjugated history. We had suddenly realized—since we were never taught such a history in the schools or at the universities—that our people had been going through the American school system for a number of generations without reading a single story, poem, or anything else written by or about Chicanos. Those of us who remember such times ought to recall what living was like without having a written legacy that we could point to as belonging to Mexican Americans and other American Latinos. That is why the Chicano experience of the early 1970s enormously raised our spirits about what the future promised, and why the current post-*Hopwood* era with its dismantling of affirmative action programs is so disturbing and alarming to a people who have not yet made sufficient progress.

Nearly thirty years ago, in 1971, those yearnings gave birth to Tomás Rivera's first Premio Quinto Sol winner . . . *y no se lo trago la tierra*, which was translated as . . . *and the earth did not part*, though a literal translation would be " . . . and the earth did not swallow him." Ernesto Galarza also published his autobiography, *Barrio Boy*, that same year. The following year, Corky Gonzalez released *I Am Joaquin*, that exhilarating, gut-level Mexican American poem of hurt and assertion that for several years was belted out at almost every conference organized by Hispanics. In New Mexico, Rudolfo Anaya weighed in with a winning book entitled *Bless Me, Ultima* in 1972. The following year, Rolando Hinojosa published *Estampas del valle*; and in 1975, El Paso's Estela Portillo penned *Rain of Scorpions*, the first longer work we then thought had been published by a Chicana writer.

In those days it seemed that the future would be as good for our people as the beautiful little rose-colored two-bedroom home that my wife and I bought for our two babies in Albany, next to Berkeley. I witnessed a number of what we might appropriately call garage presses emerge to publish Chicano authors. However, after the euphoria of publishing a book or two, most of these presses closed because there was no distribution or dissemination system to advertise, market, and promote Chicano books. The mainstream publishers were not willing to help, and the Chicano presses did not have the personnel or wherewithal to update the address lists of potential book buyers. Mainstream publishers were reluctant to endorse the work of unknown Mexican American writers who understandably wrote rather haltingly, feeling their way through the unknown print and reader terrains, much as Virginia Woolf describes the first unsure efforts of the early women writers she analyzes. The enterprise of constructing a literature from what our writers knew, from the oral materials and *corridos*[2] that were available in the barrio communities, was alternately a hopeful and a frustrating endeavor. Everything in such ventures usually turned, of course, on the quality of the work produced, and, at a more rudimentary level, on whether there were enough funds to publish, promote, and disseminate works by Chicanos. There were also no established ways of marketing and distributing Mexican American writing, other than the address lists that editors of the Chicano presses constructed as they traveled and gave talks about the budding, nascent literature. Behind these endeavors there was always the nagging knowledge that mainstream reading audiences and even our own people, who were not especially known to be book buyers or readers, would not be interested enough in buying Chicano books. The little extra money that Mexican American families might bring in necessarily went for more pressing needs. These fears and concerns turned out to be justified, and publishers and authors endured all sorts of woes, rejections, discriminations, recriminations, and other unsavory experiences during those years.

The editors and readers of Berkeley presses like Tonatiuh, Quinto Sol, and Editorial Justa Publications, other publishers like Pajarito Publications in Albuquerque, Floricanto Press and Dezkalzo Press in San Antonio, and the few presses that we still have today, such as Arte Publico Press in Houston and the Bilingual Press in Tempe, turn out, in effect, to be the main creators and perpetuators of Chicano literature. These publishers decided which manuscripts, all initially from unknown writers, would become the early texts of Chicano literature. Publishers and editors like Octavio Romano, Herminio Ríos, José Armas, Angela de Hoyos, Gary Keller, Nicolás Kanellos, and even Ishmael Reed were and have remained in many ways the unrecognized champions behind the emergence of Chicano writing.

From the start, these literary entrepreneurs have identified and then created the leading Chicano authors who have written and promoted their literature wherever enlightened Americans and international *literati* have expressed enough interest to invite them. Romano and Ríos, two academicians turned publishers, published a number of the earliest Chicano texts together, then went their different ways to set up separate presses. They are unrewarded, committed people who generously effaced themselves for many years in order to advance the cause of Chicano literature and the new authors like Anaya, Rivera, Hinojosa, Burciaga, and many others, some of whom eventually turned elsewhere for their livelihoods.[3] Of these early entrepreneurs, only Kanellos and Keller have been able to marshal the necessary financial support from a variety of sources to stay in business all of these years.[4] Keller continues as the publisher of the Bilingual Press in Tempe; Kanellos heads Arte Publico Press at the University of Houston, which is correctly advertised as "the oldest and largest publisher of U.S. Hispanic literature."

Other than an occasional lone maverick who has since been discovered by archival research and published, usually by Arte Publico Press, like novelist Jovita Gonzalez and short story writer Cristina Mena, there were no widely known Chicano authors or publishers to speak of before 1970. Writers previous to this watershed period tended to see themselves as Mexican writers or as educated American writers who were unsure about how to render and dramatize Mexican American speech, thinking, and action. José Vasconcellos, a leading Mexican intellectual who coined the phrase *La Raza Cosmica*, literally, The Cosmic Race, by which he meant a type of Whitmanesque unity for all *educated* Latinos, did not think well of Mexican Americans, mainly because he mistakenly saw Chicanos as uniformly vulgar and uneducated. He was a friend of Diego Rivera, Mexico's best-known proletariat artist; yet, Vasconcellos could not reconcile American Hispanics to Rivera's theories and his wonderful presentation of the indigenous people of the Americas. We have since learned to place Vasconcellos's thinking next to that of Nobel laureate Octavio Paz, who, unfortunately, also was not interested in understanding Mexican Americans. Paz mistakenly saw the *pachuco* as the representative Mexican American, an image he found so unappealing to the Mexican national soul that he could not withhold his distaste. Although Paz clearly understood why Chicanos in Los Angeles became *pachucos* or "zoot suiters," as they were fashionably called later, Chicanos remained objectionable to these two leading Mexican intellectuals. Their perspective certainly did not help how the leading social classes in Mexico see Mexican Americans even today.

Chicano critics initially thought and hoped that Vasconcellos might fill the useful and much-needed role of intellectual leader to the emerging literary movement. But, as Juan Bruce-Novoa demonstrated in his essay "Chicanos in Mexican Literature," Chicanos are not especially attractive to educated Mexican citizens either. To the elitist Vasconcellos, the Mexican Americans of San Antonio appeared "repulsive and despicable" because they were uneducated and spoke vulgarly. According to Vasconcellos, who ironically expressed a view rather prevalent among Latinos who have had the benefit of good educations, Chicanos massacred the Spanish language. Like Paz, Vasconcellos apparently did not care to notice that *pachucos* took great pride in inventing their own language, in coining new words to designate the mundane realities that depressed them and which continually informed them that they were not part of the American society in which they were born, lived, and would die.

The view that prevailed in the two decades before World War II was that Chicanos were neither Mexicans nor Americans. Vasconcellos, like Paz, asked: What are the Mejicanos who live over in the United States? Apparently we have been seen and continue to be seen as half-and-half people, who are not sufficiently appreciated because we are part Mexican and part American. We clearly have a separate and distinct culture, but exactly what that culture is and what our sense of ourselves and our contribution to American society is remains indistinct and fuzzy. Vasconcellos's verdict was that we were not likely to develop into anything to be proud of; that in our writings, as in everything else, we would not likely match the impressive work of Hispanic masters such as Quevedo, Cervantes, or Unamuno. Since mainstream Americans did not expect much of us either, should we be surprised when other Chicanos and Latinos sometimes thumb their noses, ironically, at our efforts to "improve" ourselves?

In a way the *pachuco* that Paz so disliked represents not only an extreme version of the Mexican national character, but also how many Chicanos actually feel in the United States. Displaced and feeling like outsiders in our own land, many Chicanos, like the *pachucos* that Paz describes, opt to turn themselves into pariahs, fashioning grotesque ways to live that call attention to our situations. Many Chicanos are suspicious and uncomfortable in American society because the iconography of the United States does not allow us a space to define ourselves. Several years ago, one of my uncles (captured as a child in the picture in the frontispiece of this book), sitting beside me at the wake of his ninety-seven-year-old mother (my grandmother, who is also in the photograph), turned and abruptly asked me, Do you really like living over there with the Gringos? It was the first time he had really spoken to me in years. He was in his seventies and had endured a life of hardship in the fields as a young man and in the many auto repair shops that he owned and worked at later. The answer I gave him was that not all of the Gringos were as bad as he remembered them any more. What else could I have said that he would understand? I would need to write this book, I said to myself several days later, which then I would have to read to him so that he might understand how race relations keep changing. Or, better, I would have to explain it to him over a beer in whichever *cantina* he preferred these days in McAllen or Edinburg, a pleasure not easily managed from College Station where I now teach.

This personal reminiscence brings us to the different postcolonial constraints on the imagination under which Chicano and Irish writers both labor. Chicanos in some ways are like the Irish, whom the British people have not been able to change all of these years. Some Chicanos, like my uncle, tend to focus on our separateness, on the fact that we are just different, irreconcilably so. Others, though, believe that we have more similarities with other Americans, and that our common future requires us to make more of an effort to work together. As with any culture, all sorts of positions and opinions exist and are possible among Chicanos, so it is difficult to generalize. Looking at the literature that we have so far published, I suspect that an enterprising scholar could, with some difficulty, nonetheless successfully categorize us. We have, the litany goes, Chicano or Tejano music, a mixture of northern Mexican music or *musica nortena* and the German polka; and we have our *corridos*, our legends, our *cuentos*. Most of these stories are communicated in the language of the common people with little reason for or desire to capture them in the best possible words to impress scholars or posterity.

Both literatures arise from the desire of people to talk, to record their lives, to express the largely oral qualities and characteristics of their existences. Chicano literature obviously falls short of Irish literature. But Irish literature has a history of over a thousand years, and Chicano literature can only offer one scant generation of sustained effort. Except for Rivera, the best-known founding authors of Chicano literature, like Hinojosa and Anaya, as well as lesser-known ones, like Angela de Hoyos, are still writing. Yet despite its long presence, Irish literature had not amounted to much throughout the eighteenth and nineteenth centuries. It was not until the twentieth century that it emerged to shape the world's literary field. Before that, the literatures to read in English were British, for even American literature was looked at suspiciously. But twentieth-century Irish literature now looms large on the literary landscape. For what writers, from Marquez, Borges, Cortázar, and from Fuentes to Allende, have not been influenced by the likes of Joyce, Yeats, Shaw, and many other lesser-known but very good writers?

Sean O'Faolain died at ninety-one years of age. When he passed away he was widely regarded as the Irish Chekhov for his beautifully crafted stories. Subsequent writers will measure themselves against the likes of O'Faolain, but how long did it take for an O'Faolain, or a Joyce, or a Yeats, or a Shaw to appear and move Irish literature forward from the folklore that dominated it before? Much has been made of the genius of the Irish imagination, of Lady Gregory and the Irish theater and literary world. That assessment is all the more justly deserved for its being long desired, hard earned, and eventually won. But for how many generations did hundreds of lesser-known Irish writers labor to bring forth the O'Faolain who wrote the excellent *Bird Alone?*

In writing the previous section, I suggested that Chicano literature has not yet come of age, that it is still in its formative stages, and that, if supported and encouraged, it may yet flower more fully. There are, to be sure, people who claim that true writers will write, whether supported or not. This is true, but the better literature will be longer in emerging and that path will likely require more travail.

So where is Chicano literature headed? Clearly we have already constructed a type of sociology of Chicanos, but we also need to explore other areas of the Chicano life and imagination. Chicano writers have

successfully communicated our woes to the public; we have laughed at,
disregarded, and risen above our troubles, and satirized our ills and
tribulations. We need, however, to be more inventive, less barrio-
centered. We need to be more responsive to—in fact, to consider writing in direct opposition to—the larger postmodern American trends of
the day. Our writers need to expand into areas that are riskier. It is acceptable to write about Chicano people in our own familiar environments, but what about working in more open-ended terrains where
both the nature of the experience and the outcomes are less certain?
Such a path would create more interest in American Latinos. What if,
for instance, we were to examine our daily lives for possibilities that are
not as far-fetched as they once were? I know a colleague, for example,
who left teaching after nearly thirty years, sold his home, and applied to
a law school in the Midwest. Now here is a story that, if written well,
might engage attention. Did his wife follow? Did she want to? And what
about their two sons, an engineer and a welder, and their divorced
daughter, who is an accountant in San Francisco? My mother used to
say that every head is a separate world. These lives are all separate but
related worlds, and they warrant and invite dramatization by imaginative writers. I think we ought to ask Chicano writers to risk entering the
consciousnesses of a number of our people whose stories are not being
dramatized and presented as Chicano literature.

It may seem that I have used the title as a ploy to lure the reader toward an interest in Chicano literature. Perhaps a good way to end this
chapter is by suggesting what I, for one, would be interested in seeing.
In 1979, a student of Joyce, Yeats, O'Faolain—in fact, of all things literary and Irish—published a great novel that made the world of fiction
readers take notice. The novel was called *The Year of the French* and the
writer was Thomas Flanagan. Flanagan is a scholar of Irish literary history, a former chairman of the English department at the University of
California at Berkeley, the same department that hired me in 1974.
Flanagan's historical novel was marketed as "the year's most glorious
best seller," and it won the National Book Critics Circle Award in 1979.
Well versed in the history and literature of Ireland, Flanagan's magnif-
icently conceived novel imaginatively re-creates an aborted revolution
that occurred in Ireland in 1798. Anyone who has read the work knows
that to open the pages of this novel anywhere is to encounter a superb
prose that immediately transports readers to the urgency of those anxious times in late eighteenth-century Ireland.

Why, I have asked myself, do we not have Chicano writers who can write like that? Quite simply because our writers have not yet had the education and experience that will allow us to write such books. Does that mean that Chicano literature is not worth reading? No, I think Chicano literature, like Irish literature, or any other literature, is worth reading precisely to see how writers progress, to see what they *are* saying, and *how* they are saying what they feel should and must be said at this point in our history. For certain books, as we know, are clear departures from previous works, while others are elaborations of previously broached ideas and issues, since all literatures are like a long, interminable conversation with the past and the future.

So why hasn't an ambitious Chicano author written something like, say, a historical novel about the story of Juan Cortina? We do, of course, have the novel that I analyze in Chapter 6, Americo Paredes's *George Washington Gomez*, completed in 1940 but lamentably not published until 1990. Here the historical misdeeds of the Texas Rangers are brought out in the early pages of the book, stories that our folklore has turned into a number of Texas Ranger jokes.[5] But I would also love to see a novel on José Antonio Navarro, or on Juan Cortina, a narrative that might capitalize, for example, on the rich history that José T. Canales, Charles Goldfinch, Armando Alonzo, and David Montejano, among other historians, have brought out.

Cortina was the son of a rich landowner in Brownsville, Texas. In 1859, he came to the defense of a drunk servant and *ranchero* who had suffered a beating from a Brownsville Marshall named Bob Shears. In self-defense, Cortina shot Marshall Shears in the arm and hid the *ranchero* in his own ranch to protect him. Cortina was charged with attempted murder by the American authorities. When attempts to compromise were refused, Cortina and his supporters retaliated by raiding and capturing the city of Brownsville. Montejano, whose *Anglos and Mexicans* won the 1988 Frederick Jackson Turner Award, says that Cortina issued a proclamation to the Mejicanos of Texas, saying: "Many of you have been robbed of your property, incarcerated, chased, murdered, and hunted like wild beasts, because your labor was fruitful, and because your industry excited the vile avarice" that motivated our enemies. In less than a month, Cortina gathered a substantial force of five to six hundred men. A six-month war ensued. Imagine being a Mexican or a newly created Mexican American, given the 1848 Treaty of Guadalupe Hidalgo, in Brownsville in November of

1859, and hearing a proclamation like that? What would Christmas be like that year? What would happened if one joined Cortina's force? What would happen if one did not join? How long would the fight with the Americanos last? Were you an Americano, too, or not? Can you or your family afford to fight? Can you afford not to? Should you go with Cortina or lie low?

Such predicaments were the stuff of real life, and they can be the material for great fiction, too. Such uncertainties, in the hands of a seasoned writer like Flanagan, can be turned into first-rate literature. Flanagan's work, we should realize, does not emerge or occur in a vacuum. A work like *The Year of the French*, as Virginia Woolf amply made clear when discussing the writings of the women before her, does not emerge full-blown out of nowhere. Every work or masterpiece, she suggested, has a long apprenticeship somewhere, somehow—either in the public eye or, more often, away from the public spotlight, in some garret or forsaken room where a writer has read and thought and dreamed, until finally one day a world is created that captures the spirit of a people, a nation. After Yeats, Shaw, Joyce, O'Faolain, and Flanagan, Irish writers know where the mark is; they know some of the stories that have mattered. At this early point in Chicano literary history, who will next produce the best Chicano work? Readers who know where Chicano literature has been now need to work to create the future that we want to shape. But first we need to understand how Chicanos have wrestled with and waited for education and the American media to help tell our stories, too.

3

Latinos in
American Culture

ince the 1950s, when I grew up, I have periodically observed that pictures of Hispanic people are not selected for the covers and inside pages of the national and regional mainstream magazines, advertisements, and promotional brochures in the United States. This is the kind of statement, of course, that may challenge some people to prove I am wrong. But even if a handful of pictures could be found, and I am convinced that they cannot, the fifty-year dearth I have witnessed is but another sign of the 150-year exclusion that Hispanics in the United States have endured since the Treaty of Guadalupe Hidalgo was signed in 1848.

This salient demonstration of our absence from the national consciousness has always bothered me considerably, but it is the kind of fact that I suspect very few Americans have ever noticed. Had I not started to dwell on the psychologically destructive interrelationship between (1) how the media either fail to depict us or portray us negatively when they do, (2) the education that Latinos tend to receive, and (3) the Chicano literature that we have produced, I do not think the absence of Latinos from the American cultural screen would stand out as prominently as it does.

For a number of years, beginning in the late 1960s and early 1970s, there was a hope among Hispanics, as among African Americans, Asian Americans, and other ethnic Americans, that as a people we would be more noticeably embraced by the media and American culture. Indeed, following the 1964 Civil Rights Act and the awakening to the social realities that most American minority people lived in, some mainstream media started promoting a greater inclusiveness. Pictures of African Americans began to show up in the more prominent national newspapers and magazines. But other than occasional images of the Mexican Americans that Cesar Chavez's marches attracted, or the Cuban people whom Fidel Castro dispossessed, little appeared in American culture that made Mexican Americans and the larger population of Latinos feel good about how the media represented and interpreted our lives. Nonetheless, those of us who knew the history of the past and looked for signs of change were optimistic.[1] For *raza* people used to long hours of work for low wages in the less desirable jobs throughout the United States, seeing pictures and witnessing discussions of Hispanic issues in the mainstream media was downright exhilarating, for such cultural reifications suggested that the future would be considerably better than the past had been for our own fathers and mothers. So where are Latinos today in American culture?

Some advances, of course, have been made and have obviously changed the nature of the Hispanic presence in the last thirty-five years. There is no denying that life for Hispanics has improved. But progress, we also need to say, has been so slow as to be almost insignificant, especially when we consider the demographic prediction that Hispanics will become the largest minority population in the United States by the year 2010. One can even argue that the progress that has been made has been the result of forces that have emerged and have not been sufficiently curtailed, since curtailment has been evident, I think, in reduced educational opportunities.

At this point in American history, a very small fraction of the more than 32 million Latinos living in the United States have achieved professional status. The great majority of Hispanics remain unprovided for in this great country, and most Americans remain either oblivious or indifferent to signs of progress among Latinos. Hispanics have one of the lowest, if not the lowest, per capita income level of any group of people in the United States.[2] Yet we also have one of the faster rising middle classes, which means that, with the proper help and encouragement, we have shown that Latinos can succeed. To dramatize this fact to the world, for instance, each year since 1990 *Hispanic* magazine has published a list of the one hundred American companies that regularly provide "the most opportunities for Hispanics." This list is produced by people who yearly monitor and benchmark the progress of Latinos in the United States. But, regardless of what Spanish-speaking Americans accomplish, I think it is fair to say that the advances made by Latinos rarely receive notice in the larger American society. In the January/February 1997 issue of *Hispanic*, for instance, editor and publisher Alfredo J. Estrada, in apparent frustration, wrote, "In many ways, Hispanics came of age last year, both politically and economically. However, corporate America failed to keep pace with our growth." Estrada specifically had in mind, among other races, Victor Morales's November 1996 run for the U.S. Senate against Phil Gramm, as well as a number of other state and larger urban political races that clearly showed that Hispanic voters will increasingly make a difference in many future elections.[3]

Economically, the story is much the same. In one of the few reports that has covered the issue, a 1995 *Entertainment Weekly* article entitled "The Latin Factor: Hollywood Plugs into a Burgeoning and Profitable Ethnic Market," Richard Natale observed: "There are 26.6 million Latinos in the U.S., a figure that's expected to increase to 40.5 million by the year 2010. According to the Motion Picture Association of America, Latinos now buy as many movie tickets as African Americans (12 percent of the national total), even though blacks represent a larger portion of the population (12 percent versus 10 percent)." In the February 1997 issue of *Hispanic Business*, Alyssa Glass similarly identified twenty-two occupation-based groups of Latino professionals who now comprise a growing middle class that has increased Hispanic buying power by three times that of the rest of the American citizenry since 1990. The organizations singled out for attention in her article have sizeable, growing memberships that regularly meet and hold annual conventions. But, again, the point is that the dominant media seldom cover the activities and plans of even the more prominent Latino professional associations.[4]

The Hispanic National Bar Association, for instance, boasts a membership of 22,000 lawyers; the Society of Hispanic Professional Engineers has 8,000 dues-paying members; the National Hispanic Academy of Media Arts and Sciences has over 3,000 affiliates; the National Hispanic Employee Association has 10,000 members; and the National Association of Hispanic Journalists, to name some of the larger, more prominent organizations, has 1,800 Latino reporters and media professionals. The American Association of Hispanic CPAs has 800 accountants; the Interamerican College of Physicians and Surgeons includes 4,500 physicians; and the Hispanic Organization of Professionals and Executives, with the appropriate acronym HOPE, has 200 members. The Hispanic Public Relations Association also has a membership of only 200, suggesting that Latinos at this point in history are not proportionally engaged in the business of serving as image representatives for American corporations and firms.

In a country with 31,365,000 Hispanics out of 272,878,000 Americans as of July 1999, according to the U.S. Census Bureau, such professional association numbers, while significant, are still so minuscule as to be downright shameful when compared to the total Latino population.[5] Even then, without support, further awareness, and encouragement for such young organizations, the prospect for the continued professional development of Latinos in the United States does not appear promising, especially when we consider the educational problems discussed below.

Regardless of what people think about affirmative action policies, for example, we need to understand that a good number of the advances made during the last two generations have been prompted by this contentious federal government policy.[6] Since 1965, when affirmative action began, this Washington initiative has sought to induce reluctant state governments to extend higher education admission and employment opportunities to minorities. Women were added to the list of underrepresented people during the Nixon administration. Such directives, nonetheless, were not meant to be panaceas; affirmative action was instituted to open the door of opportunity to minorities and women who previously would not have been able to prove their worth to employers.

But on March 18, 1996, the Fifth Circuit Court of Appeals in New Orleans ruled in *Hopwood v. State of Texas* that consideration of race as a factor in college and university admissions would be prohibited. Three and a half months later, on July 1, 1996, the Supreme Court correctly chose not to hear an appeal that would have sought to defend the University of Texas's indefensible two-system law school admissions policy. For a number of years, we have learned, the University of Texas School of Law had been making use of two different admissions systems, one for minority students and another for white students. A law school, above all other kinds of institutions, should have known that such a practice was unconstitutional. *Hopwood* showed that the Fourteenth Amendment's "equal protection of the law" principle guarantees equal treatment to every citizen. In my view, however, this decision went further than the Constitution requires and outlawed the use of race as a consideration in all higher education institutions in Texas, Louisiana, and Mississippi, the three states under the jurisdiction of the New Orleans federal court. Because Louisiana and Mississippi have been under separate desegregation court orders from the federal government, Texas is the only state that cannot currently consider race in its admissions decisions. In Texas, Attorney General Dan Morales extended this ruling to encompass all race-based scholarships and financial aid programs, enormously disabling minority students from pursuing higher education in the state's more selective universities. Except for California, which passed Proposition 209 in a statewide November 1996 referendum doing away with affirmative action, the other forty-eight states at the time of this writing are still allowed to follow affirmative action. Although the future regarding this decision is uncertain, judicial signals seem to indicate that the *Hopwood* opinion—based, ironically, sed on the Fourteenth Amendment, which was originally passed to help African Americans—is likely to prevail.

Prior to the *Hopwood* opinion, no other human quality or trait had ever been so anathematized by the federal courts as race had been. Since the beginning, when the framers of the Constitution struggled with how, if at all, to count African Americans, the United States has recognized the legality of race. Apparently, the color of people's skin continues to cause problems, so now the Fifth Circuit has decreed that Americans have to be "color blind" and "race neutral" when considering candidates for higher education and likely for employment, too. For the courts to neutralize and eliminate the importance of race at this point in our history is to go against the needs of American society today. The United States has a history of consciously using race to deny African Americans and other minority populations some of the basic, most fundamental rights spelled out in our Constitution. That, indeed, is what we learn when we consider minorities and education in *Plessy v. Ferguson* (1896), *Missouri ex. rel Gaines v. Canada* (1938), *McLaurin v. Oklahoma State Regents for Higher Education* (1950), *Sweatt v. Painter* (1950), and *Brown v. Board of Education* (1955), among other landmark Supreme Court cases. For *Hopwood* in 1996 to tell Americans that we cannot take a person's race into account when considering a candidate's suitability for a position is a complete reversal that once more disadvantages people of color. The historical reality is that race has been at the center of American culture since George Washington presided over the 1787 Philadelphia session that gave us the Constitution, and race has always been used to advantage whites.

Any person's experience of living inside his or her *skin* cannot be obviated, ignored, or neutralized. That is what novelist John Howard Griffin learned and dramatically communicated in his best-selling *Black Like Me* (1960), a memoir about his experiences after he temporarily darkened his skin to pass as an African American in the Deep South. Race is an essential, inextricable component of who we are as American citizens, and all of our experiences from the day that we are born to the day that we die are inevitably shaped and influenced by this truth—a reality that cannot be wished away or disregarded. This truth can be called the reality of the streets and of the world, for, although the courts of the United States may now legally opine otherwise, saying that we believe that people can behave according to the ideal of not seeing race will not automatically create that reality.

When considering and evaluating candidates for college admissions and employment, race will continue to be a factor, as much as a candidate's record and an applicant's personality and way of presenting himself or herself. Race, for this reason, should not be excluded from consideration, because it is an inseparable part of every American's identity. The objective should be not to give anyone preference because of his or her race, but to consider the entire person without willfully subtracting anything that properly belongs to an applicant. The Ninth and Tenth Amendments protect the rights and property of all Americans. The Ninth Amendment holds that "the enumeration in the Constitution, of certain rights, shall not be construed to deny or disparage others retained by the people," and the Tenth Amendment states that "the powers not delegated to the United States by the Constitution, nor prohibited by it to the States, are reserved to the States respectively, or to the people." These two Amendments comprehensively seek to buttress the ideas contained in the Preamble to the Constitution, which wonderfully says: "We the people of the United States, in order to form a more perfect Union, establish justice, insure domestic tranquility, provide for the common defense, promote the general welfare, and secure the blessings of liberty to ourselves and our posterity, do ordain and establish this Constitution for the United States of America." Finally, the Fifteenth Amendment, which was passed during the Reconstruction period following the Civil War, also recognizes the existence of "race" and "color," whereas the words "color blind" or "race neutral" are nowhere to be found in the Constitution.

Beginning in 1964, Americans made a communal, conscious decision to try to put a highly racialized past behind us by doing what we could to see and to interpret race as a positive attribute, instead of the liability that the dark skin of a person of color used to impose on people before the Civil Rights watershed. Whereas many Americans of all races have worked for the last thirty-five years to allow people of all ethnic backgrounds to represent themselves and their races proudly, the *Hopwood* opinion, in correctly enforcing "the equal protection of the laws" clause of the Fourteenth Amendment to the Constitution, abruptly reverses that sensible social necessity. *Hopwood*, indeed, asks Americans suddenly to forget about consciously working to make people feel good about the personal property of their skins, and to pretend instead to be "color blind." The new legal directive is not to notice a person's race; now the courts ask us to be "race neutral" in business decisions and, by extension, in everything else that we do. But how realistic is this requirement, however desirable it may be to people who are not themselves directly affected by such a law and social policy?

Instead of creating an America where some citizens feel insecure because of the color of their skin, it would be better to have an America where all citizens are encouraged to feel good about themselves. Feeling good about oneself includes feeling good about one's skin in all situations and conditions. Since our social infrastructure has long made some people feel insecure about themselves, because the values and mores of our mainstream American culture have already effectively zeroed them out, why not help all people to build their self-esteem and pride? Why not provide all citizens with "the equal protection of the laws" clause of the Fourteenth Amendment, as *Hopwood* correctly does, while also insisting on seeing and treating race as a positive attribute, instead of reverting to and emphasizing a negative racialized view of minority people by asking every American to pretend not to notice race? That experience is precisely what Ralph Ellison dramatized in *Invisible Man* (1947) when his black protagonist says: "I am an invisible man, I am invisible, understand, simply because people refuse to see me. . . . All my life I had been looking . . . for myself and asking everyone except myself questions which I, and only I, could answer." The convoluted self-doubts that Ellison's invisible man entertains are prompted largely by the refusal of people around him to see and to have commerce with him *because* of the color of his skin. *Hopwood* now *requires* Americans not to see and not to notice a person's skin. But what will such a federal court opinion do psychologically to the nearly 70 million Americans who are not white, given the personality damage that Ellison and Griffin, among other writers, have trenchantly captured?

My sense is that *Hopwood* in time will be overturned by the courts, since that is the arena where such changes have occurred. It will only happen, however, if the courts recognize and acknowledge the importance of race in a person's makeup and perspective. This position is constitutionally supported by the First, Ninth, Tenth, and Fifteenth Amendments, where race can be seen a part of the identity and an undeniable, inextricable possession of all Americans. Since race is inseparable from everything else that any one person is, why should it be the only aspect of a person that is singled out for denial, to be outlawed and erased, as *Hopwood* does?

As Chicano literature shows, Mexican Americans tend to be troubled by the same kind of invisibility that society imposed on Ellison's protagonist and on Griffin in *Black Like Me*. This psychological reality causes inner turmoil and uncertainty, as we will see in many ethnic minority narratives, including the texts analyzed in this study. Although Latinos who are now members of the professional organizations cited above have benefited from the Kennedy-Johnson decision overtly to extend civil rights protections to African Americans, further progress needs to be made and promoted, if the growing Latino middle class, like the African American one, is to counter successfully the assessment that Carey McWilliams made thirty and fifty years ago.[7]

In spite of the obstacles, some progress has been made. In a recent article in the *Austin American Statesman*, for example, Victor Landa, news director at KVDA-TV in San Antonio, Texas, pointed out that "between 1987 and 1992 Hispanic-owned businesses grew at three times the rate of that for all firms in the United States. Receipts rose by 135 percent, twice the overall rate, from $32.8 billion to $76.8 billion." Using the latest Census Bureau Report, which is published every five years between the ten-year official census counts, Landa identified the following trend-setting developments of the Latino business community:

Four years ago, the last time they were counted, there were 863,000 Hispanic-owned businesses in the country, making a lot of money and a lot of noise, paying taxes and salaries and helping the economy grow.

The majority of Hispanic-owned businesses are in California, with 250,000 firms. Texas is second with 156,000 businesses, and Florida comes in third with 118,000.

Nearly half of all of these businesses are in the service industry, which is outstanding when you consider that this unprecedented growth comes in the face of proven discriminatory lending practices, insurance red-lining and a growing and unfounded resentment across the country against a Hispanic community accused of "not wanting to assimilate."

U.S. Hispanics are making a lot of noise, contributing, and building a better nation despite the odds against them, and still not a word about it in major media outlets.[8]

Why, readers may ask, should such commercial activity and the continued population growth of Latinos matter? Why should non-Hispanic Americans develop and promote interest in Hispanics? Mainly because the nearly 32 million Latinos now living in the United States constitute the beginning of a different society for which all Americans ought to start preparing.

According to Steve Murdock, the U.S. Bureau of the Census projects that between 1990 and 2050 "ethnic diversity will increase substantially."

Due to higher rates and levels of immigration, roughly 9 of every 10 net additions to the U.S. population from 1990 through 2050 will be members of minority groups. Under the middle scenario, by 2050 the total population is projected to increase by 53.9 percent, but the Anglo population by only 7.3 percent; the Black population would increase by 96.2 percent, the Hispanic population by 260.9 percent, and the population in Other racial/ethnic groups by 375.4 percent. From 1990 to 2050, the proportion of the population that is Anglo could decline from 76 percent to 53 percent, while the Black proportion increases from 12 to 15 percent, the Hispanic proportion from 9 to more than 21 percent, and the Other racial/ethnic groups proportion from less than 4 to more than 11 percent.[9]

Most Americans, commentators have observed, do not especially feel affected by the fact that Latinos consist of a younger population that is already substantially shaping American fertility, mortality, and immigration rates. But preparing for the future requires everyone to develop a different perspective and to change their attitudes. For, although examples of progress can be found in the Hispanic community, the great majority of Latinos face difficult economic futures. Such prospects could considerably lower the standard of living for all Americans, if different social and political public policies are not soon developed to meet the changes that demographers like Murdock predict:

> Average annual per-household income could decline from 1990 levels by more than 5 percent by 2050 and the proportion of all households in poverty could increase by roughly 3 percent. Although the higher proportion of minority populations living in family household types that generally have higher household incomes will partially offset such patterns, it is evident that, if the relationships between resources and minority status do not change, the projected patterns of change will lead to general stagnation in household income in the United States and to increased rates of poverty.[10]

Demographic projections of this nature, reported by the media for more than a decade, are not being sufficiently factored into planning for the future. The actions of American society amply tell us that such population forecasts are still not part of our current national and local plans, leaving Latinos to deduce that mainstream Americans simply have too many other competing interests that they consider more important than the growing needs and realities of Hispanics. What is clear is that these needs, in one way or another, will still significantly alter and shape the future of the United States.

So where are Chicanos and Chicano literature today, as we close the twentieth century, and how do we explain the relative failure of Mexican American literature to communicate more successfully with the American citizenry and with a larger Latino reading audience? The answers to these questions lie in the natural links between Chicano literature, the low-expectation educations that most Mexican Americans now receive, and how the American media normally represent Chicanos. Education and the media—whose businesses, respectively, are to educate and to prepare people for the future, and to depict us in ways that facilitate and encourage success—are the two principal forces that have influenced and shaped Mexican American lives and behavior throughout the twentieth century.[11] Although Chicano literary scholars like Juan Bruce-Novoa, José Limón, Genaro Padilla, Ramon Saldívar, and José David Saldívar among others have emphasized different theoretical and new historicism approaches that illuminate the contours and parameters of Chicano literature, Mexican American writers have also consistently highlighted (1) the connections between Chicano aspirations and daily realities; (2) the images that the world knows, and which we ubiquitously see of ourselves, wherever Chicanos are represented by what has to be called an unsympathetic media; and (3) the wide failure to connect school experiences to opportunities for social growth for the great majority of Latinos in the United States.

Most non-Hispanic Americans have little or no response to both the absence of Latinos and the unattractive representations of Spanish-speaking citizens in American culture. Very few citizens, indeed, are even aware of the issue. The media daily shows us that little if any attention is given to how Latinos are represented because we are not seen as people living in the United States, but are often presumed to reside in Spanish-speaking countries. American Latinos respond in one of two ways to being socially constructed as foreigners: either we tend to overlook and dismiss such representations of ourselves, failing to challenge them, or we become irked enough to angrily clarify our status. The latter response often raises surprise and even astonishment among mainstream Americans. Either way, we lose, since most Latinos do not appear to know how to assert our presence in ways that will provide us with the type of attention and consideration that we deserve as resident American citizens.

Since we are conflated with and widely, though incorrectly, perceived as citizens of Mexico or as Hispanic immigrants to the United States, the role and place of Latinos in American life has never been properly established, acknowledged, or accepted, regardless of the efforts by Hispanic spokespeople and writers. Not being publicly represented as full-fledged Americans is an injustice that generation after generation has locked out many of our people from fully participating in all facets of the American experience. As Mexican Americans, we have effectively been shunted off into anonymity, and since our surnames, like our people, are not generally treated with much respect in America, except as a way to single us out as Hispanics to whom less attention can be paid, we are for that and other discriminatory reasons interchangeably mistaken one for another, sometimes raising humor if we justifiably insist on the linguistic integrity of our often mispronounced names. American society simply has not taught itself to expect much from Hispanics. For most Americans, we barely exist and then only when we are forced to call attention to our presence and needs. Most of the rest of the time, Latinos live in another America that here and there intersects with the rest of mainstream America.

Is it any wonder, in such a cultural environment, that many of our youngsters end up as nonproductive, self-denigrating, unwilling and unresponsive members in society? Most things in the United States clearly tell and show them that they do not fully participate in the challenges that engage other Americans. Again, when Chicanos have sought to raise awareness of these discouraging psychological realities, non-Hispanic Americans have generally been surprised. Perhaps they are too busy with their daily lives to be interrupted by the idea that America has reneged even on the run-of-the-mill promises that it holds out to its citizens. The Preamble to the Constitution, which the courts unfortunately dismiss as being too general to be useful, nonetheless specifically itemizes the following list of purposes, each of which ought to be relevant when we consider how minority people ought to be provided for: "establish justice, insure domestic tranquility, . . . promote the general welfare, and secure the blessings of liberty to ourselves and our posterity."

A society that does not provide these rights across the board for Hispanics, too, effectively tells us to go away, not to ask for help or support from the dominant American community. Because Latinos, like other minority populations in the United States, have not felt that these constitutional protections have been extended automatically to us without our having to fight for them, we have developed a self-sufficiency that prevents both mainstream Americans and Hispanics from finding common ground where we ought to be working to help each other more. Barring significant changes in how Latinos are educated and socialized, the United States is far from establishing the type of social and cultural commerce that fellow Americans of different races and cultures can share, benefit from, and enjoy.

Criminal justice statistics and any visit to the prisons tell us that our jails are disproportionately populated by minority people. Since education does not provide minorities with enough self-actualizing opportunities, too many minority youths turn to criminal activity. Surveys continually conclude that most Americans remain more interested in supporting incarceration than education. Is the media mainly responsible for making the reduction of crime the number one issue on which politicians continue to run for office year after year? On March 4, 1996, for example, the Center for Media and Public Affairs reported that throughout 1995 the three major network evening news shows aired "a record 2,574 stories about crime" out of 13,617 news stories broadcast. News programs are competing more and more with entertainment programs like *Hard Copy*, which have gradually outstripped their popularity. Because of their sensational appeal, crime reports have progressively become the main staple of the news business. "Crime received more coverage in 1995 than any news topic in recent years," reported the center, leading the "national news agenda."[12]

Although Mexican American leaders and writers tour the country advocating better educations and speaking against crime and gang activity, school districts have continued to provide the very same types of educations that have amply been proven to fail minority students. Instead of working with concerned Latino citizens to design more engaging, successful academic programs, school districts and the media regularly choose to placate the fears of the dominant white population, who tend to see minority populations as threatening a dwindling American pie, committing crimes, and being engaged in disruptive or subversive activities perceived as attempts to undermine the status quo hegemony.

Many calls from members of the Hispanic community for positive images to counter the negative stereotypes of Latinos fall on indifferent ears in the United States. Nowhere in American culture or on the educational landscape do we see the kind of images that sensible, educable young Hispanics would want to emulate.

Selena, the young Tejano music singing star from Corpus Christi, was a wonderful exception. The first Chicana to hit the top of the pop record charts with a combination of salsa, cumbia, polka, and conjunta music, she brought Mexican Americans to the forefront of the media. Chicanos proudly saw her as the next Gloria Estefan, the famous Cuban American singer. But, Selena's business manager tragically shot her to death on April 30, 1994, and with her went the dreams of many young Mexican Americans who had been indescribably excited by her music and by her growing presence on the larger American stage before her untimely death.[13]

At one point in the movie *Selena*, made three years after her death, Selena's father, played excellently by Edward James Olmos, has the following conversation with his daughter and her younger brother Abe, as the three Quintanilla family members drive in their van:

SELENA: So cool to go to Monterrey!
DAD: I'm not so sure right now.
ABE: You said everything's a risk, right?
DAD: They don't accept us over there. They never have.

SELENA: Hello?! We're Mexican!
DAD: No, we are Mexican Americans! They don't like Mexican Americans.
ABE: No, it's all the same . . .
DAD: They can be mean. They can tear us apart over there. Selena's Spanish is . . .
SELENA: What about my Spanish? I've been singing in Spanish for ten years. It's perfect.
DAD: Singing, yes, but when you speak it, you speak a little funny . . . I have been there. You've got to speak perfectly or the press will eat you up; spit you out alive—I have seen them do it.
SELENA: Oh, Dad, you're overreacting again . . .
ABE: Dad, the music will speak for itself, Dad.
DAD: Listen, being Mexican American is tough. Anglos jump all over all if you don't speak English perfectly. Mexicans jump all over you if you don't speak Spanish perfectly. We've got to be twice as perfect as anybody else. [*Abe and Selena laugh.*] Why are you laughing? What's so funny? I am serious . . . Our family has been here four centuries, yet they treat us as if we just swam across the Rio Grande. I mean we got to know about John Wayne and Pedro Infante. We got to know about Frank Sinatra and Augustin Lara. We got to know about Oprah and Christina. Anglo food is too bland; yet when we go to Mexico we get the runs. Now that's too embarrassing. Japanese Americans, Italians, German Americans, their homeland is on the other side of the ocean. Ours is right next door—right over there. And we got to prove to the Mexicans how Mexican we are; we got to prove to the Americans how American we are. We gotta be more Mexican than the Mexicans and more American than the Americans! Both at the same time! It is exhausting! Man, nobody know how tough it is to be a Mexican American![14]

Here we have one of the best expressions available anywhere in American culture regarding the differences that one generation sees and a younger one does not. Either the attention of members of the next generation is not sufficiently focused on realities that are widely known, or they already are experiencing another kind of reality.

In the eyes of Selena's father, the life of a Mexican American is a very taxing endeavor because the expectations from American culture and Mexican society pull Chicanos in different directions. Neither mainstream Americans nor Mexicans sufficiently understand or appreciate the fact that Mexican Americans are strongly shaped by the tension that the two cultures create. For this reason, Chicanos tend to show signs of irresoluteness, ambivalency, and what might be called, for want of a better term, imbalance. Revealing, too, is the view that Mexican people are not especially sympathetic to the problems that Mexican Americans face, a perspective that complicates relationships between the two, although this is not always the case.

The theory that might be constructed here is that on a spectrum between mainstream Americans and Mexican society, Mexican Americans can be found anywhere between the two larger societies—some closer to the American end, and others closer to Mexico. In either case, the issue is personal and sometimes psychologically uncomfortable for Chicanos, especially since our ideal is to be comfortable in the American society where many of us live. What we see in Selena's father, for example, is a high degree of discomfort, though that does not appear to be the case with the younger generation, so long as they are encouraged to feel good about themselves. This is why we can say that on the strength of a Chicana singer from south Texas, the doors of the American media have been opened by a film like *Selena*. Another important motion picture that has advanced Latino education is the 1988 film *Stand and Deliver*, starring Edward James Olmos and Lou Diamond Phillips. It remains to be seen, however, whether relations between these two cultures will be comfortable or as troubled as they have been in the past.

What is important to note here is that except for Selena, who achieved fame in an unprecedented way for a young Mexican American woman, most of our youths, like African American and Native American youths, are not aware of enough successful Hispanics in the United States to emulate. This lack of models tends to discourage youngsters, often so much that they give up on themselves early in life. Such a reality is not due to culture and upbringing, as some commentators, like University of Texas law professor Leo Graglia, have posited. Rather, it is because our young people are seldom exhorted and worked with to exert themselves to the best of their abilities. Mexican Americans, instead, are not expected to excel in any area requiring sustained endeavor.

If the parents themselves are not educated enough to be in a financial position to support and encourage Latino youngsters, then the task necessarily ought to fall on the schools, an idea not sufficiently embraced by educators. Consequently, most Hispanic students are simply passed from school grade to school grade, most without ever being challenged, in a positive way, to reach their full potential in an academic discipline, in sports, or in much of anything else. Because of this, many Chicanos end up abandoning education, the main road to generational change and success in America.

Rousseau and Foucault saw education and crime as closely related realities. Both paths offer opposing life avenues for minority youngsters, as Luis J. Rodriguez's 1993 book *Always Running: La Vida Loca: Gang Days in L.A.* amply makes clear. A more contemporary version of Piri Thomas's *Down These Mean Streets* (1967), *Always Running* dramatizes the harrowing, deadly gang life of Los Angeles Chicanos, a natural extension of a long-established barrio way of life, as we will see in Anthony Quinn's *The Original Sin*. Like Pat Mora, Carmen Tafolla, and Gary Soto, who write and promote Latino children's literature, since writing *Always Running* Luis Rodriguez has committed himself to encouraging Latino youngsters to express themselves with words and not through violence. But these dedicated writers have their work clearly before them. As things now stand for many young Latinos, the lure of a financially more rewarding life of crime outshines a boring, seemingly purposeless schooling that leads to a deadend, low-paying job. Perhaps that is why too many minority youths opt for crime. Education offers Latinos and other minorities no viable goals and it fails to promise them anything that, as they clearly see life, is worth their efforts.[15]

Happily, exceptions can be pointed to that counter this grim scenario, but as Douglas Kellner brought out in his book *Media Culture*, the representational world is ubiquitous in creating, determining, and sustaining the dominant mores and values of a culture. Little, in short, remains untouched and unaffected by the images and signals that newspapers, radio, television, and movies give to people to help us navigate through American culture and the world. Represented reality, in fact, often overshadows other daily realities, since, by comparison, the latter appear mundane and less exciting than life as represented on the tube, the radio, or the internet.

Since technology allows us to focus attention on what we want and to filter out what is less desirable, certain perspectives, people, attitudes, and ways of life are continually being strengthened and nourished, while others are assumed to be dead, dying, or *passé*, based largely on the amount and the quality of the media exposure they receive. The American media frequently diminish or downright erase Latinos, thereby telling everyone the kind of people who are valued and appreciated in the United States and what kind are not. Emerging realities that might be used to enhance the self-esteem of Mexican Americans and Latinos are routinely constructed and reshaped by the media to render, not the new professional class of Latinos, but the older, stereotyped representations that American audiences expect and like to ridicule or laugh at. Stereotypes, indeed, call for mindless, known representations that invite dismissal, but dealing with a new emerging reality calls for reconceptualization and recasting.

Instead of hiring a Mexican American actress to play the part of murdered Tejano music star Selena, Hollywood impresarios chose a Puerto Rican actress to portray her in a movie about the singer's life. Given Selena's success, everyone knew that the film would be a box-office hit, as it was.[16] This choice told Chicanas, who also vied for the role, that the film industry and its audiences are still not favorably disposed toward Mexican American women. Hollywood, in short, continues to prefer other types of Latina women whom movie moguls have traditionally employed. In what might be called the mediafication process—that is, the creation or the transformation of people into acceptable images for advertising, marketing, and cultural consumption—Mexican Americans continue been seen as undesirable, as Ana Castillo scintillatingly demonstrates in *Massacre of the Dreamers.*

In addition to being erased by both Hollywood and *Hopwood*, American Latinos continue to be culturally deleted in all sorts of other ways. The constant media message is that we need to change ourselves in order to fit the images that most Americans have or would like to have of Hispanics.[17] In the 1995 film *The Perez Family*, for instance, neither Mexican American nor even other Latino actors were chosen to portray Mexican Americans. In this instance, studio magnates let it be known that American audiences, in their cavalier estimation, would not likely pay to see real Latino actors. Hispanics did not object; some of us even went to see a movie that employed American actors unfamiliar with Latino customs, but who had more name recognition, portraying Latino men and women on the big screen. By not being selected, of course, Latino and Latina actors are denied the opportunity to become name actors whom the public will recognize and pay to see.

These types of experiences continue to typify the nature of Latinos' interaction not only with the entertainment industry, but also with other American media. Publications written by and about Chicanos, similarly, often are not reviewed, because editors and publishers wonder, sometimes even aloud in the 1990s, exactly what they used to wonder in the 1930s, "Would anyone be interested enough to buy books about Mexican Americans?" That, we may recall, is what the British critics asked about American literature in the 1820s, when a similar remark from his wife prompted James Fenimore Cooper to write his first romance, *Precaution*.

Not affirming the presence of Hispanics in American life and mass culture causes both disaffection and ambivalence among Latinos toward ideas and things American, feelings that sometimes even lead to the Mexican American hostility that Octavio Paz observed and analyzed in his 1959 book *El Laberinto de la Soledad*, translated as *The Labyrinth of Solitude*. Chicano books, like the four texts analyzed in this study, describe the troubled adjustments of Mexican Americans to American culture. The semi-autobiographical stories of Guálinto Gomez and Esperanza Cordero and the autobiographical narratives of Anthony Quinn and Ana Castillo amply dramatize conflicted personalities that often leave Hispanics psychologically wounded. A host of poems too long to mention here and other Chicano books, like Oscar Zeta Acosta's *The Autobiography of a Brown Buffalo* and Richard Rodriguez's *Hunger of Memory: The Education of Richard Rodriguez* also show that the personal cost of succeeding for Mexican Americans and Latinos in the United States is high and often quite traumatizing.

If Latinos in the United States are to feel accepted and comfortable enough to help contribute to our country's economy and our communal future, the nature of our experiences must be improved until our lives are on a par with those of other Americans. Instead of growing up to be perceived as a burden or drawback to the larger American community, I believe all American Latinos ought to strive to be educated well enough to pay our own way, allowing everyone, in turn, to contribute to society's progress. But without genuine efforts both by other Americans and by Latinos to improve the barrio lives captured in books like Rudolfo Anaya's *Heart of Aztlan* and Sandra Cisneros's *The House on Mango Street*, Hispanics will continue to live uncertainly, facing bleak prospects, and failing to provide the United States with a growing population that can serve as a considerable resource to sustain and improve America's role in the world.

The little information about Latinos that is now nationally, regionally, and locally disseminated in the United States is usually included on a "space-filler basis" on television, newspapers, radio, and the internet. Such peripheral acknowledgment only underscores the marginal place of Hispanics in American culture. Crime, killings, robberies, drugs, and other negative news items should not be the main way to portray Hispanics to other citizens of the United States. When mainstream America's attention is secured, say, by a one-hour, one-night television program like the generic *Latin Night,* which aired in July 1995, media coverage should not ignore the event the next day. Latino media activities and positive news items, when communicated at all, are given brief treatment or are trivialized by commentators and columnists. Radio talk-show host Howard Stern, for example, comfortable in his iconoclasm, recently reminded listeners that things Hispanic are "foreign" and not really part of American culture.

Negative portrayals of Latinos are so frequent in the American media that they amount to drive-by shootings, or hit-and-run media events. Hispanics are seldom mentioned or acknowledged, and when we are it is usually in negative ways. Thoughtless, nasty, and even unethical representations, when permitted by the people who manage the media industry, reveal pervasive media attitudes and perspectives that inhibit cooperation between Latinos and other Americans. On such occasions, mainstream audiences are quietly being invited to enjoy ethnic stereotypes, and we seldom hear objections or dissent from American leaders, responsible media sources, or other citizens of the United States. Such unethical drive-by tactics besmirching ethnic populations need to be called to the attention of the media and educators.

Negative responses to Latinos and Hispanic cultures in the United States can be traced at least as far back as Francis Parkman's 1847 text, *The Oregon Trail.* Before that, attitudinal differences and downright dislike between Anglos and Hispanics gave rise to the American war with Mexico of 1846, to the Alamo (1836), and perhaps can even be traced back to the 1588 defeat of the Spanish Armada.[18] Such legacies continue to influence people, making racial frictions difficult to overcome, but that is exactly what the current challenge requires. Parkman is singled out here because this Harvard history professor seldom mentions Hispanics in his book, but when he does, he immediately depicts Spanish-speaking people as "swarthy ignoble Mexicans" with "brutish faces" (Chapter 7). Parkman and his fellow historians are important because they helped to shape the opinions of many leading Americans of the nineteenth century, as David Teague has brought out in *The Southwest in American Literature and Art.* In *Gente Decente,* Leticia Garza-Falcón has also shown how in the twentieth century Walter Prescott Webb's histories distorted realities to emphasize the Manifest Destiny ideas championed by Parkman and his contemporaries. These influential historians represented Mexicans as people who were to be scorned as much and as openly as Native Americans were, even though Parkman also claimed to admire the latter.

The Oregon Trail has been taught in higher education institutions throughout the United States for more than one hundred and fifty years. As a perennial favorite among American readers, Parkman's book is one of the most popular first-person historical narratives that attractively communicates the matter-of-course, *educated* person's belief that it is acceptable behavior to treat Mexicans, Blacks, and Native Americans with contempt and disdain. These minority people are anthropologically cast as too different to be assimilated into American society, encouraging armchair historians interested in the progress of Manifest Destiny ideas to look down on the strange ways of "these people," an offensive, patronizing way repeatedly used to designate minorities. Books promoting jingoistic views of such ilk prompt and continue to encourage ethnic and racial divisions, producing untold psychological damage to all citizens who are encouraged to engage in the practice of devaluing other people, making it easier for such populations to be overlooked, disregarded, and then turned into disadvantaged Americans.

Since before the mid-nineteenth-century war with Mexico, which appears to have fanned the dislike that Parkman and many Americans have held toward people of Mexican and Hispanic descent, non-Hispanic Americans have not looked kindly upon Latinos. In Texas, for example, Hispanic landowners were gradually dispossessed of property, as the census records following the fall of the Alamo in San Antonio show: "Although incomplete, the 1840 census showed that Tejanos owned 85.1 percent of the town lots at San Antonio, along with 63.8 percent of land claims with completed titles. On the 1850 census, however, they owned only 9.1 percent of real estate values claimed, and only 7.8 percent on the 1860 census."[19] Despite the 1824 Monroe Doctrine, which was arguably ratified to keep foreign countries from acquiring land in the Americas as well as to promote control of the economies of Latin America, the United States has not developed the type of commercial and social ties that, for instance, we have developed with Canada, our northern neighbor. Not until the 1993–1994 North American Free Trade Agreement (NAFTA) has Mexico been offered favored economic treatment. American views of Latinos, in short, have been pretty consistent for many years, and improving how Hispanics are seen will not be easy, but that is what the current situation requires.

Only after the 1927 founding of LULAC, the League of United Latin American Citizens and the 1948 founding of the American G.I. Forum, both in Corpus Christi, Texas, did Latinos start to receive some reluctantly accorded recognition as contributing members of American society. Even so, today the majority of Latinos are still widely perceived as menial laborers, as employees who care for the custodial and physical plant facilities of America.[20]

What response, indeed, should Hispanics have toward their country when their fellow citizens' behavior repeatedly underscores the fact that Americans seldom think of or include Hispanics in conversations, commercials, research, and education when the future of the United States is addressed?

4

Hispanics and the American Media

When we study the representation of Latinos in the American media up to and throughout the 1990s, we find what reluctantly has to be characterized as insistent disregard for most things Hispanic. Such neglect, as suggested in the previous chapter, psychologically damages both Latinos and the larger American population, since the former have to adjust to being consistently excluded and the latter remain ignorant and unaware of the progress and remarkable efforts of Latinos in the United States. This charge has been leveled against American society by Hispanics since the late 1960s and early 1970s. The American media has made it clear that mainstream society does not have time, space, or inclination to focus attention on Hispanic matters. When Latinos are given a little news space in the American media, the issues are usually illegal immigration, crime, low educational attainment, or demographic projections that raise anxiety in the rest of the population. This type of news coverage of Hispanic affairs, in effect, alarms the larger population of the United States into wondering if, by paying attention to Hispanics, American society will be turned into a Latino culture. Since the 1980s, demographic studies have projected a Brown Wave, that is, substantial increases in the growth of the Hispanic population. If the United States were to develop a commonsensical interest in Hispanics in order to prepare for our country's future, an attitudinal change would also be enormously helpful to all Americans and to our policy-setting entities.

Two related news items received a little national attention in the mid-1990s because they dramatized how the media represent Hispanic realities within the context of the larger American society. First, in May 1994, the National Council of La Raza created a media event, covered by the *New York Times*, out of the fact that the Smithsonian Institution in Washington, D.C., has not, until very recently, collected Hispanic materials and artifacts. As far as the collections at the Smithsonian show, Americans could conclude that until the summer of 1994 Hispanics did not exist in the United States. Now that America's national museum has been made aware of our presence and has publicly acknowledged the fact that Latinos are born, raised, and live entire lives in the United States, particularly in the Southwest, the current director informed a press conference that the Smithsonian, which is devoted to the preservation of all things American, would *start* to collect Hispanic materials.

So where have Hispanics been living all of these years? Judging by the Smithsonian's collections, Hispanics have not officially existed within the United States throughout the history of this country. We have not lived in Chicago, Philadelphia, Washington, New York, Florida, Texas, New Mexico, Arizona, Nevada, Utah, California, and throughout all those other cities, villages, and towns of the northeast, the midwest, the west, and the south where our surnames pepper the phone books. I think it would be difficult to find another comparable case where a whole people, who, having so willingly served the United States on all fronts whenever called, have been so systematically *erased* from the national consciousness by the very agency commissioned by our American government to preserve the national past.

Some African Americans, as we know, left slave narratives that are still being recovered. Despite Lincoln's 1863 Emancipation Proclamation, blacks have since continued to experience outright discrimination and all sorts of other objectionable human rights abuses that, as in the case of other minority populations, have long been ignored. W. E. B. Du Bois's 1900 prediction that "the color line" would be the twentieth century's chief problem has proven correct; for, so long as we do not properly educate people to appreciate and take pride in the color of their skin, race will separate human beings. Native Americans, American history constantly reminds us, for people who will see, were decimated and consciously dispersed, breaking up community-centered lives that many Americans profess to admire. Asian Americans, every-

one knows, were also not historically welcomed. Although they helped
settle and develop the West, they were largely left out of accounts of its
history. Along with Hispanics, all three of these larger minority groups
continue to labor as our country's menial workers, living testaments to
the poor quality of the educations they received.

Hispanics, to underscore the point, have traditionally been ignored
and continue to be disregarded, in spite of considerable talk about the
professed values of "cultural diversity" and "multiculturalism." Indeed, if we pay close attention, we will observe that Hispanics are
oddly missing or only tangentially included in most dialogues about
diversity, even when the needs of "minorities" are being discussed.
When referencing Hispanics what we have—and one cannot soften
the nature of the "oversight" much—is a vast and pervasive national
unwillingness to acknowledge almost everything that is Hispanic.
Other than the Taco Bells, Taco Cabanas, and other corporate entities that are now capitalizing on selling Mexican American food, the
concerted disregard toward Hispanics that we see across American
cultural life, amply covers all facets of Hispanic life in the United
States.

That is why in the twentieth century, Latinos in the United States
have particularly turned to developing our own media avenues and our
own ways of publicizing our news, events, and accomplishments. We
have had to create our own worlds within America, our own ways of
building, asserting, and promoting the self-esteem and securing the attention that the larger American society has denied our communities
and our individual men and women. Such efforts have long existed, but
because the Latino presence and influence is increasing, we are only
now beginning to be noticed by the wider American society. For all of
these reasons, we need to talk about this division, for we have long been
one of the least noticed people in America. At a time when more Hispanics are trying to enter the professions, few people in America notice
or observe that relatively few Latinos successfully "make it." We are
very far from meeting the current needs of our people and American society, given our considerable and expected future demographic growth.
Some aspects of Hispanic culture, such as our food and some forms of
our music, for instance, are making progressive incursions into American life, though promoted mainly by non-Hispanic corporations and
entrepreneurs. But, according to most scorekeepers, we sadly lag behind in virtually everything else—and, it needs to be said, the resistance

against Hispanic progress seems to increase as soon as Latinos venture out into the larger American community.

How has the American public media served us? The Center for Media and Public Affairs in Washington, D.C., held a September 1, 1994, news conference to publicize its report titled *Distorted Reality: Hispanic Characters in TV Entertainment*, prepared by S. Robert Lichter and Daniel R. Amundson, announcing what arguably may well be the most startling fact regarding Latinos in the United States—that television blatantly ignores Hispanics. The report, which received coverage only in the less prominent pages of some of the country's newspapers, also noted that when television occasionally deigns to turn the cameras on Hispanics, invariably we are portrayed negatively—often very explicitly as downright criminals—or as background space-filler people.

Consider for a moment what such coverage would likely do to a group of people who for nearly fifty years have been daily rendered as undesirables before the national mirror. Why do we then wonder that our children often drop out of school? Worse, how can some members of the larger American citizenry self-righteously blame the parents of Hispanic and other minority youths when they fail? Why do we fault Hispanic adults for ignoring and often refusing to participate in the highly touted competitive "American way of life" that so offensively excludes almost all of our people?

When I saw the Center's report in the local paper, I immediately went out to seek what I hoped would be better coverage in the *New York Times*. But there was nothing about Latinos in that day's issue. The National Council of La Raza, which also called a news conference to publicize the Center's *Distorted Reality* report, apparently failed to create enough interest to make the country's most important paper that day, and I lost interest in seeing what other newspapers in the United States covered this significant Hispanic media milestone during the next few days.

Why should all Americans pay attention and wonder what might be done when television is characterized as a "vast wasteland" for Hispanic Americans?

It is a little satisfying to hear that research centers and institutes have finally begun to take note of what some Hispanics have been saying for years about the media representation of Hispanic life in the United States. For, in different ways, Hispanics have been requesting, perhaps too politely, more attention for our people for three or four generations. But it was not until the *Distorted Reality* study, which relied on the social science method of content and quantitative analysis, that the media was made officially aware of the fact that the nature of Latino culture in this country needs dire improvement if Hispanic Americans are to be embraced as Americans instead of excluded as assumed foreigners. For Hispanic Americans, everything remains to be seen; we are carefully watching how both the rhetoric and the actions of the media and the American nation respond to the growing Latino presence.

The Center for Media and Public Affairs found the following quantifiable facts:

- That Hispanics comprise only 1 percent of all characters on entertainment TV today; forty years ago, in the 1950s, to compare, 3 percent of the characters on American television were Hispanic.
- Forty-five percent of Hispanic characters on "reality-based" TV programs commit crimes, compared to 10 percent of their white counterparts. The study found "that whites are shown enforcing the laws and minorities breaking them." Does this representation resemble reality too closely?
- Although very few Hispanics appear on TV, the few who do are portrayed negatively. Forty-one percent are portrayed negatively, compared to 31 percent of whites and 24 percent of blacks.
- Twenty-two percent of Hispanics are represented as unskilled laborers, compared to 16 percent of Blacks and 13 percent of whites.
- One out of every five Hispanics on TV is a criminal, as opposed to one out of every nine whites and one of every fourteen blacks.

That is exactly the way that Hispanics are represented by television for our youths to admire and emulate, and for all the world to see. Need we wonder why so many Hispanic parents and youngsters are unengaged and feel like rejecting some aspects of "American life"?

If we look at how newspapers, radio, and advertising depict Hispanics, we see that these widely disseminated negative images directly shape and influence how Hispanics are treated and responded to not only in the United States but everywhere in the world. Next to the outrageous misrepresentations of Native Americans, how the media continues to portray America's Latino population is the biggest case of communal traducement and misrepresentation perpetrated against a people.

African Americans have spokespeople such as Jesse Jackson and the NAACP who continue to speak out against the distortions and misrepresentations. With two or possibly three not very widely known exceptions, Latinos have not had the benefit of being defended or promoted by known voices or champions. Cesar Chavez spoke out for the California field and migrant workers in the 1960s, but the leaders envisioned by enlightened intellectuals like Carey McWilliams and other less known Chicano activists in the late 1960s simply have not materialized during the last thirty years. Chicano leaders have not developed largely because of the poor education available to our people, the images of ourselves that we have variously internalized, and, as Chicano literature shows, because we have not been sufficiently able to disassociate ourselves from the negative stereotypes that everywhere surround us in our own homeland, the United States.

Since Hispanics tend to speak Spanish, or combinations of English and Spanish, too many unsympathetic Americans simply assume that Hispanics can be ridiculed for the way we speak and represented in all sorts of demeaning ways. Rarely are we imagined sympathetically and as useful, productive citizens, even though most Americans know us as a people who have shown that we are willing to work to improve American society. Careless treatment of anyone in America, we are too slowly learning, has a way of affecting everyone. Regarding the long perpetuated misrepresentation of Hispanics, Raul Yzaguirre, president of the National Council of La Raza, has said:

> The toll it has taken on our population in terms of image and public goodwill has been enormous. Every day, we watch television programs that show we are not a part of the American community, that the only Hispanics visible to the mainstream population are drug lords, illegal immigrants, and criminals. Television exacerbates the stereotypes we face every day at work and throughout society; and it profoundly impacts the self-images our children develop.[1]

This information, to be sure, is not new, but the warranted disturbance that Hispanics seek to create by calling attention to these facts is. Scholars like Americo Paredes, Alfredo Mirandé, and Carl Gutiérrez-Jones have long discussed how Latinos have been consistently criminalized, with little or no observable improvement.

The Center for Media and Public Affairs study examines television programming in the United States from the 1950s to the 1980s, and it ends by focusing attention on television programming in the early 1990s. To drive home its conclusions, the study goes further and actually presents report cards on the major television networks. ABC, for example, receives a grade of F; CBS is rated C−; NBC earns a solid D; and FOX, the newest network, earns a solid F. It is instructive to see that the youngest television network feels that it can totally omit portraying Hispanics.

The Center for Media and Public Affairs has announced that it intends to conduct yearly studies to monitor the representation of Hispanics on television. I looked forward to these reports, wondering how the American media would respond. However, no reports have appeared for 1996, 1997, 1998, or 1999. I suspect that, when the report first came out, journalists simply wrote perfunctory stories, then returned to their regular issues. I was also interested in seeing, indeed, if this first report would make any difference to the television executives who plan the television programs. Marketing and financial considerations, I knew, would have to be examined anew, since the media are used to telling us how to view the different age and ethnic groups in the United States. The point is that the leading networks now know—even if the newspapers and much of the general public seems to have missed the important news—that the growing awareness of ethnicity during the last three decades has completely bypassed Hispanics in television land as it has on the big silver screen, and Latinos are awaiting improvements.

But does television mirror reality, or does reality mirror television? The answer, of course, is that both mutually shape and influence each other, as politicians who seek good press coverage have amply demonstrated. For this reason, what happens in television is extremely important for Hispanics, American society, and the world. The situation that needs to be addressed is that Hispanics and the general population are not being helped by either television or reality, as things now stand.

Hispanics are starved for some models worth admiring, emulating, and holding in some comfortable regard. The current state of the media's representation of Hispanics, as suggested earlier, is the primary reason why both our adults and our young people are disaffected and remain uninvolved. We are almost totally unappreciated in American life. Hispanics, however, are not uninvolved by choice, for, as most people know, individually and communally we Latinos tend to be warm, caring people. My personal view is that Hispanics have been socialized and very effectively taught not to participate, not to believe and to feel that our views count. We have consequently learned—too well, I would add—to walk away from activities that have traditionally left us out; and, to avoid being excluded again and again, we now go about excluding ourselves. For this reason, many of us are now disinclined to participate in many American activities, like voting, enrolling in local clubs, and joining and supporting educational groups. Some of us, to be sure, participate in the work of our communities, but most Hispanics do not because have been taught and have learned to stay away. We simply do not feel comfortable joining the Rotarians or the Lions Club or other local, regional, and state associations. Like other ethnic groups in this country, namely African Americans and Native Americans, Hispanics have consequently chosen to create our own worlds where we are more comfortable. Many of us are reluctant to involve ourselves with people who continue either to demean or to represent us in unattractive ways. Who enjoys being misrepresented or patronized all the time?

I believe I am correct in saying that Hispanic allegiance and respect for almost all things American is well known, especially during moments of crises such as war or threats of war. Yet, if anybody was to base his or her sense of America on what the Smithsonian collects, on what the American media represent, or on what appears in advertisements, that person would likely conclude that Hispanics do not exist or have not long lived in the United States. Whenever Hispanics are allowed visual or print media presence, it is generally to support Anglo Americans who represent the more "American" positions or issues. Who speaks out to say that Hispanics are also born in the United States and that we are as American as Bob Hope? Instead of being regarded and represented as Americans, too many of us are subtly or directly excluded, disregarded, and then treated as inconsequential people. Does this type of treatment continue to make sense in the face of the fact that all demographic projections expect Hispanics to be the largest minority in the United States by the year 2010?

The complaint is not new. In 1983, for example, Raul Yzaguirre appeared before a federal congressional subcommittee on telecommunications to make much the same point:

> It has become widely accepted that the electronic media, and especially television, are a major socializing force in the United States. Consciously and unconsciously, viewers tend to adopt many of the perspectives presented on the screen, and to see the Nation as it is portrayed not only on the evening

news, but also in the situation comedies, detective shows, and other fictional programming.

It is also widely recognized—at least by specialists in the field—that the current portrayals of minorities on television tend to reinforce ethnic and racial stereotypes. . . . Non-Hispanics who take their cues from the electronic media are likely to perceive all Hispanics as poorly educated, semiliterate, unable to speak clear English, employable only in menial jobs, unassertive and probably lazy, yet extremely prone to gang violence and the commission of felonies with knives.[2]

Such words have apparently continued to fall on deaf ears in Washington and in the media industry, but if the trend continues, if we continue to fail to make full use of the human resources offered to the United States by Latinos, our country is going to be hopelessly enmeshed in the racial and social problems that we are already beginning to experience.

The *Distorted Reality* study conducted by the Center for Media and Public Affairs found that today "Hispanics are less visible in prime time than they were in the 1950s." At that time Latinos were supposed to be thankful for Desi Arnaz, who played the role of Ricky Ricardo, the one Cuban entertainer on American television, and for Bill Dana's portrayal of Jose Jimenez. Did we then and have we ever had even one Mexican American person, male or female, about whom we as a people could actually feel good and claim as our own? Frankly, at this late date I still cannot name a single TV person or personality who is universally known. Even Edward James Olmos, Paul Rodriguez, and Eric Estrada do not command the type of recognition that any number of other mainstream American movie stars do. Among women, one can only think of Rita Moreno and the rising Jennifer Lopez, both Puerto Rican actresses.

Have Hispanics ever had a laudable, high-profile television actor or actress who has made us feel that we are part of America and that we can expect successful futures in this beautiful country? Again, no name readily emerges. Guy Williams, the actor who played Zorro in several Disney productions in the late 1950s and early 1960s, appeared Hispanic, though he actually looked more like Errol Flynn, that other flamboyant swashbuckler who made amorous Casanovas out of most Hispanic male teenagers at one time or another. But the Hispanic Casanova, like the legendary prototype, also follows many of the stereotypes that we see on television, mirroring and helping to explain unattractive Hispanic realities. Who, for instance, would be interested in growing up to be like Bill Dana, who used to say "My name's Jose Jimenez," other than comedians wanting to laugh at how Hispanics mispronounce words?

Regarding women, I cannot honestly say that I remember even one Hispanic woman on the big or the little American screen. When I vaguely recall one, I see her as one of those morally loose, provocative vixens luring men into disreputable actions or situations. I do, on the other hand, remember Marga Lopez, Lola Beltran, Sarita Montiel, Libertad Lamarque, Maria Felix, Flor Silvestre, and some other older women who peopled the Mexican films that we used to see in south Texas when I was growing up. But very few Americans saw these films, and gone are the days when they peopled movie screens with actresses more worthy of emulation.

According to the Smithsonian, apparently our Chicano childhoods never happened, since we have not officially existed in the United States, even though Latinos have been living throughout the Southwest since the sixteenth century. Who knows, for example, that 1748 is the year that the Spanish land grants of Nuevo Santander opened up south Texas, leading to the settlement of the area? This fact remains to be brought out in a way that will register culturally in the American psyche.[3] Despite the work of David Montejano, Gilberto Hinojosa, Richard Griswold del Castillo, Leticia Garza-Falcón, and other Chicanos who have written histories ignored by school textbooks, here in Texas, for example, historical accounts dismiss events before the fall of the Alamo. The Native American Texas past or the founding of Nuevo Santander in south Texas, as brought out by Armando Alonzo in his book *Tejano Legacy*, needs to be championed more. Everyone knows the John Wayne Alamo story and the defeat that the victorious Mexicans soldiers suffered after in San Jacinto. Even today these events are reenacted at the San Jacinto Monument in southeast Houston every year, lest Texans and Mexican Americans forget the Alamo. "But how *can* anyone forget?" Chicanos say. This celebration is as unifying as those in which southern whites bring out the Dixie flag whenever possible, unmindful that such a symbol blatantly reminds today's African Americans of slavery and oppression.

We need to consider which historical events ought to be commemorated, and why we need to remember certain occasions. For not all historical occurrences are worthy of commemoration. We also require events and occasions that show positive Hispanic images on television, in the newspapers, and in films, images that can constructively both shape Hispanic lives and be transmitted to the world.

At the individual level, throughout my forty years in academic life, I have been met with a type of educated but nonetheless condescending curiosity which, in effect, subtly says again and again: What can a Mexican American think about? What could a Mexican American say that would be worth our attention and time? "Our," of course, refers to the media and to the high-brow professors who openly used to quip about others like them, "Oh, he's one of us"—professionals, of course, who politely said nothing if the person was not "one of us," such things having been visibly understood.

Nowadays people say less brazen things. And that has changed because minorities have had to insist on improving practices. In too many quarters Latinos who speak up for their civil rights are seen as pushy, aggressive, and downright rude or crude when we stand our ground or assert a different view. Some of us have had to be strongly persistent, since little has been handed to us, and almost everything else naturally assumed by the dominant society is usually withheld or not sufficiently and effectively communicated or made available to us. Life today is a little different, but the old biases tend to remain, altered, but nonetheless present.[4] Differences among Latinos will thus elicit a variety of responses, shaped in part by bifurcated political allegiances, the conservatives and the liberals.

On the political spectrum, Hispanics are continually lured by one party on one issue, then encouraged by the other party on another issue. The upshot of such courting, if courting it is, is only good until the next racist faux pas occurs to stop progress anew. Like other minority groups, Hispanics still encounter considerable intolerance in one form or another almost everywhere in America. Since we do not have an acknowledged, visible, communal presence that represents us in a positive way, negative experiences are a regular part of life. When we remind ourselves that the current generation has been exposed to events mainly since the passage of the 1964 Civil Rights Act, we have to observe that racial consciousness is still too tentatively ingrained, even in the supposedly educated Americans, to offer Latinos and other minority people much of a different world.

The last thirty-five years have not made as much of a difference as we thought and hoped they would.[5] People of different races are still quite uncomfortable when dealing with each other. Comfort zones seem to be the most important consideration when people from different races interact. People are either comfortable or they are not, and much of everything else appears to depend on the racial chemistry that occurs between individuals. I suspect that the thing to do now is to outlaw racism, and then to cure it, much as we have considerably reduced hazing, sexual harassment, and even smoking—all practices that people once thought could never be significantly curtailed or eliminated. I mention such an option because we need to start with the majority of our educators, who seem to have chosen not to emphasize the beauties of learning to live across, among, and next to people from different cultural and racial backgrounds. Educators talk a good talk, but youngsters in the schools are not taught how to like and how to appreciate people who are not like them. As a consequence, the racial divisions remain and the discomfort felt with people of other races continues to shape reality unabated.

Unfortunately, what we have emphasized in our schools, neighborhoods, and communities is the harmful idea that we are all better than our neighbors. We continue to teach our young that they need to learn to rely on themselves and not to pay as much attention to their peers as they do. In American schools, I was essentially taught to rely on myself, and to need other people mainly when there was little choice. This notion is part of the American Creed, and, despite the good, strong qualities of individualism produced by this most American of philosophies, I am also convinced that the idea wreaks havoc on the development of our people, young and old, and, ironically, on our way of life.

We can see this socially detrimental view at work almost everywhere if we look carefully. Take a bus station, a restaurant, or a ball game, to name a few of the places where people congregate. We tend to visit these places with friends, usually with people who look like us—unless, of course, we happen to be with fellow employees and thus are making the best of the situations under which we work. But when we have choice, we frequently choose to be with people with whom we feel comfortable, with people who could be our race and blood relatives.

What about the rest of the world? Disregard it, we are in effect told, largely because other people do not generally promote our interests, or because they do not directly affect us, except unfortunately as obstacles, nuisances, or as sources of inconvenience. The perspective is decidedly unchristian but quite widespread. I am talking now even about educated people, people who should have been taught otherwise and who supposedly know better. Which is also to say that the disregard and lack of consideration for others is increasingly becoming a way of life. But what is the excuse of the educated, who know better and yet continue to disappoint us as leaders and shapers of life and public policies?

Where has education failed us? Everywhere, when we consider human relations. Psychology, business, and a number of other disciplines have marked out "human relations" arenas, but how people deal with and treat others cannot and should not be compartmentalized in specific disciplines and markedly ignored by other areas of study that directly impact daily life in America.

As the twenty-first century approaches, what I see are "human relations" classes or course components where African Americans, Whites, Hispanic citizens, Asian Americans, Native Americans, and people of many more ethnic groups sit incommunicado. Each of us is in his or her own separate world, supposedly respecting each other's privacy, but actually too carefully and actively engaged in disregarding people of another culture or group. Often, we should see, an enormous amount of human energy in such gatherings is invariably spent on cautiously ignoring the "other" groups of people, without necessarily being impolite, though nowadays downright impoliteness is not out of order either.

When the professor or coordinator of our hypothetical class appears, carrying the textbook for the class, it soon becomes clear that the objective of College Course 101 on "Human Relations" is to mix, to be human. The idea for this class, says the professor, is to treat other people who do not look like us as if they are actually human beings. The admirable idea that needs to be communicated, expounds this imaginary professor, is that people need to feel comfortable about approaching others to discuss issues of supposed mutual concern. There is a basic, fundamental humanity that unites all of us, that minimizes the differences between us, that connects us to the human lot, and that brings out our common humanity. While the class or the lesson on "how to be human" lasts, interactions occur that are genuine or that may at least look heartening. But when the class ends and the student representatives of American culture filter back into the streets of America and the world, the prevalent disregard for people of other races that existed at the beginning of the class returns. That disregard essentially says, "I would prefer not to deal with you because you do not look like me. I do not feel comfortable talking to you, and, since I do not have to, I will instead talk to others who make me feel more comfortable for that reason."

The point is that the education of Chicanos, which is influenced and undermined by the images constantly presented on television and by the ways that Hispanics are treated in real life, needs to be addressed. Current educational practice is not meant to change for the better the real world in which we play out our days. What we teach in the schools and universities is not genuinely useful for Hispanics. Education does not consciously seek to change attitudes that are detrimental to the welfare of all human beings. Our educational lessons and materials do not attempt to improve how we see and treat each other. As educators, leaders, and parents, we do not try to transform people who need to be taught that all human beings should be approached with respect—if we are to build better relations with other members of the human race.[6]

The hypothetical professor or class leader dutifully tells us how we should be, how we should treat other human beings, and, while the camera lens of the class is on the course members, while something is gained by the participants, the admonitions prevail. But within, we also know that the niceties that we should be paying to people who do not look like us all too often turn out to be mainly surface conventions reserved for certain occasions, rather than heartfelt convictions. Authenticity is hard to come by, but isn't that what America also needs regarding race relations?

There are no easy solutions to the human dilemma of desirable racial relations. We ought to begin by widely acknowledging that we have so far failed. Then we need to draw up local communal plans designed to change attitudes so that we can all understand that true human relations do not consist of a course or two, but that true regard for other human beings is a full-time twenty-four-hour endeavor that should be practiced everywhere we go. The bottom line is that Americans need to change how we view, think about, and respond to people who are different, who are not like us.

5

Love and the Mexican American School Experience

hicano authors have not especially dwelled on the idea of love, and neither have the critics. The medieval writers discussed by C. S. Lewis in *The Allegory of Love* continue to hold the literary imagination when we consider the issue of love. Of course, writers like Cervantes, Turgenev, Constant, Stendahl, and Flaubert, as well as modern practitioners such as Ford Madox Ford, Carlos Fuentes, and Lawrence Durrell have also extended the concept of love, a subject that has now turned the hot love of the Harlequin romances into a popular genre at the grocery store checkout counter. Since the 1605 publication of *Don Quixote*, writers have moved far beyond Plato's perennially engaging *Symposium*, which has it that somewhere in the world there is only one person of the opposite sex meant to be the other half of the person looking for love. But love, Benjamin Constant showed in *Adolphe*, has more to do with a lover's state of mind, with the anxieties experienced by the person who loves and who would be loved, than with the loved object. Love stories have since focused on the discombobulations suffered by a lover desiring another. When we thus hear that love has smitten someone, usually we are interested in how this person reacts to the unsettling, destabilizing effects of love, a state of mind that generally eclipses almost everything else in life.

If there is one half-positive image that Hispanics stereotypically conjure in the American imagination it is that of Latin lover, even if the model for this type was the eighteenth-century Venetian lover, Giacomo Casanova. In Chicano life, love appears to emerge suddenly and uncontrollably, generally during the teen years and in early adulthood, as Sandra Cisneros's *Woman Hollering Creek and Other Stories* (1991), among other works, shows. Love is particularly important to the Chicano psyche, because much of life for Mexican American youths early begins to revolve around the need to be accepted and loved, as we shall see, for example, in Anthony Quinn's *The Original Sin.* Teen-age love is a widespread American reality, but based on what I have seen, being wanted by another person of one's age group appears especially important to Mexican Americans. School is so much more unfulfilling and boring for most Chicanos and Chicanas that finding that special person of the opposite sex becomes an enormously exciting substitute for education. Although there are few useful studies that follow the growth and psychological development of Mexican American children, beginning about the fifth grade many Chicanos and Chicanas become concerned, not with learning and extending their knowledge of the world, but with locating that other person who will most desire and appreciate them for the person they are or the person they are becoming. There are, of course, exceptions, that is, students who do not succumb to the desire for a love object at this early stage of life, but I am now speaking about a sizable number of young Latinos.[1]

During the middle school years, most Mexican American youths attempt to blend in with others to avoid possible humiliation or ridicule by teachers or peers, while simultaneously, in effect, freeing themselves for the task of finding that significant other. Most teenagers, of course, pass through such a stage successfully, but once young Chicanos begin this process, the search for the loved other tends to become the central school concern for a great majority. School helps to supply the necessary time for finding that wonderful boy or girl who will love what soon becomes the educationally disenfranchised Chicano, who searches for personal self-esteem in the eyes of the other. The title of one of Luis Valdez's first plays, *No Saco Nada de la Escuela* (He Didn't Get Anything out of School), makes the most trenchant statement possible about this pervasive, sad reality. Usually, what Chicanos *do* find in school is that other person with whom love and, possibly, marriage occurs.[2]

Why mention Plato, Cervantes, C. S. Lewis, and the other authors alluded to when connecting junior high and high school Chicano love to the growing-up experiences of Mexican Americans as represented in literature? In part because no widely known or appreciated psychological literature exists to help Latinos navigate our way successfully to the adult world. A known set of guidelines or expected milestones might help articulate the different stages of the maturation process that Hispanic youths undergo in more positive, stabilizing ways. But other than the love stories that we have in our *conjunto* music, polka music, and *corridos*, most of which end violently, young Chicanos are not discernibly supported or psychologically encouraged by the available curricular materials in school or by an American media that seldom notices or takes our youths into account. The absence of such an infrastructural scaffold in American society does not preclude some Mexican Americans from passing through this stage of life successfully, but this lack of support explains why the majority of Hispanics are disenchanted with an assimilation process that does not actively embrace us, in effect abandoning our youngsters to lonely school existences that are usually countered only by finding a lover. Such realities help clarify why Mexican Americans are children one day in school and overnight find themselves entering the adult work world, in need of marrying and finding employment—all complicated responsibilities that shape the rest of their lives and that of their children.

Since much of our music is written for married or soon-to-be married Chicanos facing love difficulties, the cultural images our teenagers absorb tend to revolve around bipolar happy/unhappy and fulfilling/frustrating gender relationships. Latinos do not have regular rite-of-passage dating rituals, monitored by parents and educators, that help our young people to safely navigate the difficult school years. That is why many female students become pregnant, why males leave school to work, and why members of both sexes drop out of school for "personal reasons," as the files of these students perfunctorily record the facts. Since local customs and expectations differ, Chicano writers from Texas, Arizona, New Mexico, Illinois, California, and other states feature experiences that show how Mexican Americans are treated in different parts of the country.

Growing up in south Texas, for example, I well remember deriving a sense of identity not only from my parents and the adults that my brother and I were fortunate to have, but, as kids will, from other sources. The fortifying psychic force in our lives, aside from the stabilizing influence of our Catholic upbringing (against which we naturally chafed), were the Mexican films brought to the big screen every Sunday afternoon in the neighboring town of McAllen. While other people in the United States were enjoying the films of Jerry Lewis, Doris Day, John Wayne, Frank Sinatra, Bette Davis, and other comparable American movie stars, my brother and I were taken to see the films of Lola Beltran, Luis Aguilar, Pedro Infante, Carlos Montezuma, Pedro Vargas, Margo Lopez, Jorge Negrete, Augustin Lara, Jose Alfredo Jimenez, and a host of other Mexican movie stars remembered now only by dedicated aficionados of the Mexican film.[3] Each of these Mexican actors brought in a whole world. We knew almost every film that featured them, and looked forward to their future works. For comedy we saw Tin Tan and Cantinflas, the latter long regarded as the Bob Hope of Mexico. A little later there were other comic film stars, such as Clavillazo, Resortes, Mantequilla, and other *sonsos y mensos*, slapstick comedians who thoroughly entertained us through the years as we moved up the grades of the American school system.

Ours was a type of residential Chicano life commonly available to Mexican Americans who did not follow the seasonal crops in other parts of the country. We were what might be called the lower middle class, but other than the unemployment that plagued the south Texas communities of Edinburg, McAllen, Pharr, San Juan, and Mission, which regularly has one of the highest rates in the country, our experience was not typical of other Hispanic communities in other parts of the United States. Growing up Chicano in the barrios of Albuquerque, Los Angeles, Chicago, or even San Antonio offered Mexican Americans and other Hispanics different kinds of lives. One cannot thus say that Chicanos or other Latinos have normative, standardizing experiences in common—even if going *a la pisca*, that is, to pick cotton or other crops either locally or in other states, might be advanced as the essentializing experience of Mexican Americans older than forty. Picking cotton was a way of life for some Mexican Americans who *had* to work in the fields. Others in the early 1960s earned hourly wages of $1.25 or so in the department stores and businesses of our communities. Differences, though, have not been sufficiently rendered by our writers, and our texts do not capture the wide diversity within Chicano culture, offering what in effect is a skewed picture of the actual lives that Latinos went through and now live.[4]

Hispanics who are not Chicanos will have had even more varied experiences shaped by altogether different growing-up circumstances. Both groups, however, are likely to have in common school experiences, joined by the struggle to learn and master the English language. The different and often difficult socioeconomic circumstances that Hispanics face shape relationships, including the search for love among the young.

When growing up, my brother and I felt loved by our mother, father, grandmother, and other relatives. Our grandfather had died of a heat-stroke working in the cotton fields in Buda, outside of Austin a little be-fore the frontispiece picture in this book was taken. In the 1950s, we lived in the barrio, in *la vecindad*, as our adults referred to the west-side Edinburg area that we called home. We loved to play in the safe con-fines of our neighborhood with other Mexican American kids who looked like us. The Anglo population, which roughly comprised only 15 percent of our town, lived in the better-constructed, larger brick homes near the country club. That part of town also contained the city's hospital, which was near the new high school that we knew we would attend someday.

The desire to be loved made its presence known when we learned that Martita over in the next block had eloped with Jaime and that Mary was going steady with Juan. The drive-in was the place for making out or necking, for expressing the love that occurred when a couple was un-der the Texas stars in the summer with a warm night breeze blowing through the parked cars and pick-ups. When the songs of Little Richard's "Lucille" and Elvis Presley's "Are You Lonesome Tonight?" were played during the intermission, we knew who was doing what, and who had actually been watching the double-feature Mexican films that made the drive-in rounds in the Rio Grande Valley. When Elvis sang "Love Me Tender, Love Me Sweet," we swooned in exaggeration, puckering our lips to smack the air, laughter erupting at the loving go-ing on in the parked cars. Other than on the Spanish-language radio sta-tions played in places where Chicanos worked—the fields, gas stations, and town buildings, and in the cantinas where Chicanos drank Lone Star, Pearl and Falstaff beer, particularly on Friday and Saturday nights, Mexican music was not then played on the American side of the border, though we constantly heard all the Spanish radio programs from Mex-ican cities along the Rio Grande border. The Spanish radio stations played boleros, cumbias, and corridos, and they advertised local sales all day long. What is now fashionably called "Tejano music"[5] was success-fully promoted in the Chicano community by mainstays like Johnnie "You Got It" Canales, Little Joe and La Familia, and Los Dos Gilbertos. *Conjunto* music was known to *raza aficionados*, but hardly to the rest of America.[6] Freddy Fender, I believe, remains the only musician who successfully crossed over into 1950s American rock-and-roll and kept his ties with Chicano culture.

During the summer, love was on exhibit in many ways in many places. Would one rather love or be loved? Metaphysical considerations were not our forte. The issue was to have a girlfriend or a boyfriend, and that she or he be "cu-ute," as Toni Morrison captures the word in *The Bluest Eye*. The baseball season at the local park served teenagers well. Although we chose to sit through or participate in many community activities, we alternately ran hot and cold to everything in our world because, even though we freely participated in sport activities, many Chicano youngsters soon came to see that social progress in the world was controlled by Anglos and that we could only be as "American" as we wanted to push that option. We went through the seasons of baseball, football, and basketball during the summers of our young lives—before we became too cool to go to the park first to play and later to watch the games like the adults that we uncertainly yearned to become. During our earlier years, there were few things to which we looked forward to with more anticipation than a baseball game under the lights in the park. Later, baseball offered the dating and kissing excuse for going to the lesser-lighted areas of South Park, but, after that, the prospect of adulthood was fuzzy because we all wanted to succeed but we did not have any notion of how "success" was achieved from the barrio.

Such was the Mexican American world before Chicano literature began to emerge in the late 1960s, and I relate such experiences here because this whole world did not appear to be part of the American picture captured or promoted by the media, and yet we knew it was. Where are such hot long days and fleeting pleasures remembered or represented in print, in art, or in the American media or culture?[7] Most of the Mexican American experiences that I allude to are not readily recognized as "American," and I mention these vignettes to provide a glimpse of just how American and how Mexican American our world was, as well as to contextualize the two Chicano stories I want to discuss. Exploring the idea of love in the Mexican American community is not commonly seen as part of American civilization, but students of American culture would do well in recognizing the new, emerging, poor Americans in the following stories.

Tomas Rivera's "Eva and Daniel" and Saul Sanchez's "Esperanza y

'Turo" are two little-known stories that wonderfully capture some archetypical realities of Chicano love that are repeated wherever Chicano teenagers live. "Eva and Daniel" was left out of Rivera's well-known 1971 novel . . . *y no se lo tragó la tierra* on the advice of Herminio Rios and Octavio Romano, the editors and publishers of Quinto Sol Publications. "Esperanza y 'Turo," on the other hand, is part of Sanchez's 1977 novel *Hay plesha lichens tu di flac*, the Chicano phonetic transcription of the opening words to the Pledge of Allegiance. All Texas students learn the pledge as part of their first grade curriculum, but Sanchez's Chicanitos learn the sounds without knowing what they are reciting. Mexican Americans youngsters, indeed, often carry out school activities that are seldom sufficiently explained either to students or their parents. Chicano youngsters are also often expected to tolerate mainstream Anglo American youngsters and to move aside to allow the latter to take center stage—largely because there are other, more important agendas afoot in schools that, intentionally or not, end by excluding Mexican Americans and other Latinos. Rivera's and Sanchez's Chicanos make what accommodations they can, given the unattractive avenues available to them.

Eva and Daniel and Esperanza and 'Turo are the kind of Chicano couples we never see represented in the American media, but are very likely to see walking home after school in south Texas, San Antonio, Dallas, Houston, Tucson, Chicago, Seattle, or San Diego. Eva and Esperanza are both attractive, eye-catching young women, Rivera and Sanchez tell us, and therein resides most of the capital that they have to make their way in the barrio worlds they know. The wider American world, which is effectively closed to them, is best represented in these stories by an environment that surrounds them but which rarely has a positive effect on their lives. There are no good, viable prospects or opportunities for Chicanos or Chicanas in the America that these characters inhabit, mirroring the realities of many Mexican Americans today. All four characters are allowed to drop out of high school, undisturbed and unapproached by any responsible adult. Daniel is drafted, trained in California, and sent to Korea to defend America. Having twice failed to secure permission from his superior to visit his ailing Eva, Daniel goes AWOL, arriving too late to comfort his dying young wife.

In Sanchez's story, 'Turo is the love of Esperanza's life. Arturo is a musician who has to work in the fields for their livelihood. As a migrant worker he follows the crops out of state, leaving Esperanza alone in

Texas. The barrio neighbors watch her steps closely, so closely that she cannot even work because doing so would provide opportunities that might lead to other men. Pressured by the constraints of her life in the barrio, the many travails of Esperanza's frustrated love life end in her poisoning herself with pills. When 'Turo learns about Esperanza's fate, he drinks himself into a stupor and dives into a river. The community later recovers his body.

Both stories are presented as matter-of-fact elegies, oral ballads intended to be recited in commemoration of these grim tales. The stories are transposed into print by narrators who do not want to see the stories of Eva, Daniel, Esperanza, and Arturo forgotten. "Eva and Daniel" and "Esperanza y 'Turo" were written to keep these sad but all-too-common high school experiences from fading in the memory of the Chicano community, which both Rivera and Sanchez construct as a supportive but hands-off chorus. The two stories are related to many *corridos*, which draw both culturally and emotionally from the form and content of the *cuento* tradition. Both stories, written bilingually in Chicano Spanish and English, attempt to communicate the substance and the impoverished life patterns of Texas Chicanos in the everyday, unadorned language of a people who make their living by working in the fields. These stories can be connected to the wonderful songs composed by Jose Alfredo Jimenez or sung by Pedro Infante and heard in the classic Mexican love films that we knew so well. But, other than a handful of Chicano scholars, what American critic or scholar is going to know or appreciate such efforts? The cantinas where Daniel and 'Turo drink would have played Jose Alfredo Jimenez's "Ando Volando Bajo" or Pedro Infante's version of "Historia de un Amor," references that even the Chicano authors do not include, since much of Chicano literature leaves out important contextual experiences and thus impoverish our stories.[8] The statements that Rivera and Sanchez seek to make with these and other comparable stories point elsewhere.

Rivera and Sanchez endeavor to capture quotidian love relationships into which few people from the larger American society would likely inquire. These dedicated Chicano writers are both very much concerned with detailing the unfortunate developments of tragic love affairs for the edification of anyone who will read about what the Hispanic community knows all too well. A young couple that marries without *porvenir*— that is, without the wherewithal to construct a good future—will live out another sad story begun by love and destroyed by the couple's failure to make it in the long run in a tough American economy that offers few places for uneducated Chicanos. Motivating both writers is a clear desire to depict a world that reflects the realities that keep Chicanos working in the fields and in other dead-end jobs.

"Eva and Daniel" and "Esperanza y 'Turo" implicitly raise questions about society, particularly about schools that serve essentially as holding tanks for Latino youngsters until, frustrated and dejected, they drop out at sixteen years of age, simply because they legally can. School administrators have failed to take significant measures to make a difference in the lives of young Mexican Americans, who are released unprepared to cope with American social and economic realities. In the Preface to "*Let All of Them Take Heed*," Guadalupe San Miguel, Jr., informs us that "we know little about the socioeconomic and cultural characteristics of Mexican Americans and how, over the last 150 years, public schools have responded to them or to the issues of cultural differences raised by their presence."[9]

The stories of Eva, Daniel, Esperanza, and 'Turo underscore the message that such characters have been told, in many ways over the years, that they are not important enough as human beings to matter. Consequently, many Chicanos develop an "I don't care" attitude that manifests itself in a great variety of ways that educators and legislative leaders have not successfully addressed. By the time such Mexican Americans reach high school, if not middle school, they have been so disregarded that when they drop out they are, in fact, acknowledging that they have long suffered from immense educational neglect. A similar message emerges in the 1987 film *La Bamba*, which chronicles the unhappy life of the Chicano rock-and-roll singer Richie Valens, born Ricardo Valenzuela, who died tragically at the age of nineteen in a plane crash with singers Buddy Holly and the Big Bopper. Here Richie's brother, Bob, drinks heavily and is depressed and pessimistic, since he sees no future for himself. He has no skills or talents that have been developed and little interest in education. Shunned by society, he predictably ends up in trouble with the law.

This type of trenchant statement, found again and again in Chicano life, Chicano literature, and in recent films about Latinos, has not heightened awareness about a very serious problem. Although the stories I have been discussing were written in the 1970s, the same message continues to be expressed in the Hispanic films of the 1980s and 1990s. Mexican Americans know that we have Evas and Daniels and Esperanzas and 'Turos and Bob Valenzuelas all over Texas, California, Arizona, New Mexico, the Midwest, and throughout the rest of the country where Latinos live. But I have seen no discernible interest from educational institutions, legislatures, or other established institutional entities to improve the lives of young Mexican Americans and other Latinos who see no futures for themselves.[10]

In *Under the Feet of Jesus*, a novel filled with images and metaphors that show how young Mexican American field hands are spiritually sustained in the face of harsh natural and environmentally hazardous working conditions, Helena Maria Viramontes revealingly depicts the migrant experience through the eyes of women who have not previously been central characters in Chicano fiction. Under the guise of love and marriage, many of today's real-life Hispanic couples prematurely leave school, cutting themselves off from the type of futures that are more available to mainstream Americans who have enough parental encouragement and financial support to continue studies that eventually turn into degrees that lead to better-paying positions.

Through such lives, Rivera, Sanchez, and Viramontes reiterate the fact that parental, communal, and psychic sustenance and support are exactly what Chicano youths lack. These are qualities clearly not supplied by the K–12 educational pipeline. Mexican American students, it has become increasingly clear, at most have been merely tolerated in the schools since 1848, when the war with Mexico ended with the signing of the Treaty of Guadalupe Hidalgo. Except for a few well-known cases of Chicano success, to which the American media point in an otherwise disastrous education record, it is difficult not to avoid concluding that the overall impact of the schools on Latino lives has been and largely remains a negative one. If the schools do not make the discernible positive difference that Hispanic youths broadly require, parental influence alone will not help. If educators and policy leaders do not make a difference, little else will significantly improve the lives of today's Latinos.

Due to negative education encounters, Chicano students very early tend to cut themselves off from school and then from American society by falling in love with each other in attempts to sustain themselves in a psychologically difficult socioeconomic environment. The generally unhappy results of such early love unions are widely known because we hear about them in the local newspapers or on the evening newscasts on television and radio. These are the stories that tell us that someone with a Hispanic surname shot another person; that alcohol, drugs, or both resulted in some kind of altercation. Several weeks later we may hear that a grand jury has indicted a Hispanic man or woman on a charge that upright, tax-paying citizens with steady jobs and good incomes just cannot understand.

What Rivera, Sanchez, and other Chicano authors write about is the nature of the miseries faced by couples, individuals, and families in stories pulled from the everyday tragic lives of down-and-out Latinos in the United States. The problem, of course, is that there are simply so many other issues in this country that there is never time to address the lives, dreams, and needs of Mexican Americans and other Latinos. This, at any rate, appears to be the message continually sent to Latinos, who, finally, are always left to live within our own insufficient resources in the United States.

6

Enhancing the Visibility
of Chicano Literature

ven though Chicano literature has its followers, our books
still need wider appeal throughout the United States and
abroad. For Chicano literature to continue to develop in a
healthy direction, we need to ask ourselves why a literature
that some readers have been following for nearly thirty years
is still not known by most Americans. Other than in course
offerings of a few colleges and universities in a few areas of
the country and in Europe, Chicano literature today seems
at an impasse, suggesting it is time to take stock of this important Latino enterprise.

When Chicano literature made its little-heralded appearance in the late 1960s and early 1970s, many Chicano writers and critics believed that we would finally be heard, that
the largely unarticulated Hispanic presence in America had
awakened. Many of us believed that a carefully crafted literature would help usher in a new social reality not only for
Latinos but for the entire United States. The view among
Mexican Americans in particular was that we would be publishing views that would be widely disseminated, and that
discussion of our issues would help improve our realities.
Despite some initial resistance and skepticism, on the whole
Chicano literature was encouraged by academics who had
enough foresight to see that in order for Mexican Americans
to live better, access to opportunities had to be provided for
the Spanish-speaking population of the United States.
There was a sense of social justice and commitment associ-

ated with the effort, an ethical component that has remained part of this worthy literary endeavor. Change was palpably in the air, and that atmosphere helped launch the initial books written by Chicano authors and promoted mostly by Latino publishers. At the time, Americans seemed more compassionate, inclined to help fellow citizens who showed signs of wanting to be more visible and influential in the American community.

Although the ways and views of society change slowly, the signals received by Chicano writers was that the established presses would consider new writings for publication. For a number of years, the actual size of this potential new reading audience seemed unclear. Because we had different stories to tell that had not been available, some of us naively believed that the American reading public would now start buying Chicano books. Chicano authors soon realized that engaging the attention of both Chicanos not used to regular reading and established reading audiences unfamiliar with Mexican American culture was a complex challenge.

No single factor adequately explains why Chicano literature and American culture did not develop mutually beneficial terms for a better relationship. What appears to have happened is that in the excitement of being heard, Chicano authors did not pay enough attention to the reading habits of the American public, since they were, of course, focusing attention on how to engage Latino readers. Chicano writers also had not lived like other American authors and therefore could not and did not want to write like other writers, for their expectations and reasons for writing were different. The larger American reading public, on the other hand, did not know what to expect. When Chicano anger and *raza* pride appeared in their works, the established presses turned away from Chicano authors, faulting content and style. Then there was the uncertainty about how to respond appropriately to the lives of people whom society had previously disregarded with widely posted "No Mexicans Allowed" signs. Such signs, which now, fortunately, have been forgotten, dotted the American southwestern landscape until the end of World War II.[1] The initial inclination to be receptive to Chicano literature was soon dashed by the inability of both groups to find common ground to resolve past differences. Whereas the mainstream presses, representing American readers, would have preferred positive success stories about growing up Hispanic in the United States, most Chicano and Latino writers could not write without taking the American way to task, an option that many Mexican Americans believed was exactly what pent-up frustrations required.

Chicano literature at that juncture was somewhat in the position that American literature as a whole was in during the early part of the nineteenth century, when most readers felt that writing by Americans was not literature worth reading. Today some literary people who sampled and were turned off by early Chicano books may still believe that Chicano writing has not yet reached the point when it can be taken seriously as literature. Chicano writers and critics, to be sure, cannot dismiss the fact that Chicano literature is not as actively pursued as, say, Latin American writers have been during the last thirty years. Chicano literature has not yet produced a Gabriel García Márquez, Jorge Luis Borges, or Julio Cortázar, but the prospect for ushering in comparable writers is nonetheless closer. This reality and the efforts made by writers to create Chicano literature suggest that it is useful to consider issues that Chicano writers might also undertake. For writers, thankfully, are independent and feel free to choose both the subjects and the forms for their writing. But, since Chicano literature is part of a larger community effort to establish a dialogue among ourselves and with other Americans, suggestions aimed at minimizing the ill will that has dominated discourse between the two cultures ought to be useful.

Chicano literature is moving in several directions today. Which paths appear more interesting and engaging will depend on what authors and commentators are asked. Regardless of the roads and ideologies embraced, at the risk of upsetting some critics, I believe that Chicano literature has not yet found its main path or purpose. A number of works have caught the eager attention of those of us who look for signs of how Mexican Americans and Latinos want to represent ourselves in American culture. But regardless of how much we like the work of any one Chicano writer, no single work can validly claim to be the *par excellence* Chicano work, including Sandra Cisernos's highly popular *The House on Mango Street* or Rudolfo Anaya's earlier *Bless Me, Ultima*. Each of these novels has its champions and detractors, and both works have achieved a certain prominence not accorded to other works by readers or the critics. Yet in spite of these two popular works, several other Chicano texts might also be nominated which provide readers with a useful sense of Mexican American life and culture. Even then, no single Chicano text has yet taken the larger literary world by storm.

This proposition may seem heretical to readers and supporters of

Chicano literature, but I make the claim because only a handful of Chicano books at this point successfully measure up as world literature. My purpose is not to upset anyone but to challenge prevailing discourse on Chicano literature. We need to recognize where we are and to encourage the writing of the great Latino American novel, the same shibboleth that has usefully advanced American literature. The nature of the experience of Chicanos in America is the presumed subject matter for a communal story, but before examining several Chicano texts that illustrate our relationships with the media and our experiences in education, several remarks are helpful.

Most books of Chicano literature are good, useful texts that help us talk about the role and place of Mexican Americans and other Latinos in American society. Some works are more illuminating than others, but we also need to recognize that most Chicano literature actually provides little guidance for Chicanos and other Latinos, given where most of us are sociologically and educationally today. One of the main benefits of literature, aside from providing for the social and aesthetic needs of a people, is to offer readers a clearer sense of the kind of people we are, and the people we want to be. From these perspectives, I think we can say that we have not had enough novels that begin with the type of people we are, and we have virtually no novels that point out what we might be or want to be as a people. When we have broached this desideratum, the product has been a novel like Anaya's *Heart of Aztlan*, which ends with Chicanos becoming a new proletariat fighting against a large industry that keeps Mexican Americans subjugated in the barrios of Albuquerque. Given the destructive educational and media realities daily faced by our people, Chicanos need books that raise questions and offer resolutions that we do not usually consider.

In our literature we still do not have the type of characters, for example, that American literature has developed, featured, and established in the minds of readers. Aside from Tony Marez in Anaya's *Bless Me, Ultima*, there is, for instance, no Isabel Archer, no Huckleberry Finn, no Natty Bumppo, no Nick Carraway, that is, no featured character whom we automatically associate with specific books or writers. We also do not have any memorable objectionable or infamous characters who have left an indelible mark on readers, like Herman Melville's Bartleby. Rather, so many of our characters tend to be ephemeral or, worse, anonymous types whose names we hardly care to remember ourselves. As a people, I think we are already nameless enough. For our writers to use names or characters that do not matter or that do not long stick in the imaginations of readers is not going to help to increase the visibility of Chicano literature. We do have, of course, Cisneros's Esperanza Cordero in *The House on Mango Street*, whose literary stock continues to rise, but what characters have so far reached the level of a Billy Budd, an Edna Pontellier, an Ahab, or even Ernest Hemingway's Santiago?

Character construction, some writers and critics might argue, may not be the way that writers want to leave their mark in these postmodern days. But, lacking better models that might include the Latin American writers mentioned above, we need to recognize that Chicano literature has not done as well in its first thirty years as American literature at its outset. We can rationalize and explain the differences in all sorts of ways; the point is that the parent literature has since become one of the most read literatures in the world—largely by focusing attention on what an American is, and on what an American is constantly in the process of becoming. Perhaps by developing a known gallery of characters, incidents, and purposes that focus reader attention on what we are and what we are trying to be, Chicano literature can someday rival other literatures. Chicano literature, after all, is nothing more than one of the newest branches of American literature, and, as such, it should naturally receive both the protection and the encouragement of the parent. In this case, it seems that the parent needs to be reminded and perhaps even cajoled into offering support.

1

Americo Paredes's *George Washington Gomez*: Educating Mexican American Students

A merico Paredes's *George Washington Gomez* in many ways is
the master Chicano narrative produced by a Mexican American writer so far. Finished three generations ago, in 1940,
but not published until exactly half a century later, in 1990,
this novel by all rights should have exerted an enormous influence on all Chicano literature that has emerged since. Jose
Antonio Villarreal's *Pocho* (1959), Raymond Barrio's *The
Plum Plum Pickers* (1969), Abelardo Delgado's *Chicano:
Twenty-Five Pieces of a Chicano Mind* (1969), and the other
Chicano novels published in the period before Chicano literature emerged in the 1970s did not have the benefit of
Paredes's novel. That, indeed, is what happens when one
generation suppresses a book that should have enlightened
the following generations of writers.

For fifty years, Paredes's work remained tucked away in
the author's dresser, reportedly the object of cold rejections.
"Who would be interested in reading a novel about Mexican
Americans?" publishers asked in the 1940s.[1] During that and
the following decade, though, Mexican Americans, including Paredes, would serve in World War II and the Korean
War. It was not until Quinto Sol Publications in Berkeley,
founded by Octavio Romano and Herminio Rios, awarded
their first $1,000 fiction prize that considerable interest in
Chicano literature was created among Mexican American

writers. That first award went to Tomas Rivera's . . . *y no se lo tragó la tierra/* . . . *and the earth did not part* in 1971, the same year that Alurista brought out *Floricanto en Aztlan* in Los Angeles. While the earlier Chicano novels and collections of poems that I mention above showed us that we could write and publish, the books by Rivera and Alurista awakened Chicanos and other readers to the possibility of creating a new literature. These developments set in motion the gradual publication of the roughly 180 primary texts and 40 secondary books that today constitute the emerging field of Chicano literature.

Paredes's *George Washington Gomez* is a semi-historical novel set in the fictional town of Jonesville, humorously pronounced "Hon-esbil" by its Mexican American inhabitants. Paredes's fictional community is modeled after his hometown of Brownsville, Texas, in the Rio Grande Valley directly across from Mexico. The novel begins when World War I erupts in Europe and continues through the 1920s and 1930s. Had the work been published when finished in 1940, it should have earlier alerted educators to the disastrous educations that Chicanos tend to receive. Paredes's narrative on how Mexican Americans are educated, ironically, still ought to serve as a major point of departure for today's Chicanos. The novel is the ur-Chicano text because it carefully chronicles the spiritual, social, and psychological growth prompted by the education received by one George Washington Gomez, a young Mexican American citizen from south Texas. Although Rivera's 1971 novel also addresses the importance of education for a first-language Spanish-speaking youth whose family follows the seasonal crops, it is Paredes's text that best establishes the psychologically destructive grade-by-grade educational progress that too many young Chicanos and Chicanas experience in the schools of America.[2]

Paredes's *bildungsroman* remains unsurpassed in detailing the educational journeys of several Mexican American students. His narrative also remains timely, even though it depicts the type of education that Chicanos received when most schools in Texas were segregated according to race. For, despite some current research and dialogues on how best to educate Mexican Americans, readers need to recognize that the educational practices and attitudes revealingly dramatized by Paredes in the 1920s and 1930s still largely shape the educations that Chicanos and other Latinos and minority students experience in the United States. Educators may argue differently and may even defend current classroom practices, but Texas Education Agency and U.S. Department of

Education statistics have showed that throughout the twentieth century Hispanic students have had one of the highest high school dropout rates in the country, the numbers varying depending on how dropout students are actually counted.[3]

Literary critics have not addressed the issue of the education of Mexican Americans in Chicano literature because such subjects are assumed to be obvious and the purview of educators, the social sciences, and public policy. But since improving the educational realities of a growing population of Mexican Americans and other Latinos is important, the problem needs to be brought out in a way that it can never again be disregarded. This goal was one of the central driving forces promoting the creation of Chicano literature, but it remains at most tangentially addressed by criticism. Secondary critical texts that discuss more theoretical issues, like Ramon Saldívar's *Chicano Narrative* (1990), Juan Bruce-Novoa's *Retrospace* (1990), and other literary studies, have connected Chicano literature to identity, to transnationalism, to third world realities, and to other more literary perspectives. I am interested in raising and pursuing solutions to problems posed by Chicano life and literature about why Mexican Americans have been misserved by education for so long. Not to focus attention on the clear public educational policy transgression and misservice that most Latino youths continue to experience daily in our schools amounts to not sufficiently insisting on the rights of our people to better educations as Americans. If our needs and progress have not been altogether clear, the good will of all Americans now requires enlistment in order to offer better educations to the Mexican American and Latino youths who will soon become one of the larger student cohorts in the twenty-first century.

In Paredes's novel, "Gualinto" is how George Washington Gomez's grandmother pronounces her grandson's given name. Through Gualinto's education, Paredes presents a series of carefully chosen incidents that writers, citizens, educators, and legislative and political policy leaders would do well to study. The author's aim is to educate readers about the experiences that minority youths struggle with to secure a meaningful education in their efforts to function in American society.

George Washington Gomez strongly suggests that our education system needs to be designed to build the self-esteem of all students, regardless of ethnic background and race, for moral and character strength are best built on school and classroom activities that nurture instead of demeaning youngsters. In the novel, for instance, Gualinto is emotionally and physically abused by Miss Cornelia, his Mexican American low first grade teacher. A beating leads his uncle Feliciano Garcia to visit the principal with two lawyers by his side, a state of affairs that Mexican Americans have often had to resort to in Texas in order to improve the nature and the quality of education, as Guadalupe San Miguel has shown.[4] The visit ends in a compromise: Gualinto is allowed to transfer to finish the year in Miss Josephine's low first grade. Having shown his intelligence, the following year he is placed in Miss Huff's high second grade, where readers are told that he enters "American school at last" (147). These initial experiences show that if a young person is to grow and develop healthily in American society, educators need to engender a positive sense of self that adequately challenges students instead of discouraging them. If teachers and other members of society fail to exhibit self-esteem and care to all students, few educational endeavors, Paredes suggests, prove successful.

George Washington Gomez is concerned primarily with Gualinto's education, but through Gualinto's uncle Feliciano, Paredes demonstrates that Mexican American adults sometimes feel so uncomfortable with schools where English is spoken that they would rather not interfere, as they perceive it, with the education of Gualinto and his peers. Even though every Spanish-speaking person in the novel wants the Chicano youngsters to be educated as "leaders," none of the Mexican American adults knows how to work with the teachers to accomplish this desired purpose. As a fourth-generation "Border Mexican" (19) from south Texas living in "Gringo land" (25), Feliciano Garcia has not been educated himself, and this deficiency does not encourage him to see himself as helpful to Gualinto's schooling.[5] Feliciano nonetheless is important precisely because he is about as representative a character as we have in Chicano literature of the sensible, quiet-spoken resident Tejano or Mexican American whom educators generally avoid *because* he speaks Spanish and does not understand English.

Although Feliciano appears deceptively matter-of-fact, when we pay attention to the few words that he utters, as well as to his actions, we learn that he silently condemns his nephew's life in an education system that does not even try to understand the values and ways of Mexican American culture. This fact may elude most readers unfamiliar with Mexican Americans Since Feliciano is too smoothly effaced throughout a good part of the novel without ever fully communicating his views, the task of a careful reader is not only to understand Feliciano's deep disappointment with Gualinto's education, but, indeed, to wonder why so many Latino students have repeatedly continued to fail all of these years. Represented as a humble, low-key man, Feliciano Garcia is placed in the novel's complex social background, ironically in the very role that mainstream Anglo Americans socially encourage minority people to occupy in real life.

The message that emerges from Paredes's *George Washington Gomez* is that Mexican Americans are continually discouraged and very successfully repressed by an education system that ostensibly professes to help. Paredes's novel is useful because it shows how learning experiences encourage the unexamined, troubled internalization of anti–Mexican American beliefs and perspectives into the lives of young and very susceptible Chicanos. The novel's Chicano youngsters are psychologically vulnerable and impressionable because they cannot see that they are daily absorbing negative and debilitating ideas about themselves and their culture. No character in the novel, however, sees this educational tragedy clearly enough to articulate it for readers. That, indeed, is one of the shortcomings of the novel, though I think that Paredes meant astute readers to pick up what seems to him a self-evident fact. Even Feliciano Garcia, who is as uneducated as the Mexican American community that he represents, increasingly becomes aware that the education Gualinto is receiving is not preparing him to be a proud Mexican American and a "leader" of his people. Readers who study Feliciano will discern his progressive, though silent, disenchantment and disappointment with his nephew's American education.

Nowhere in the novel are readers explicitly informed that educators need to understand Mexican Americans better if the quality of our lives is to be improved in the United States, but that, nevertheless, is the central message of the book. The novel's third-person omniscient narrator in places is satiric and even sardonic, but otherwise Paredes maintains a matter-of-fact tone. Although Paredes periodically employs a tongue-in-cheek commentary that reveals how Mexican American students gradually become disillusioned with the education they are offered, part of the irony in representing Feliciano as a character who communicates his displeasure with Gualinto's education is to show that such a stance is part of the normal Chicano adult view of American life in general. Whereas adults in other cultures articulate their views on issues, most Mexican Americans silently seem to say that we do not like the message that there is little or no place for us in American society. Our silence often indicates that we feel powerless to reform a system that does not want to pay attention to our needs. This position is reinforced by our inclination to use words sparsely, whether in Spanish or English, a trait or quality that is read as showing personal strength. Nonetheless, readers should understand that Mexican Americans often refrain from making statements that are likely to emerge as ambiguous, unclear, or apathetic.

George Washington Gomez remains especially instructive as American society moves toward the twenty-first century. As mentioned earlier, Latinos have the highest high school dropout rates in the country, even while we are projected to become the largest minority population by the year 2010.[6] Teachers would do well to examine Paredes's analysis of the educations that the Chicano youngsters receive to discover how educators continually fail to develop the type of sympathetic stance that could help Latinos to think, speak, and write in a language that has traditionally blocked Latino success. Only when educators understand how past practices and prejudices between Anglos and Mexican Americans have shaped realities will they be in a position to prepare minority students for a better place in American culture.[7]

In the novel Gumersindo, Gualinto's father, has been shot and killed by Texas Rangers, who are known to have abused Mexican people.[8] Paredes captures the turn-of-the-century rivalry when both the *rinches*,[9] as Hispanic people derisively called the Rangers, and the Mexican Americans who lived along the Rio Grande commonly carried arms to defend themselves. Paredes sketches a state of affairs that few readers know about, except perhaps by reading specialized historical monographs.

> Some of the [American] soldiers would fall, an expression of pained surprise on their young, red faces. As if they were amazed at it all. As if to say, "What is this all about, anyway? What do we know about your fathers and brothers and the lands you say you lost?" Then as other soldiers returned fire, they would fall back through leaf-mold-covered trails to their horses. They would scatter and thread their way through the easier parts of the dense brush toward the river, trying to get to the Mexican side with as few casualties as possible.
>
> That would be all. Except the next day the Rangers would come. To kill everyone they found close to the scene of the ambush, that is everyone who could not speak English. Until the dead reached a satisfying total, and then they would go back to Jonesville and wire headquarters in Austin, reporting a certain number of bandits killed. (24)

Mistaken by the Texas Rangers for border bandit Lupe Garcia, Feliciano's younger brother, Gumersindo Gomez, is gunned down. As in countless Mexican *corrido* folk ballads that commemorate similar historical events, the reason that Lupe is regarded as an outlaw is that, as a *corrido* might express it, "Lupe had killed a Gringo who had laughed at him because Lupe looked so puny."[10]

The rest of Feliciano's days are shaped by a promise he makes to the dying Gumersindo, the father of the novel's title character, to take care of his widow and her children. His life is a vintage Chicano existence, for honest Feliciano spends the next quarter century dutifully living by his word, quietly caring for his sister-in-law Maria and her children, Gualinto and his two sisters. In Paredes's novel, Mexican American women do not figure prominently; the lives of the sisters, Carmen and Maruca, are discussed mainly as they highlight Gualinto's progress through school.

Gualinto's promise as a future Mexican American leader is at the center of Paredes's novel. If all Mexican American children were as promising as Gualinto, most of the problems investigated by social scientists who study Latinos would be easier to resolve. But since Gualinto is raised to believe that he is destined to be a leader, what happens to him on his educational journey is a story worth the attention of all Americans.

As a novel, *George Washington Gomez* could have been tightened and polished further. The work, however, grows in a reader's esteem, particularly when the seriousness of his educational experiences become apparent. The manuscript is almost certainly not a "first draft," as Rolando Hinojosa observed in his 1990 introduction to the text, for the narrative contains some superb scenes and several perceptive analyses of the Chicano condition that suggest Paredes reworked a novel that was close to his heart. Parts of the novel would have benefited from further revision, but the decision to publish the work as it was left in 1940 when Paredes was only twenty-five years old was wise, since the narrative reflects conditions in the lower Rio Grande Valley during the first half of the twentieth century.

Because no comparable Chicano work is known to have existed before the 1970s Chicano literature movement, *George Washington Gomez* pedagogically ought to hold a preeminent place in the history of Mexican American education. For Paredes's work captures a complex geopolitical world that is not recognized as part of the American experience, even though the book is as American as *The Education of Henry Adams*. To say that the entire Chicano literary movement of the 1970s occurred without Paredes's *George Washington Gomez*, indeed, is to invite readers to wonder what Chicano literature might have been like if our subsequent writers had profited from reading this youthful work.

Few histories address, other than superficially, the internecine animosity that existed between the Anglos and Mexican Americans of Texas at the turn of the century.[11] This relationship is part of a past that both groups downplay, largely because educators have not taught students to deal with this unfortunate past without raising disquieting anxieties that neither group knows how to use to promote better current relations. Not to discuss Anglo and Mexican American relations, Paredes suggests in chapter 12 of Part III of his novel, only insures that the racial animosities that have long existed will continue to influence a reality that educators need to counter consciously.

Only a handful of narratives directly deal with Anglo and Mexican American relations before Chicano literature raised consciousness about the issue in the early 1970s. Jovita Gonzalez and Eve Raleigh's *Caballero*, written in the 1930s and 1940s about events following the 1846–1848 U.S. war with Mexico and published in 1996, and María Amparo Ruiz de Burton's *The Squatter and the Don*, completed in 1885 and published in 1992, are two recently rediscovered works that articulate the complexities of these relationships. Along with other volumes, including *George Washington Gomez*, these two books were published by a University of Houston project known as Recovering the U.S. Hispanic Literary Heritage, making these publications important sociohistorical works that document a part of American life that is only now being articulated.[12]

Like Paredes's novel, these two works highlight cultural inequities and affronts between Anglos and Mexican American that have led to battles waged on a variety of education, political, and legal fronts in Texas and the American Southwest over the years. Although not the best-written works, such historical novels provide readers with a sense of Chicano life in different areas of territories that used to belong to Mexico that is little known to the larger literary world.[13] Thanks to the Robert Runyon Photograph Collection, housed in the Barker Texas History Center at the University of Texas at Austin, pictures exist of the social conditions in south Texas during the early years of the twentieth century, which in part graphically capture some of the events in these novels. But aside from the rare photographs and documents that attest to the racial strife and physical violence communicated, for instance, in the opening pages of *George Washington Gomez*, few records reveal how the people of the area actually lived during the period.[14]

Historians Ricardo Romo, Rodolfo Acuña, José Limón, and others have documented the 1915–1917 "brown scare," a precursor to California's Proposition 187, aimed at preventing Mexican immigrants from entering and staying in the United States.[15] Most of the Mexican people who subsequently joined earlier Spanish settlers in south Texas came as a result of the political disruptions caused by the Mexican revolutionary struggles between 1910 and 1920. Those troubled times, my grandmother used to say, embroiled both sides of the United States–Mexico border. It was the days of Pancho Villa and Venustiano Carranza, and those difficulties that drove her, and many other Mexican families, to seek refuge on the American side of the Rio Grande.

Situating his novel within these historical events, Paredes develops the story of Feliciano Garcia, who selflessly raises Gualinto, the hopeful future leader of the Mexican American people. *George Washington Gomez*, however, goes on to dramatize the sad separation that develops between Feliciano and his nephew as the latter makes his way from the first to the twelfth grade in the American school system.

As one of Jonesville's brightest students, Gualinto's education is not commonly experienced by most Mexican American children. Yet, because Gualinto represents one of the brightest Mexican American students who ostensibly succeeds, the novel asks readers to mull over to what extent his school experiences actually help the adult Gualinto. What readers learn is how Gualinto is slowly but very successfully conditioned, as he moves through school, to dislike and eventually even to feel ashamed of himself, ending by disassociating himself from his own race in great anger. At the end of the novel, Gualinto, who now calls himself "George," uncomfortably thinks of himself as an Anglo American, denouncing and ridiculing the very Mexican American people that his parents and friends hoped he would lead toward a new future.[16]

Unlike Ernesto Galarza's 1971 novel *Barrio Boy*, which offers a narrator who develops and sustains pride in his racial and ethnic roots, *George Washington Gomez* can be read as a precursor to a misguided book—Richard Rodriguez's 1982 memoir *Hunger of Memory*. Here, another educated Mexican American ends up feeling so ashamed of his culture and ethnicity that he professes he cannot speak to his father, whom he portrays irreconcilably as living in a Spanish-speaking world that his American education has not allowed him to access. Although Rodriguez presents *Hunger of Memory* as a document of his awakening and eventual intellectual enlightenment, the book also contains lamentable statements about his inability to coexist comfortably in the Anglo and the Mexican American worlds he has known since birth.

Since when is being able to speak two or more languages an educational drawback, especially for Americans who professes to be educated? Any reputedly excellent school system that makes students of any background feel ashamed of themselves and "educates" or allows such students to feel uncomfortable with their own parents and people cannot, of course, justifiably claim to educate young people. For education is about drawing out the best in a person, leading a student toward balanced personal growth, not toward repressing or denying any part of a pupil's essential being, as Paredes's Gualinto does, and, as we will see in the next chapter, Anthony Quinn's autobiography suggests.

When Gualinto is growing up, a *licenciado* or lawyer from Mexico moves next door with the hope of helping "poor Mexicans who have problems with the law." The example of that one lone professional adult in Gualinto's world prompts him to decide that he, too, will become a lawyer to help Mexican Americans (65). During his early years, Gualinto admires Mexican American men enormously, especially his guardian and uncle, Feliciano, whose very walk he imitates. For $230, Feliciano buys a house for himself and Gualinto, his mother, and his sisters. He secures employment at the Jonesville's saloon, El Danubio Azul (The Blue Danube), which in time he converts into a grocery store (71). Two years later, Feliciano finishes making payments on the house to Judge Norris, the Anglo politician who controls the Mexican American votes that Feliciano ambivalently delivers during elections. Since Feliciano's purpose is to provide a safe growing-up environment for Gualinto, he does what he can in a world he does not control:

> In later years George W. Gomez [Gualinto] would remember his childhood home as an enchanted place. The porch of the blue frame house was covered with honeysuckle vines that screened a corner of it entirely from view, forming a fragrant, shady cave. The front yard was full of rose bushes with flowers of many colors, which he scrupulously avoided for fear not only of the thorns but of his mother's wrath as well. Then there were the figs, the papayas, the guayabas growing by the sides of the house. (50)

In his backyard banana grove, Gualinto grows up pretending to kill *rinches*, the Texas Rangers. Since Feliciano remains true to his promise to Gualinto's father not inform Gualinto that Gumersindo was killed by the Texas Rangers (21, 31), readers may wonder where Gualinto learned to play at killing rangers. Does he learn this from his general environment, or does he somehow learn that Uncle Feliciano does not like *rinches* (67)? Gualinto's childhood is otherwise portrayed as idyllic; he has adults who care for him, and he is perfectly comfortable in his Mexican American world. Everything that Feliciano undertakes successfully contributes to his purpose: "his nephew was getting close to school age, and Feliciano would need money, much money" for Gualinto's education (82).

From the first day of school, when Feliciano walks him by the hand to register him in the first grade (108), much as John Quincy Adams walked the child Henry Adams in *The Education of Henry Adams*, until Gualinto graduates from what must be the University of Texas at Austin at the end of part IV of the novel, Feliciano steadfastly supports Gualinto. As Gualinto moves through the grades, however, he distances himself from Feliciano and the home for which Feliciano sacrifices his life (155–56). When Feliciano one day hears Gualinto's sister Maruca say that Gualinto and his sisters are downright "ashamed of this house. It's no palace, really," he is stunned and left speechless: "On the porch Feliciano sat for a long time in his rocker, thinking. He inspected his large, bony hands as if he had never seen them before. Then he looked around him, studying his surroundings. After that he sat in the rocker for a long while, unmoving, his eyes fixed in the distance. Finally he put on his hat and went out for a walk" (157).

Class and racial distinctions have begun to make the young Gualinto feel ashamed of his relatives and neighborhood. Feliciano, on the other hand, felt he could justly be proud of the house in which his family lived. It was not a brick mansion like those downtown, but except for the Lopez-Anguera house, it was the best in the whole Dos Veintidos area," (155) the Mexican American *vecindad*, the barrio. Being an uneducated, simple man, Feliciano cannot understand why young Gualinto feels bad about himself and his home, since being Mexican American has always been a source of great pride, as Paredes shows in Part II of the novel (50–105).

In a few historical background paragraphs, Paredes tells readers how the local school district deals with Mexican American students. The narrative informs us that "more than half of the low-firsters dropped out after their first year of school, and considerably less than half of the second graders made it into the third grade. It was a process of not-quite-so-natural selection, and it did wonders for the school budget, while the few Mexicans who made it through high school did so by clawing their way to the top" (117). This type of filtering system, unfortunately still more or less in place in many parts of the Rio Grande Valley and in the Southwest today, encourages only the Mexican Americans students who are adept at "clawing their way to the top" to see themselves as equal to their peers.[17] The poorer students are simply moved through the grades of the educational ladder until, frustrated or bored or both, they eventually drop out either to marry or to work, as we have seen, because they are too discouraged to continue their educations further.

Maruca, Gualinto's eldest sister, for instance, falls behind her older sister Carmen. Instead of repeating the seventh grade, Maruca is pulled out of school by her mother, Maria, because at sixteen she is no longer considered a "school child." Educators in the novel do and say nothing about her leaving school. Carmen, who "loved to study, to read and to know," dreams of graduating from high school, but when Maria accidentally falls while caring for her rosebushes, Carmen, too, is forced to leave school to care for her (151–52). Seeing his sisters and peers dropping out of school, Gualinto "felt a strange mixture of emotions. . . . Elation at what the future promised. And at the same time feelings of sadness and loneliness. Perhaps it was the weather. Perhaps it was the thought that so few of his friends remained in school with him. El Colorado, Arty Cord, and La Vibora had made it through junior high with him, but they dropped out after seventh grade and went to work" (158).[18] Gualinto is happy about his own progress, but depressed about the fact that his close friends are leaving school. At this point, we are informed, Gualinto has started to develop "simultaneously in two widely divergent paths. In the schoolroom he was an American; at home and on the playground he was a Mexican"[19] (147).

The system of education in Texas during the 1920s and 1930s, as Paredes describes it, sought to separate out a *handful* of academically gifted Chicanos from the many Hispanic students who drop out. Unfortunately, this practice continues to be the case. According to the Texas Education Agency, 47 percent of Chicanos in Texas are still dropping out in the 1990s. Because Hispanic youths are not expected to succeed, students who make it through an essentially unsympathetic school system, like the Gualinto in Paredes's novel or the Richard Rodriguezes of real life, tend to be troubled throughout their school years by psychological problems prompted by experiences connected to race.[20] Instead of enjoying their years in school, the few Latino students who do successfully negotiate the grade levels do so despite the system, and not because the schools help them adapt to feeling good about being Mexicans *and* Americans.[21] This important psychological issue has historically been downplayed, and the points raised in the following passage from Paredes's novel remain virtually unaddressed by school counselors, psychologists, and educators:

> In school Gualinto/George Washington was gently prodded toward complete Americanization. But the Mexican side of his being rebelled. Immigrants from Europe can become Americanized in one generation. Gualinto, as a Mexicotexan, could not. Because, in the first place, he was not an immigrant come to a foreign land. Like other Mexicotexans, he considered himself part of the land on which his ancestors had lived before the Anglotexans had come. And because, almost a hundred years before, there had been a war between the United States and Mexico, and in Texas the peace had not yet been signed. So in assembly, while others were singing, "We're proud of our forefathers who fought at the Alamo," Gualinto and his friends would mutter, "We're proud of our forefathers who killed Gringos at the Alamo." (148)

For Gualinto, as for many Mexican Americans, "Texas history is a cross that he must bear" (149). The Anglo Texas perspective is brought up throughout the school grades in ways that educators do not see as divisive and psychologically destructive for educating Mexican Americans and other students. This is one of the ways, the novel contends, through which Mexican Americans in the schools are "gently prodded toward complete Americanization."

Paredes's *George Washington Gomez* captures the quandary of Mexican American split-allegiance, which countless fiction and nonfiction Chicano texts have since articulated. From this moment in the novel to the incident in the novel when Gualinto courageously stands by his Mexican American friends when they are not allowed to enter their senior prom site at a Harlanburg [Harlingen] restaurant because they are Mexicans (170–90), Gualinto is portrayed as a proud Mexican American. Paredes, however, also makes it clear that formidable social pressures everywhere force Chicanos to choose between being Mexican or American. In Gualinto's progress through school, for example, we see how his Mexican culture is gradually eroded by the very education that should be building the self-esteem of all students.

From that first day when he is taken to school by his uncle, Gualinto's learning experiences pull him away from the culture and the people who have brought him up and who expect education to empower him. Mexican American students soon realize that racism exists, and that their education in the United States virtually requires them to distance themselves from their Mexican Spanish-speaking culture. Although Gualinto resists leaving his culture in order to be Americanized through the first twelve years of his schooling, he is increasingly embarrassed by his people's ways, a process that culminates in the complete renunciation of his Mexican roots at the end of the novel.

When Gualinto hears Feliciano say that he is willing to peddle vegetables in the streets if the Great Depression forces him to, Gualinto is not moved by Feliciano's willingness to do whatever it takes to help Gualinto succeed. Instead, Gualinto is seized by the humiliation that he would face if his friends were to learn that his uncle was a street vendor (192). Confronted by this totally undesirable prospect, Gualinto announces that he would rather leave school, forego college, and work. When Feliciano mentions that Gualinto's father wanted college for his son and that he has "been adding to a special cache" for this purpose since Gualinto was a baby, Gualinto unexpectedly berates the memory of his father: "My father was just an ignorant Mexican! He got it into his head I was going to be a great man. A great man! And he saddled me with this silly, stupid name!" (193). Paredes writes that "Feliciano clenched his fists and half-rose. Then his hands relaxed and he sat back into the sofa. His face was pale. 'Don't you ever again talk like that about your father,' he said quietly."

Again, Paredes again uses Feliciano as a barometer to assess the progress of Gualinto's education. Throughout the novel, Feliciano is true to his word. He generously rearranges his whole life to provide for Gualinto's education so that Gualinto will help the "Mexicotexano" people. Since Gualinto's education is Feliciano's hard-won legacy, how Gualinto is to become a "great man" to lead Chicanos engages Feliciano's interest. The difference between *George Washington Gomez* and other stories about Chicano leaders—such as *Bless Me, Ultima, Heart of Aztlan* or *The House on Mango Street*—is that Paredes's novel, buttressed by his work as a folklorist and *corrido* singer, shows an incisive awareness of the real social and educational pressures that students like Gualinto experience.

Gualinto understandably alternates between his upbringing and studying to become a leader of Chicanos, eventually abandoning his Mexican American heritage altogether.[22] Many writers since W. E. B. Du Bois have written about this "dual personality," a psychological reality that Paredes memorably renders in Mexican Americans:

> When he is called upon to do his duty for his country he is an American.
> When benefits are passed around he is a Mexican and always last in line. And
> he has nobody to help him because he cannot help himself. In the United
> States he is not the only racial group that often finds the going hard. But
> while there are rich Negroes and poor Negroes, rich Jews and poor Jews,
> rich Italians and Poles and poor Italians and Poles, there are in Texas only
> poor Mexicans. Spanish-speaking people in the Southwest are divided into
> two categories: poor Mexicans and rich Spaniards. So while rich Negroes
> often help poor Negroes and rich Jews help poor Jews, the Texas-Mexican
> has to shift for himself. (195–96)

Given Gualinto's life, readers want to know why his education leads him
away from his people. Since he chooses not to become a leader of *raza*
people, as everyone hoped, will he dash the leadership expectations of
his Mexican American community (292–93)? Paredes draws out the uncertainty so that readers can understand where Gualinto started and
how his educational journey changes the thinking of this promising
Mexican American.

As in the best novels of Henry James, *George Washington Gomez* remains engaging to the last page.[23] By that point, we have learned that
Gualinto has disappointed everyone's hopes, for he has become what
the Chicano community calls a *vendido*, that is, a person who consciously ignores his or her own heritage for another one (294). Gualinto
tells Feliciano in the novel's closing pages that he is a "first lieutenant
in counter-intelligence" for the U.S. Army, and that his "job is border
security." Without missing a beat, Feliciano responds, "Whatever face
you put on it, you're still a spy." Feliciano smiles when he hears Gualinto assert that he doubts "there will be any foreign [German or Japan-
ese] agents at this end of the border. If any spying or sabotage takes
place it will be by some of our own people" (299). Feliciano reminds
Gualinto that Jonesville's Mexican Americans expected him to be the
"leader of his people," which prompts a series of surprisingly shameful
statements about Mexican Americans from the university-educated
lawyer Gualinto:

> His nephew snorted disdainfully. "I had a meeting with them before I came
> here. They're a bunch of clowns playing at politics. And they're trying to
> organize yokels who don't know anything but getting drunk and yelling and
> fighting."
> "Then you see no future for us."
> "I'm afraid not. Mexicans will always be Mexicans. A few of them, like
> some of those would-be politicos, could make something of themselves if

they would just do like I did. Get out of this filthy Delta, as far away as they
can, and get rid of their Mexican Greaser attitudes." (300)

Gualinto here shows the extent to which he has internalized much of
the hatred that exists toward his own people, which he has absorbed
from his education in American culture and society.[24] Readers, indeed,
are startled at the unexpected anger in Gualinto's sudden denunciation
of Mexican Americans, for which the novel does not prepare us. Yet, a
closer look will reveal that all along Paredes has been suggesting that,
as Gualinto progresses through school, he becomes increasingly dissatisfied with Mexican Americans, expressing a larger American sentiment
that is expressed whenever Anglos interact with Chicanos in the novel.

Chicanos and other Latinos who would sustain our culture and language within a larger, unsympathetic society that promotes only or
mainly assimilation, are often required to both absorb *and* learn to tran-
scend that very education. Educated Hispanics often learn that the cultural empowerment provided by an American education can also end
placing limitations on minority populations who are not seen as being
fully within the mantle of American society. Sometimes even our
brightest students, like Gualinto, succeed in fully assimilating what they
learn in school without being able to go beyond that education to see
how it affects the way in which Latinos see themselves and our people.

The rest of the closing exchange in the novel portrays a Feliciano
who heroically endures his nephew's ill-mannered, sad views with admirable equanimity. Feliciano restrains himself from voicing his bitter
disappointment at Gualinto's clear betrayal of everything for which he
has worked. Feliciano's condemnation, nevertheless, is quite apparent,
for the novel ends with the realization that, despite Gualinto's outward
success, he has miserably failed himself as a person as well as the Mexican American people, who expected help from him as an educated
lawyer (292).

The novel's poignant conclusion underscores what Paredes presents
as the unavoidable separation between Feliciano and Gualinto. This
gulf, which widens as Gualinto's education progresses, ends with Gualinto's decision to embrace the same American society that has historically kept Chicano culture apart. *George Washington Gomez* thus lodges
a serious indictment against an educational system that has historically
refused to recognize or address the identity and psychological problems
that all Chicano students, like Gualinto, cannot avoid negotiating. A
careful study of Paredes's work would help educators, legislators, and

policymakers understand how Hispanic children, who are supposed to be socialized into American society, are gradually being conditioned by the schools to fail, cutting them off from subsequent opportunities for personal and professional improvement as adults. If Gualinto psychically implodes as a Chicano, failing to engender esteem and respect as an educated adult Mexican American from readers and from his community, what then can be said for the rest of Gualinto's classmates who dropped out of school and barely succeed in making a living?

Gualinto's friend El Colorado, who drops out after the seventh grade to work, endures his father's terrible abuse, as do his mother and his siblings (251–52). Orestes, who does not want to be a mechanic like his father (115), perseveres and, despite many obstacles, eventually seems to fare best, joining the middle class as a pharmacist (289). The hapless Antonio Prieto (158) and Elodia, Gualinto's classmate who demonstrates how Chicanos talk (160), graduate from high school and marry. They subsequently make their livelihood by maintaining a Mexican food restaurant (286).

We cannot forget that for Feliciano and his sister, Maria, Gualinto is the Great Brown Hope. He is one of the Rio Grande Valley's most promising young students. But can an education that produces students who feel ashamed of their Mexican American heritage truly be called successful? This is exactly what still happens to many of the best Mexican American students who journey through the school system, troubled very much by the same kind of identity problems that Gualinto faces.

These and other psychosocial issues brought out in *George Washington Gomez* require further study. There are no easy answers to the difficult minority education issues highlighted by Paredes's work. His 1940 novel tells us that these problems have been with us for a long time, and they are not the type of issues that will go away of their own accord. Half a century later I think we can say that we have not yet successfully addressed this cultural need that Mexican Americans and other Latinos continually encounter. At this point, I am not even persuaded that educators are interested in recognizing the problem, much less looking into solutions.

The future not only of the Mexican American people but of all the people of the great Southwest and throughout the United States largely depends on the nature of the educations offered to all of our youths today. Alongside the educations available or not available to African

Americans, Native Americans, and Asian Americans, I cannot think of a greater need than to provide a better education for Latinos. As a concerned Mexican American educator, I believe American society ought to make use of its great resources to avoid creating people who delude themselves about their racial or cultural roots. There is no need to "sell out," as the pejorative expression has it, to become a *vendido* like Gualinto, for no Chicano should be put in the position of having to choose between succeeding as an "American" and one's own heritage. Gualinto's cavalier dismissal of his Mexican American heritage, so remarkably rendered by Paredes, leads him to reject his own past by angrily blasting his school friends, demonstrating his self-hatred.[25]

Aside from not fully understanding what his education and cultural environment have done to him, we can say that Gualinto does not understand the plight of other Mexican Americans. His own existence has been made relatively easy, thanks largely to Feliciano. That is why at the end of the novel, Gualinto predictably succumbs to the constant pressure that his education and his whole environment have placed on him since the day he entered the first grade. He is never able to see how he has been affected by a system that effectively changes him by destroying the person he was. Predictably, Gualinto chooses the path of least resistance, abandoning his people because, as he is reminded throughout the novel, he can pass for being an Anglo American, since he is told, "You look white" (284).[26] My sense is that unless we substantially reform education so that all students in the United States are taught to appreciate and respect themselves and people of all other races, the prospect for Americans looks even bleaker than the south Texas lives that Paredes portrayed more than fifty years ago.

8

The Lives of a Chicano Film Star: Anthony Quinn's *The Original Sin*

n 1995, the year he turned eighty, Anthony Quinn published *One Man Tango*, an account of his life among the movie stars he has known during his more than sixty years as a film star and theater actor. This second published story of Quinn's life covers his relationships with Hollywood movie stars more directly than his first autobiography, *The Original Sin: A Self-Portrait* (1972). Quinn's earlier book, however, ought to occupy an increasingly significant position in the history of Mexican American thought and American culture. Whereas Americo Paredes rendered the nature of K–12 education for Mexican American students in the south Texas of the 1920s and 1930s, Anthony Quinn reveals the burden of being Mexican American in Los Angeles during the 1930s. Since that time, he has continued to make his difficult way through the film and acting industry.

Although not specifically written as a work of Chicano literature, *The Original Sin* is one of the most engaging autobiographies yet published by a Mexican American who has achieved success in America.[1] Quinn's narrative, which is now out of print but ought to be reissued for its useful insights on growing up as a Chicano male, illuminates a rags-to-riches story that movingly dramatizes and provides considerable insight into a variety of assimilation problems also raised by Paredes's *George Washington Gomez*. Students interested in learning how race, consciousness, and a Latino's personal self-image interact, and how all three of these factors are shaped both by the world in which Quinn grew up, as well as the on-and-off stage world of the cinema and media, cannot do better than to study the conflicts that *The Original Sin* underscores.

Primarily motivated by the understandable desire to shape how posterity will see him, Quinn has at different times in his life paradoxically sought both to downplay and to highlight his Mexican American heritage. His objective clearly is to shed the best possible light on himself and his considerable acting talents. In his professional and personal hunger for life, love, attention, and what has to be seen as his own search for psychological balance, Quinn has consistently been shaped by his Mexican American ethnicity, as his life and two autobiographies demonstrate. The issues he raises, his narrative strategies, his intimate and quite public tabloid relationships, and the continual chaffing he experiences when his private and professional roles coalesce are so interconnected that it is difficult to envision another Mexican American narrative that successfully competes with Quinn's tumultuously adventuresome life.

Despite the fact that Hollywood has not exactly clamored for Hispanic actors throughout the twentieth century, Anthony Quinn has achieved unimagined success for a Mexican American actor. Not that Quinn is especially known in America or anywhere else for his Latino or Mexican American roles. In fact, in his more than sixty years of acting in films and on the stage, Quinn has played an enormous variety of roles, most of which have masked his heritage and background. From his best-known *Zorba the Greek* (1964) to his many performances as an Italian, Hungarian, Russian, British, Spanish, and even Chinese actor, Quinn has very successfully not revealed that he is a Mexican American who grew up in California. It is not that Quinn has concealed his Mexican identity, but rather that the Hollywood reality is such that if he had identified or presented himself as a Mexican, Quinn would never have received leading man roles. Even then, among his numerous film credits are several lesser-known Mexican roles that he has portrayed in movies such as *Viva Zapata!* (1952), *The Children of Sanchez* (1978), and *A Walk in the Clouds* (1995). But because he is known by the surname of his Irish father, and because he has played so many different characters from so many parts of the world, few people know that Anthony Quinn, who lived in Italy for many years and now resides primarily in New

York, is a Chicano who grew up in the barrios of Los Angeles in the 1930s. He is assumed by most film fans to be from some European country, but that impression belies the fact that he has had to play whatever roles have been offered to him because Mexican Americans have never been in demand in Hollywood, nor, for that matter, anywhere else in the United States.

Published at a time when Chicano activists in California, Texas, Arizona, and other parts of the country were beginning to create a Chicano literature that would define and restructure the image of Mexican Americans in American society, *The Original Sin* arrived at a very propitious moment for the new ethnic push. Quinn's book, however, was more of an effort to take personal stock of a career that had already achieved a good number of significant professional accomplishments, rather than an attempt to provide a Mexican American model during a period when Latinos were avidly looking for media role models to emulate. Quinn was more concerned with describing the obstacles he had vanquished and championing his life than with promoting a new literature. As a visible product of America's Hispanic culture, Quinn's achievements and professional ambitions, most of which had already been realized when he wrote his first autobiography, could well have served Chicano literature. But at that time in his career, he was ambivalently concerned about lending his name and support to what appeared to him an uncertain, unclear effort to create a new literature.

Although it is doubtful whether he would have agreed with the assessment, it is now clear that his personal needs and those of the Hispanic community in America were converging. And yet, because he was hesitant about involving himself too much with Chicano activists, he once told a Chicano editor who approached him that he did not want to be connected with "separatist efforts." Still, in a fifty-five-minute television film called *The Voice of La Raza*, which aired the same year that he published *The Original Sin*, Quinn, who narrated and served as host for the film, capitalized on the publicity raised by the story of his life to focus some much needed national attention on the Spanish-speaking people. Then, as now, the sentiment among Latinos was that we were receiving short shrift in the United States and that we had to make our presence felt, if conditions for our people were to improve. Although Quinn communicated that message, his literary self-portrait, like most cultural and media events in which he is featured, came across as sui generis.

As a truly exceptional individual, Quinn had instant name recognition not only with the American media, but, indeed, throughout the world, for he was a formidable, masterful actor. Yet, he only seemed to represent the lives of other Latinos in the United States by extension, and then with some difficulty. Only Rita Moreno, the Puerto Rican actress known principally for her early and memorable supporting role in *West Side Story*, benefited from the type of fame that Anthony Quinn had already achieved, and which more recent Mexican American actors such as Edward James Olmos and Jimmy Smits now enjoy.

As a known, long-standing actor, Quinn does not seem to have been affected by the problems that other Latinos have had in securing some good and positive coverage from the American media. He was reluctantly associated with the 1944 Los Angeles "Zoot Suit" affair, which he mentions in passing in his autobiography.[2] His own mother knew the mothers of the principals in the affair, and that relationship placed Quinn in an uncomfortable position which connected him to this high-profile negative Mexican American media episode. Most of Quinn's promotional efforts, however, do not appear to have been marred by the unattractive experiences that other aspiring Latinos can relate about the American media.

The Original Sin unfolds much like a film, in places offering revealing, detailed records of his trajectory from abject poverty in southern California, touching, through flashbacks, on the nature of the international life that Quinn has long led behind the celluloid and the lights. His autobiography is written with all the verve that Quinn regularly brings to the screen and stage. Not cast in the vein of Ernesto Galarza's more modest *Barrio Boy* or any other Chicano autobiography, *The Original Sin* tells a different kind of personal life story behind the successful one that Quinn has led. Ambitiously intended more as a twentieth-century descendant of Rousseau's *Confessions*, and in a line with *The Confessions of St. Augustine*, which he read and admired, Quinn's narrative seeks to be a veritable tour de force that impresses readers with its humor and straightforwardness. Although intended as a kind of intellectual autobiography, since the book describes his growth and development, *The Original Sin* renders a modern Mexican American's search for happiness, for God, for something substantial enough to believe in when, in the late 1960s and early 1970s, everything that held social sway suddenly came to appear hollow to Quinn. The autobiography is the account of an unsure actor who, having divorced his first wife, was consciously examining how he had lived and how he was living in his mid-fifties.[3]

Among several particularly well-written anecdotes included in his autobiography, Quinn relates an early story that quintessentially shows how his racial identity shaped and has continued to affect his actions and decisions. As a twenty-year-old aspiring actor, one of Quinn's first assignments was to play an American Indian in Cecil B. De Mille's *The Plainsman*, a 1936 film starring Gary Cooper. Quinn says that, given the idea of his role in the script, he envisioned making an impassioned speech urging the Cheyenne, Sioux, Blackfoot, and Apache to declare war against the white man. Less than two hours after arriving on the set the morning filming began, Quinn met Gary Cooper for the first time. At that point in his career, Cooper was already a famous actor, whereas Quinn's only role had been as one of several prisoners in a nondescript film that he calls *Paroles for Sale* in his autobiography, but which was called *Parole!* in which he had appeared, been knifed in the back, and died, all in the space of forty-five seconds. (Fortunately, there was a close-up that showcased Quinn, and upon seeing it, his grandmother had presciently declared that young Quinn would be a great movie star like Ramón Novarro and Antonio Moreno, two of the best known Hispanic actors in the American films of the day.)[4]

On that first morning of shooting *The Plainsmen*, Quinn became anxious when he learned that he was slated to act opposite Cooper. Cooper was playing an American trying to seek peace with the Indians; as an American Indian, Quinn's character was to accuse Cooper's of being "a liar because he's a white man." When he saw what their roles required, Quinn realized that he had to develop an intense hate for Gary Cooper by 9 A.M., when the shooting was scheduled to start. How Quinn quickly achieved the heartfelt hatred for Cooper that he so successfully communicated in the film is instructive: By surmising that Cooper "probably hates Mexicans," Quinn says he quickly and easily worked himself into the proper spirit, adding that he felt "I could really murder [Cooper]" with a hate-filled Indian speech" (235–36).

In another instance, Quinn relates that as a teenager living in the Mexican American barrios near the banks of the Los Angeles River, he was asked by Irish teenagers to join them in an evening rumble against a neighboring Mexican gang. Quinn agreed to fight with the group, but when the Mexican kids shortly after also asked him for help against the Irish gang, Quinn switched and fought on the side of the Mexican boys.

Other than this and a few other anecdotes, his the teen-age years when he ran with gangs in Los Angeles do not receive much attention, but from such revealing events, Quinn suggests the extent to which his Mexican American background, his physical looks, and spirit have repeatedly shaped his acting, his life, and his thinking. How Quinn has seen and represented himself both personally and professionally, however, has not always been as clear, as these stories and others in his autobiography make clear.

"Is it true?" asks his psychologist "Are there moments when you can tell that you're being Mexican or Irish?" "Yes," answers Quinn. "Which is easier to live with?" pursues the therapist. "The Irish," answers Quinn unequivocally, adding, "but then nobody ever called me a dirty mick. I never had to take a beating because I was Irish. I only had the shit kicked out of me because I was Mexican. So I decided to be it [Mexican] most of the time." Being "a Mexican in southern California," Quinn informs his therapist and readers, "is not exactly an open sesame. For years, they used to have signs at dance halls and restaurants: 'No Mexicans allowed.' Mexicans were lazy, thieves, greasy; they were either zoot-suiters or Pachucos, marijuana smokers" (9).

When speaking to disadvantaged youths, Quinn has often successfully employed his memories of belonging to an unwanted racial and cultural group from the poorer class. But, like many Mexican Americans brought up in the United States without the benefit of a school system that builds sufficient Chicano self-esteem, Quinn understandably has ambivalent feelings about issues that keep Spanish-speakers from achieving their full potential.[5] Due to his own substantial stage presence and impressive good looks, Quinn has been extraordinarily successful in living a different type of life from most American Latinos. But in both his films and his life, Quinn has often championed underappreciated characters through his fine acting, successfully communicating the complexities of the lives of people who are held in less regard by societies against which he has defined himself, both on camera and off.

Anthony Quinn was born in Chihuahua, Mexico, on April 15, 1915, of a poor Mexican mother named Manuela, who raised him. His Irish father was "a dreamer who thought that Pancho Villa and his revolution had the answer. He and my mother both fought in the revolution," writes Quinn. Years later, when the famous actor visits his mother, prompted by a desire to learn more about those early days for his autobiography, she says, "I never knew where your father was" Quinn's father apparently stayed home when he wanted, and then disappeared for extended periods. "A life isn't exactly like a story," his mother adds, expressing a view that also happens to describe Quinn's own narrative. "It's never 'once upon a time,' " she tells her son. "In life, time gets all mixed up. No sooner does one thing happen than something else comes in. My own life, even though I lived it, it's hard to say it happened like this and like that" (48).

In writing *The Original Sin*, Quinn confronted the type of difficult questions faced by most autobiographers: What matters or instances should be included, and what perspectives and attitudes should be emphasized? What parts of his multifaceted life should be incorporated into the text to provide a consistent, smooth story, and what incidents should be left out? Having finished the book, a reader may well ask: Since Quinn is such an accomplished actor, why does he mainly allude to his successes without discussing them? And why does he keep returning to his ethnicity, particularly to his early Mexican American days? It is clear to everyone familiar with his career that he has moved a considerable way from his younger days, and since he is so good at representing such a broad range of roles, why does he continually circle back to incidents that deal with his Hispanic identity, even though he does not use such terms? Why is he so anxious and uncertain about himself as an actor when he is without a role? Why does he clearly think of himself as a Mexican American, when he could choose instead to think of himself as the world-renowned actor Anthony Quinn? In a life inordinately filled with fact and fiction, these questions and others like them are more easily asked than successfully answered by his text.

Quinn has performed in nearly 250 films and enough stage productions to satisfy the lifetime ambitions of most theater actors. As a highly regarded movie star whose dominating presence on the screen and stage has always called attention to his skills, it is interesting that in his own story of his life Quinn repeatedly focuses on what has to be called his essential self. In other words, stripped of all the trappings that accrue from being world famous, what is Anthony Quinn's essential nature as represented in *The Original Sin?* After reading his book, one would conclude that Quinn's essential, basic self, for all of his cinematic exoticism and cosmopolitanism, is cast as his ethnic, Mexican American self.

In *The Original Sin*, Quinn undertakes to reveal some of his more personal views, especially the nature of the mental life that he has had behind the famous movie actor and public figure. His travels throughout the globe, most of which audiences remember through the memorable images of his films and the news items that periodically make the tabloids, apparently do not sufficiently satisfy the always restless Quinn. He finds some solace in such accomplishments, his narrative suggests, but he cannot seem to rest easily with himself, with his life's uncertainties, a good number of which his autobiography either discusses or suggests. He informs us, for example, that he became a voracious reader in his late teens when Sylvia, an attractive woman who was old enough to be his mother, became his lover. Sylvia introduced him to the works of Santayana, Schopenhauer, Fielding, Smollett, Baudelaire, Balzac, Dante, D'Annunzio, Ford Madox Ford, Sinclair Lewis, F. Scott Fitzgerald, Thomas Wolfe, Ernest Hemingway, and a number of other writers and thinkers (183). Although he does not mention other hobbies that occupy his time when he is not acting, aficionados who follow Quinn's career know that he is also an accomplished painter and a sculptor who has exhibited his work, and he is a recognized art collector. Readers sense that Quinn is the type of person who consciously seeks out experiences, who absorbs and assimilates much of what he encounters. But his life and his acting are never far apart. Once, for example, while crossing the Atlantic by ship to play Quasimodo in the 1957 film *Notre Dame de Paris* (*The Hunchback of Notre Dame*), Quinn tells us he developed blotches on his face, which inexplicably swelled beyond recognition. Failing to find a remedy at the hands of European specialists, Quinn was eventually cured when a homeopath informed him that due to his grotesque swelling he now knew what it felt like to be the bell-tower monster he would be playing in the film. Quinn absorbed that trying, unnerving experience and then turned that intimate knowledge of what it is like to be seen as a hideous monster into a masterful Quasimodo performance. That version of Victor Hugo's classic work is still universally regarded one of the best black-and-white motion pictures ever made.

People who immigrate to the United States frequently seem to value success more than Americans born here. Although he failed to provide for his son, Quinn says that his Irish father memorably imprinted the importance of being "Number One" to him. Judging from the experiences related by Quinn, the ambitious boy's life seems to have been driven by this paternal injunction. Living by a filial directive from a largely absent father was particularly difficult because their early life in California required them to struggle. Quinn's Mexican mother cleaned Anglo homes, took in laundry, and undertook what jobs she could to provide for her son and daughter. As a consequence, Anthony was largely left to go about becoming Number One as best he could in the barrios of Los Angeles in the 1930s and 1940s.

From such inauspicious and unpromising beginnings, few would expect Quinn to achieve the stature and artistic regard he has since secured. Without *The Original Sin*, who would know that, as a baby, Quinn's mother carried him across the bridge from Juarez to El Paso, from their homeland in Mexico to the United States, for the total bridge fee of two pennies? That was August 2, 1916, and that is Quinn's immigrant story, of which we aren't told much else. Can we connect that story to the Anthony Quinn who that is today known throughout the world for a great number of wonderful films, too numerous to list here? In the eyes of many knowledgeable movie fans, Quinn belongs in the company of the best-known English-speaking performers, actors like Sir Lawrence Olivier, Richard Burton, Sidney Poitier, Katharine Hepburn, and Sir Ralph Richardson. Yet, as in most very public lives, there have been occasions, both on and off the stage and screen, that Quinn confesses he would rather forget.

In a life inordinately filled with cinematic and theatrical events, it would be psychically necessary for Quinn periodically to take stock of his career. *The Original Sin* is the product of such a mature self-inventory, one that is carefully designed to provide readers with a casual sense of Quinn's more personal life through the years. At other junctures in his enormously full life, Quinn would likely have written another type of autobiography, one structured and narrated differently. Nonetheless, at whatever age he chooses to emphasize in his life, it is clear that Quinn always thinks of himself as an impatient, irascible, macho, chauvinistic, self-centered, and, certainly, ethnic Chicano in his thinking and constitutional makeup.

Like many Mexican Americans of his generation, he does not embrace the term Chicano because it was used in opprobrium when Quinn was growing up, forty years before the Chicano movement of the early 1970s reconstituted the term and made it politically attractive. To his credit, though, Quinn, however ambivalently, has since consistently championed Mexican American and Latino causes because he understands from experience how Spanish speakers have had to struggle in the United States both to secure attention and to succeed.

Quinn tells us that he does not always behave in real life as admirers think great actors live, or expect them to. In his book, the emphasis is always on his human side, on life's temptations and uncertainties and how he has coped and both failed and prevailed. There has always been an air about Quinn that says he feels underappreciated, and this attitude has bothered admirers who would easily grant him the stature of an Olivier or a Richardson. Such admirers have not been fully aware of Quinn's early struggles and his Mexican American background, issues which, of course, Quinn has not emphasized but which help explain the different nature of his problems and challenges. Yet, when we read about his intense desire to succeed as an actor; when we hear him describe his relationships with such famous people as Frank Lloyd Wright, John Barrymore, Carole Lombard, Mae West, Gina Lollobrigida, W. C. Fields, and a host of similar people; when we think about the type-casting difficulties he has endured, and the personal demons and ghosts that have dogged his life, as well as his Chicano past, which pursues and apparently haunts him incessantly—readers and fans have to recognize that Quinn's life, as depicted in *The Original Sin*, is a record of considerable turmoil and achievement by a great soul-searching Mexican American actor.

Anthony Quinn's background seems to have alternately empowered his success and to have been his bane. Our understanding of this important aspect of his personality, depends, of course, on what Quinn selectively offers, on how he casts and constructs the story of his life. *The Original Sin* begins with Quinn telling us about his success: "I was living in New York, surrounded by possessions, family and position. I had three pictures running simultaneously on Times Square and I was appearing in a play at the same time. Everywhere you looked on Broadway you saw my name in lights." To celebrate that success and to recognize the nature of his achievement as an actor, says Quinn,

> Some lovely ladies from a drama society gave a luncheon for me. They invited prominent personalities from many fields to pay me homage.
>
> When I was called upon, I tried to thank them. I started haltingly. I looked out at the sea of friendly faces before me, waiting expectantly. Then I heard myself mumbling that I felt like a total failure. I can still recall the shock and dismay that greeted my words.
>
> Everyone wanted a light, gracious talk and there I stood declaring that success to me did not mean a thing.

> When I finished, my hosts applauded politely, but I had hurt them. I had
> made a resounding *faux pas*, using their forum as a confessional. (1)

Quinn's reconstruction of the occasion highlights a trait that periodically appears in his book. Surprised by what he hears himself say, especially when he does not fully know his own mind, Quinn repeatedly
shows us that he often chooses to separate himself from his own actions.
This narrative tactic allows him, in this instance, to take the edge off his
faux pas, while analyzing his behavior, much as if he were a professional
performer studying a character's role, providing Quinn with the necessary distance to study himself.

Although the event requires him to speak as the famous actor, on this
occasion Quinn suggests that a voice he does not fully control inter-
venes and speaks for him. Quinn knows he should appreciate the
homage and thank his supporters. But to his surprise, he hears himself
say that he feels like a failure. A young actor in the audience impulsively
upbraids Quinn on his way out: "You shit! I have never been so ashamed
of anyone as I was of you today. I have never heard such phony humil-
ity. If you're not a success, who is?" (1). That young would-be actor expresses Quinn's very sentiments. Quinn confesses failure for something
that he feels is inexplicably amiss, but since he cannot pinpoint the trouble himself, he ends by dashing the natural expectations of fans just
when New York's high society is celebrating his success.

Why would Quinn say that another person, apparently within him,
has stepped to the microphone on that festive occasion to confess him
a failure? His autobiography suggests that despite Quinn's clear successes, an important part of his person does not allow him to enjoy his
triumphs, even in the perfunctory ways that other actors take their successes in stride.

Following the young actor's stinging rebuke, Quinn walks toward his
expensive six-story town home on Seventieth and Park Avenue nearby.

> Each floor was filled with fine period furniture, with paintings, sculptures,
> and rare books. The thought of these possessions gave me no comfort. As I
> walked down Fifth Avenue, the towering buildings seemed to be falling in on
> me. I crossed over to Central Park. I began running. With each step my
> panic increased. I ran until I thought my lungs would burst. Exhausted, I fell
> down on a grassy mound overlooking the reservoir.
>
> I longed to cry, but my throat wouldn't respond. I felt the greatest sorrow
> I had ever known, but I couldn't produce a tear. On my knees I called to God
> for help. There was no answer. I waited with my eyes closed. I waited but He
> must have been busy elsewhere. (2)

Quinn's words suggest a classic emotional breakdown. "When I opened my eyes," he continues, "the lights of the city were blinking on all around me. It was then that I saw 'the boy.' He was under a tree. I got up and struggled toward him. He turned and ran. 'You little sonofabitch, you made me do it! If I ever catch you. . . .' But he was gone" (2).

In the scheme of the autobiography, "the boy" is an apparitional construct employed by Quinn, for the first time here, to allow readers to see a part of his essential nature that seeks attention and which Quinn does not know how to represent otherwise. Objectifying a part of himself to carry on a self-dialogue, to be sure, is a risky business, but Quinn's straightforward language allows him to carry off the strategy without unduly putting off his readers. The repeated appearances of this imaginary boy pique readers' curiosity, allowing Quinn to attempt communication through a simple device that clearly suggests a complex psychology. Just in case the reader's credulity is strained, Quinn employs expletives in the hope of downplaying the theatrics of an exchange with a younger version of himself.

Once the initial uneasiness of the bifurcation strategy is clear, the reader begins to understand Quinn's dilemma. The idea behind his autobiography is to objectify a part of himself that he hopes to examine— an aspect effectively embodied by the love-hate responses of the twelve-year-old boy who inexplicably shows up to taunt the adult Quinn. The figure of the boy, which materializes at crucial points in Quinn's life when he moves or threatens to move away from his ethnic roots, readers soon realize, is a pretty clear symbol of his dissatisfaction, of the price he feels he is continually forced to pay for his rare success. The boy usually appears in Quinn's life when the actor least expects him, when the adult Quinn is involved in some pleasant activity that is tellingly distasteful to the Mexican American youngster that Quinn was when he lived in the barrios of Los Angeles. In such instances, the boy's behavior, which consists of grimaces, sudden derisive laughter, or marked apathy and indifference, so irritates Quinn that the actor's peace of mind is disturbed enough to make him forget whatever he is doing. In these cases, he then has to attend to the boy, who will not be overlooked, who will not let Quinn rest or continue with his life.

Most of the passages cited above appear in the preface to the book, announcing Quinn's subject, his own dilemma. The first chapter of *The Original Sin* is set in the office of a tweed-suited therapist, a "shrink," who comfortably smiles while the ill-at-ease Quinn eyes everything before him: "the twin pens that never worked, the fake leather blotter, the marine brass clock, the rotating calendar." (5) Anxious, Quinn asks whether he should lie on the couch. The meter is running, and he is fairly certain that seeing a therapist will not help. "A few days ago, I saw you in an Italian movie," says the therapist. "That last scene of you crying on the beach was moving as hell." Quinn writes: "Shit! Here I was paying this sonofabitch fifty dollars an hour and he was just another fan" (5).

Quinn's levity helps him deflect his anxiety and insecurity. The therapist begins by inquiring into what inspires the actor, and as Quinn reluctantly explains that crying for the scene required drawing from the accumulated pain in his own life, he finds himself thinking of the character in the film.

> I was thinking of the poor bastard I was playing. He had lived a rough, meaningless life. He had never felt love. When he finally found it, he hadn't known what to do—except destroy it. There on the beach, he felt the immensity of space. The eternity which he would have to face alone. It was probably the first time he had ever really seen the stars, and what they represented to him was an eternity of loneliness. "Do you believe in love, Mr. Quinn?" asks the psychologist. (6)

The character Quinn dispassionately begins to discuss happens, as he learns, to fit Quinn's own life. He, too, "had lived a rough, meaningless life." He, too, had felt unloved and, when he finally found love, hadn't known what to do—"except destroy it." Quinn thinks about the "eternity of loneliness" experienced by the character he was playing, providing the psychologist with the opportunity to raise the issue of love in his patient.

With this question, the therapy session abruptly arrives at the heart of *The Original Sin*, the central issue for Quinn in resolving of events in his life. This theme in part is heralded by the autobiography's dedication, which revealingly reads, "To Mama, who forgave me the day I was born." Women and love in Quinn's world are invariably connected. There are many stories about Quinn's relationships with the women in his life, from the influential Sylvia, who introduced him to great writers and artists and whom he almost married, to the secretary in her thirties who gave birth to a baby fathered by the eighty-year-old Quinn, because, he told the tabloids, the young lady wanted his baby. There is a Mrs. Harris, who sought to detain him when the young Quinn left Los

Angeles and headed east, traveling through south Texas, and out on the roads of the world, bent on acquiring experience about life, as Sylvia had urged him. Then there are his Hollywood women and the stories that the media has been playing up in the gossip columns for more than half a century. His first and widely celebrated marriage to Katherine De Mille, which lasted twenty-eight years, ended in divorce in 1965, a few years before he published his autobiography. Some readers are even tempted to say that some form of guilt regarding women is at the center of *The Original Sin*. But Quinn himself early confesses and contextualizes his relations with women: "With women I had failed utterly. There my conditions were unbending and archaic, the result of my religious training and heredity. The Indian blood in my veins was too strong to allow for any jazzy modern concepts. With women no flexibility was possible" (7).[6]

Quinn is clearly more interested in the nature of his own personal experience. "Had I ever been able to love unconditionally?" he asks. "I certainly loved my children, and yet, I had imposed laws even on them." He is more concerned, it seems to me, in finding and securing what he considers the panacea of "unconditional love." All of the love he has ever received, except for his mother's, Quinn maintains, has always been tied to conditions that he has been able to enumerate. That includes the love he received from his father, his wives, and the people who have known him. What Quinn has desired is love that is untied to conditions.

There are places in Beijing where every New Year's Day the people of the city traditionally gather to scream out their frustrations, thus unburdening themselves of whatever has bothered them during the previous year. Having publicly yelled about their dissatisfactions and shouted out the problems that have beset them, people return home, supposedly in better spirits for having relieved themselves so publicly and, oddly, so anonymously. Such a public expiation of frustrations sounds strange to the Western world, but the practice apparently serves a good social purpose.

In the case of Anthony Quinn, his voice dies at the very moment when he wants to scream for help. He is further disconcerted when the psychologist assures him that there is physically nothing wrong with his throat. Either there is a "growth on your chords, which I can't see or you have a lie caught in your throat," the therapist calmly informs him. "There were a thousand lies caught in my throat!" retorts Quinn.

"Which was the one that was crippling me?" (2). Lies, of course, are desired fabrications, the stories we make up for the realities we would rather avoid. Lies are part of the cost that we knowingly exact for our personal comfort, and they end as the price we pay for trying to create the worlds we want. Since lies are the stories that we consciously miscreate, they take a toll; they psychologically burden the desired, sought self, ironically distancing us from the very goals we seek. *The Original Sin* is Anthony Quinn's attempt to justify his progress by assessing his past. By most criteria, his life has been an inimitable success. However, Quinn himself knows that the twelve-year-old boy who periodically shows up is telling him that all is not well.

Choosing an imagined boy to help tell the story of his personal and public life is risky and significant. This fictive mechanism allows Quinn to communicate the true nature of his inner life. The boy appears at the most unexpected moments to taunt and to harass Quinn. To be sure, the youngster is not Irish. He is Mexican American, and he is not at all impressed by Quinn's success, his macho prowess with women, or his social and cultural achievements. The boy, representing Quinn's own skeptical, cynical teenage persona, is unaccommodating, uncompromising. He is not seduced by the trappings of social position, nor by success, fame, stature in Hollywood, or everything else through which the adult Quinn defines himself. By his haunting presence, the boy suggests that none of Quinn's accomplishments make much difference. What the boy apparently seeks is Quinn himself, stripped of all of the accouterments that make him the famous person he is. The boy, it seems, would prefer to have Quinn as he might have been, had he never achieved renown. Of course, if such a wish were realized, Anthony Quinn would not be a well-known actor, and there would likely be no boy, since Quinn would be just one more nondescript Mexican American male in American society. In such a case, there would be no alter ego, no Quinn who cynically keeps record of the concessions, compromises, and adjustments the adult Quinn has had to make in order to succeed in the film world.

Quinn, the text makes clear, wants the boy to embrace what he has become, what he has experienced and accomplished. But that is exactly what his Mexican American teenage counterpart will not accept. Rather, he seems to want—for he does not initially talk—Anthony Quinn as he might have been had he stayed in the Los Angeles barrios where they both grew up and cannot forget, as Cisneros's Esperanza cannot. For these reasons, Anthony Quinn and the boy share common ground as well as being at odds with each other, making conciliation or appeasement difficult.

Where does the unhappy Mexican American boy who does not like the successful adult Anthony Quinn emanate from? Although the boy in Quinn's autobiography can be seen as the archetypal Mexican American youth who is dissatisfied with everything in American life that leaves him out, in *The Original Sin* Quinn eventually locates the boy's moment of birth from an odd incident with his own father. In talking to his therapist, Quinn recalls a particular day when he was twelve years old and sold newspapers on a street corner in Los Angeles:

> Every afternoon I looked forward to the ritual of selling a newspaper to my father. I loved the easy way he jumped down from the streetcar. I admired the hugeness of him. He towered over everyone. He'd walk over to me, look at the headlines. He'd put his hand in his pocket and pull out a five-cent piece. The paper was only three cents, but he'd say, "Keep the change, boy." (94)

Earlier that same afternoon, Quinn had been pitching pennies with other newsboys, which had led to a fight. The moment the young Quinn heard the streetcar, though, he brushed himself off as well as he could and returned to his post by the pile of newspapers. When his father approached, he inexplicably looked over young Quinn's head "as if he were searching for someone [else]. Then he walked away without once looking at me." When Anthony got home, his father was already at the supper table, and his mother and grandmother were "setting plates of meat, beans and tortillas in front of him." After young Quinn washed his hands and face and returned to the kitchen, his father asked where he had been. Selling papers, as he always did, Quinn answered, "But, Papa, you walked right by me. I went up to you and you acted like you didn't know me."

"I didn't see you," responded his Irish father. "I saw some dirty little Mexican kid who asked me if I wanted a paper. He looked a little like you, but he wasn't my son. My son might be poor but he is never dirty. No matter what he does he stands proud and always looks like a prince" (95).

This dialogue between an Irish father who claims one day, for whatever reason, not to recognize his own Mexican American son left an indelible impression on the young Quinn. For, during the session with his therapist, nearly forty years later, the actor breaks down and weeps, rhetorically asking his absent father: "Does your loving me depend on the way I look, on how I behave? Don't you love me for me, for myself? My mother makes no demands on me. She doesn't care if I am filthy dirty."

One need not be a psychologist to see that the fight-bedraggled twelve-year-old Quinn who stood at the corner and eagerly awaited his father's return home is very much the same twelve-year-old Chicano youth who refuses to condone Quinn's successful adult life. How far Quinn is from being the prince that his father would have, and how much he wants his father's approval is suggested by the impact that his father's insensitive remarks had and continue to have on Quinn the rest of his life. Indeed, almost all Latinos have at least one story to tell about how once they were discriminated against, whether seriously or in jest.

Nothing in the text itself tells us whether Quinn's autobiography is ghostwritten, and in interviews Quinn has never answered this question one way or the other.[7] *The Original Sin* nonetheless is particularly significant in the history of Mexican American thought. It is Anthony Quinn's unflinching Rousseauvian search for personal truth about what his own father must have meant when he said, "I saw some dirty little Mexican kid," given that his father represents the larger American culture context in which Quinn uneasily exists.

Despite the clear fact that many times Quinn himself would apparently rather not face the disturbing presence of the twelve-year-old Chicano boy, the beauty of the book is that Quinn does not shrink from confronting a personal truth, even though it would be have been easier to avoid the issue. Although Quinn treats the experience as a personal matter, Quinn's traumatization at the hands of his own father is representative of the whole troubled presence of Latinos in American society. Living a life consisting of an uncommon mixture of reality and fiction, Quinn courageously chooses to represent a desperately unsettled man, who, despite his many successful films and stage roles, paradoxically feels unfulfilled and dissatisfied. His autobiography captures a man who has not been allowed, despite his own full life as an actor, the luxury of comfortably enjoying his achievements because his own father once called him a "dirty little Mexican kid." This racist epithet is underscored in other places in the book by other Americans (187, 299) often enough to make Quinn counter assumed racism by employing racism himself, as we saw in the film he made with Gary Cooper. Though Quinn does not formulate the issue this way, no matter what he accomplishes, he feels hurt by being disparaged as a "Mexican," which, as we have seen in Paredes's *George Washington Gomez*, was a pejorative a term to their generation. Quinn seems to have gone through life waiting to see if he will be similarly identified or insulted by other mainstream Americans, a disconcerting proposition that no one should wish on another person.

What Quinn is after is the person that deep down he seems to believe he is, because his life understandably has not allowed him to be the person that he comfortably ought to be. There appears to be, in other words, an Anthony Quinn who wants out, another person who would emerge, if such a self could be reconstituted satisfactorily without including the very experiences that have made Quinn so successful an actor. Part of the dilemma is that the adult actor and the self-monitoring author of *The Original Sin* cannot easily settle just *who* this different Anthony Quinn who did not get past twelve years of age might be. Unlike Gualinto or Richard Rodriguez, who choose to anglicize themselves and reject their cultural roots, Anthony Quinn uncomfortably seeks to maintain his heritage within his successful adult self. The psychological challenge this desire constantly presents in his life as an actor, however, does not make living any easier.

The real Quinn, the one who remains when all the other personas he has played on stage and screen have been pared away, is not easily envisioned or articulated because Quinn the author protectively suggests that he can, of course, actually be no other than the sum of what he has been. To be sure, Quinn knows that he is not just another ordinary person, so he cannot settle for that. His father told him to be "Number One" and to be a "prince," and that has guided him. Although the incident with his father can be read as yet another instance of American prejudice toward Mexican people, deep down Quinn's goal appears to have been to overcome, to conquer and to excel in order to become "Number One" and the "prince" that his father wanted. For there is, we know, great ambition in the man, a strong desire to continue to be more than the type of man who simply meets the challenges that he encounters. There is, in short, considerable pride in Quinn. The presence of these qualities is autobiographically justified—for *The Original Sin*, despite its ostensible desire to reveal the real Anthony Quinn, is undeniably among his best performances. "My God," says his therapist, apparently overwhelmed at the thought of having to sum up Quinn, "I've never met anyone who is such a contradiction. You love life and you hate it, Tony. You believe in life and yet you go about surrounded by the dead," by past ghosts who shape his life.

The Original Sin is a portrait of a conflicted Mexican American actor who suffers from a fundamental inability to reconcile his known media self to the poor, obscure ethnic roots that ironically seem to have powered his ambitious drive to fame. The book brings into relief a troubled self-portrait by an actor who could well have focused attention on his many successes. That he chose to reveal and dwell on some of his shortcomings in a public effort to embrace his ethnic past is quite telling, for the endeavor to find and articulate an important part of his truest self is a measure of Quinn's desire to embrace *lo propio*, everything that is part of his essential nature. His autobiography clearly bifurcates Quinn's personality, for his twelve-year-old Chicano self simply will not approve or endorse anything that the adult Quinn embraces. This conflict captures a stalemate—the adult Quinn is justifiably infuriated by the youngster's adamant refusal to sanction what the adult considers necessary decisions and actions. The central quandary is that the twelve year old sees the adult Quinn as a fraud, suggesting that the adult Quinn has given up some unarticulated principles, positions, or beliefs—no doubt associated with being Mexican American—in order to pursue what he desired. The youngster initially refuses to talk, further infuriating Quinn, who argues, without receiving the satisfaction of a response, that the rewards warrant what he left behind. The seriousness with which Quinn treats the boy raises issues that keep a resolution in abeyance.

The adult Quinn cannot easily satisfy his youthful version of himself, and therefore neither psychologically complex entity can find endorsement or approval in the other's perspective. What we have in *The Original Sin* is an actor's personality split into two opposing, irreconcilable versions, the younger one taunting the adult, suggesting that, like Paredes's Gualinto, the adult Quinn has sold out or is, again, a *vendido*.

Quinn's autobiography wonderfully reveals the nature of some of the anxieties that unquestioned success can raise in ambitious minority people. A good number of the books concerning the experiences of minority Americans deal with the unexpected problems of being successful, of actually achieving goals pursued. Much of the anxiety that minorities experience comes from having to negotiate with the people or social

forces that end up shaping our lives. Often, we find psychological turmoil imbedded in protagonists, as we do in Quinn's *The Original Sin*. In
such cases, the issue is one of squaring the minority person with a
known public image, a process that exposes the self-doubts and concerns that arise from the pursuit of the different ideological or social
goals that are central to learning acceptance.

At the end of Quinn's *The Original Sin*, the adult Quinn and his
twelve-year-old alter ego abruptly and rather unexpectedly drive out to
a desert in southern California. "What is it you really want?" the adult
Quinn asks the boy.

> He looked directly into my eyes. I studied his face, and the high Indian
> cheekbones and the tousled hair coming down over the forehead. I felt I was
> seeing myself for the first time. "I want you to love me, to accept me. I don't
> want to be a ghost, I want to be part of you." (306)

"Get in," says Quinn, "let's head for the desert, man. Let's see if God is
there."

Our childhood selves, Quinn suggests, continue to shape our attitudes
and perspectives throughout our lives. But other ancestors from before
our own time also make what we might call spiritual claims on our lives.
At one point in an interview with Tino Villanueva, Quinn unexpectedly
connected himself to the indigenous Indians of Mesoamerica:

> I don't know why, but I associate myself more as an Indian with, not pride,
> but almost pride, than I do as a Mexican. My deep affection, real sincere deep
> affection for the Indian in Mexico, Guatemala, Peru, Colombia, every place,
> is towards the Indian. I feel very, very close to him. I don't know if it's
> because my mother's name was Oaxaca, or why, but I feel, very, very close to
> the Indian. I don't feel very close to what I am, a *mestizo*, as I do toward the
> Indian. And I'm very proud of having Indian blood in me.[8]

Quinn says that he does not feel close to what he truly is, "a *mestizo*,"
or "a man of mixed European and American Indian ancestry," as the
dictionary defines the term. Given his life experiences as a Chicano,
that is understandable. As he said: "I never had to take a beating because I was Irish. I only had the shit kicked out of me because I was
Mexican." Chicanos have a mixed ancestry, and being Mexican American, his autobiography amply shows, is exactly what has caused some
of his troubles throughout life, even for a person of Anthony Quinn's
stature. I sense that Quinn, as a romantic, believes that if he is going to
be rejected by society or by anyone, it is better to be "an Indian," since
one can then be "proud" at being truly repudiated.[9] As Quinn sees the

indigenous *indio* of Mexico, this person has no resort, no recourse, and therefore has every reason for being proudly blameless of the exclusion he or she has received.

On the last page of *The Original Sin* the boy suddenly disappears, abruptly subsumed, we are left to believe, into the adult. "I knew I'd never again be alone," writes Quinn, rather quickly and too neatly, given the complexities raised by the troubled self in the text. Because he plays out most of his life against his Mexican American self, Quinn provides a remarkably engaging story about the selves he battles against, and the basic, essential self this book has allowed him to recognize. The legacy of Quinn's autobiography is that of a troubled Mexican American man who has suffered from uncomfortably living with a public self that the rest of the world cannot easily reconcile to the poor and obscure Mexican spirit that has powered his life.

9

Rape and Barrio Education in Sandra Cisneros's *The House on Mango Street*

T hinking about the connection between Esperanza Cordero's education in her barrio neighborhood and her rape in Sandra Cisneros's 1984 novel *The House on Mango Street* can be a disturbing and enlightening experience.[1] When this most popular of Chicano novels is discussed, invariably some reader will inquire if a rape actually occurs in the text. That such a serious violation requires several looks at the book is significant, for this traumatizing experience ordinarily shapes the form and the content of a narrative as much as rape affects a person in real life. The fact that readers feel the need to ascertain whether Esperanza is raped in *Mango Street* invites attention because that is not the case in other American texts. In Maya Angelou's *I Know Why the Caged Bird Sings* (1969), for example, rape shapes the protagonist's life. The incest rape of Pecola by her father Cholly in Toni Morrison's *The Bluest Eye* (1970) also ushers in and determines not only Pecola's insanity but most of Claudia's memories about growing up in Medallion, Ohio. Much the same can be said for the textual importance of the sexual assault that is rendered in Alice Walker's *The Color Purple* (1982). These books, all by leading African American women writers, locate rape at the center of the experiences narrated. Once the rape has been dramatized, these novels understandably deal with the stages of recovery that the violated characters endure.

Cisneros's *Mango Street* is different. This multifaceted novel deals with so many important barrio issues that even normally careful readers can miss the fact that Esperanza Cordero, Sandra Cisneros's first-person narrator, is raped toward the end of the book in the vignette entitled "Red Clowns." Why her rape is tumultuously presented and then abruptly dropped from further consideration in the text is one of the more interesting issues in the novel. I suspect the event is glossed over because reporting such a violation appears futile in Esperanza's world. There are also more than enough elements in Cisneros's novel work to draw attention away from an act of violence that enormously upsets readers more interested in seeing Esperanza succeed.

Discussing such a vile act in one of the most popular American ethnic books is difficult. Most readers are so excited by the young Esperanza's wonderfully engaging language that it is not easy to talk about the violent experience that occurs to the most attractive Hispanic girl that many readers have ever met in print. How readers react, of course, depends very much on the knowledge each brings to the text—that is, what readers have been taught to think about Latinas and the Hispanic community and culture in the United States.

Mango Street appears deceptively innocent, for Esperanza's narrative is written using the pleasing voice of a young girl who is alternately full of verve, self-reliance, compassion, loneliness, confidence, fear, strength, anxiety, and interest in her future. Esperanza's voice, in fact, is so beguilingly charming and so much more attractive linguistically than most of the voices found in other ethnic narratives that it innocently illuminates the violence against the other women in the novel while strangely glossing over Esperanza's own rape, her miseducation, and the inferiority complex that she has regarding her name and image.

Women in the book are represented as the property of men, a fact dramatically communicated at the beginning of the novel when we learn that Esperanza's great-grandfather "threw a sack over her" great-grandmother's head and carried her off to be married against her will, "Just like that, as if she were a fancy chandelier" (11). Continually seeking escape and a better life, the women in *Mango Street* invariably end marrying into similar kinds captivity. Most exchange the overly and unnecessarily protective, watchful eyes of their fathers for possessive, jealous husbands and lovers, who are too anxiously concerned that their women might be out with other men while they work.

Since much of the novel examines the generally sad lives of the women in Esperanza's world, the women in the novel clearly serve as female models that Esperanza is expected to avoid. Like Ana Castillo's *Massacre of the Dreamers*, *Mango Street* seeks to get at the inner lives of Latinas, mainly Puerto Rican women in this case, whom American society does not know. When Esperanza's rape is angrily related toward the end of the book (99–100), some readers will be puzzled by the fact that there is no follow-up, no apparent consequences either openly contemplated or even privately considered or debated. Esperanza, indeed, does not tell anyone—including her parents, her friends, or the police—that she has been sexually violated.

The difference between Cisneros's handling of Esperanza's rape and the ways in which Morrison, Angelou, and Walker handle rape in their texts is instructive. I believe that the Latina's inclination or cultural disposition not to make an issue about highly personal, negative experiences, both within and outside of the larger Latino community, is at the center of how Hispanics endure, how we have taught ourselves to survive countless injustices, rejections, and violations. By keeping negative experiences to ourselves, by swallowing inequities and outrages that we experience, as men or as women, we ironically encourage abuses of Latinos and seldom make issues out of matters that ought to be addressed.

By keeping such experiences within the insularity of our own consciousnesses, Hispanics also express a reluctance to reveal ourselves to and connect with the larger barrio community and Hispanic world, as well as with American society. Indeed, each one of these community environments presents different options and alternatives, most of which we have to assume Esperanza does not pursue because to reveal her rape would likely mean to lose control of what is left of most of the rest of her life. If she were to mention her assault to anyone, it would bring in the police, likely the media, and the American legal system, which would take the whole experience out of her world and into an arena that would be difficult to predict and from which a positive outcome would be unimaginable. By keeping her victimization to herself, Esperanza chooses to deal with her experience in her own way, avoiding having to deal with a larger American culture that would likely report the incident and file the necessary papers without, finally, doing much of anything to help her cope with the consequences or aftermath. Indifference to reported assaults in large urban areas, to be sure, are perpetrated against Latinos not only by people from outside the barrio but also by Latinos on other *raza* members, as both Cisneros and Castillo show.

Chicago is not widely known for having a large Latino population made up mainly of Mexican Americans, Puerto Ricans, El Salvadorans, Nicaraguans, and other Spanish-speaking people. I attribute this lack of information to the fact that most people living in the United States and throughout the world simply do not know that Hispanics also live throughout the Midwest and Northeast. Since the American media pays little attention to Latinos who are not in one way or another connected to immigration, crime, or low educational achievement, most Americans do not know the daily particulars of how Hispanics live in America and how we persevere. When I travel to the Midwest or to the Northeast, people there are constantly surprised to learn that a Mexican-looking person like me, in fact, is a born American. Such fellow citizens are surprised to learn that, since all of my education has been in the United States, I therefore speak and write mainly in English, though I also speak and can write in Spanish, and that I have only visited Mexico as a tourist, much as I have visited Europe, Hawaii, and Central America.

The media of this country, including the publishers of history books and other general and sociological studies, seem to have consciously conspired to leave out as much information as possible on Latinos in representing American life and civilization. *Mango Street* is a wonderful case in point, for this short novel has enjoyed an enormously wide readership precisely because so many readers have been pleasantly surprised by the fact that a Mexican American girl can live and talk about her poor life in the barrio in such an interesting and engaging way. As with Rudolfo Anaya's *Bless Me, Ultima* (1972) and other Chicano texts, the message in Cisneros's book is that Chicanos have long existed in the United States, but that we continue to live our lives very much in a vacuum, away from the notice of much of the rest of American culture. The media should now do what it can to showcase Latinos, since, as the fastest growing part of the American population, Hispanics direly need to be educated better and properly included in the larger American family. Coverage is needed that makes us more familiar, more recognizable to the rest of American society and the world. Media coverage is currently provided mainly when Chicanos and other Latinos are involved in illicit or countermainstream activities. Cisneros, in contrast, mentions the police only twice in *Mango Street*: once when a youngster takes Esperanza and a few of her friends for a ride in a Cadillac that turns out to have been stolen by his Puerto Rican neighbors (23–25), and once when Mr. Benny warns Esperanza and her girlfriends that pretending to be grown-up women in the street in front of his store will prompt him to call the police (39–42).

What readers ought to notice about *Mango Street* is that the education of Chicano and Puerto Rican youngsters does not take place in the schools. What education there is occurs mainly in the streets, since "Papa said nobody went to public school unless you wanted to turn out bad" (53). Private education, on the other hand, is mentioned only in passing, mainly at the beginning of the text, and always as a negative experience that pointedly demoralizes and even makes Esperanza cry. Instead of building her self-esteem, Esperanza significantly states that her teachers "made me feel like nothing" (5, 45), corroborating the school experiences of too many Mexican Americans and other U.S. Latinos, as we have seen in previous chapters. Esperanza is not simply making a passing statement; she is speaking, and quite forcefully, for all of the Hispanic children who do not have a forum and do not know how to communicate the negative education experiences that too many Latinos endure in our own country.

Negative education experiences cause Hispanic children to question their very presence in a land that does not recognize or acknowledge them in its images or in the ways it represents itself both at home and abroad. Such treatment causes Esperanza to question even the appropriateness of her name, which means "hope" in Spanish. Esperanza says her name is too long, that people cannot pronounce it, that she does not like it. She clearly has an inferiority complex about the wonderfully appropriate name that her good and hard-working parents gave her. Living in the Mango Street barrio, she appears to believe that she would rather have the name of a tough *pachuquita*, a girls' gang member. Of course, as a parochial school student (a fact that alludes to the even poorer quality of teaching in the public schools), Esperanza is not inclined to join a gang. Nonetheless, the youngsters around her do get into all sorts of life- and limb-threatening trouble and disciplinary problems, so Esperanza informs us that she would like "a name more like the real me, the one nobody sees. Esperanza as Lisandra or Maritza or Zeze the X. Yes. Something like Zeze the X will do" (11).

There *is* an Esperanza that "nobody sees," just like all of the poor, forgotten Latina women in Ana Castillo's *Massacre of the Dreamers*. What Latinas are looking and yearning for is some way to be recognized as powerful, new women, as the name Zeze the X suggests. That is why it should not surprise us to learn that Esperanza dreams of growing up strong and independent, as she says in the passage titled "Beautiful and Cruel" (88):

> In the movies there is always one with red lips who is beautiful and cruel. She is the one who drives the men crazy and laughs them all away. Her power is her own. She will not give it away.
>
> I have begun my own quiet war. Simple. Sure. I am one who leaves the table like a man, without putting back the chair or picking up the plate. (89)

Esperanza considers herself "an ugly daughter. I am the one nobody comes for." From American society and the media she has learned that her sex can be employed to secure and to demonstrate power. Sex, however, is also the one trait through which Latinas have traditionally been defined. Is that why Esperanza's mixed fantasy is to become like the men who oppress the women, to leave "the table like a man," like the John Waynes that no doubt she has seen in American films? That, she suggests, is power and control, the two qualities that the Latina women she sees around her wish for and pursue.

School does not factor into the lives of most of the other women in the novel, either. Although one would expect education to be extremely important as one of the best ways to leave the barrio, for Cisneros's Chicago Latino community education simply is not even in the picture as a possible option. Alicia, who is "young and smart and studies for the first time at the university," has to take "two trains and a bus" to reach the campus, but only after she awakes very early every morning to make the family's tortillas. Her father tells her that, as the eldest daughter, this task is her responsibility, since her mother has died. Her father also tells her that she imagines the mice she periodically sees running about the kitchen; they "do not exist," he says, suggesting that because she "studies all night" something may be wrong with her head. Like Marin, who sells Avon products, Alicia is "afraid of nothing." The prospects of both characters look grim. Cisneros represents them as forgotten women who valiantly struggle for a different type of existence away from the barrio, but they do so without any support or attention from anybody. What education is secured by Hispanics in the neighborhoods around Mango Street, Cisneros's narrative shows, is obtained not in the schools, where education ought to occur, but in the populous, dangerous streets of Chicago's Latino communities. On these streets— Mango, Loomis, Keeler, Paulina, all the streets where Esperanza has lived—educations for urban Hispanics are fraught with people preying on others, and with influences and options that do not offer attractive jobs or the life-changing opportunities available elsewhere in America.

As Cisneros's novel illustrates, next to Los Angeles, Houston, and San Antonio, Chicago has one of the largest concentrations of Hispanic people in the United States. During the Vietnam protest summers of 1967 and 1968, I had occasion to visit the Latino sections of south Chicago. Since she was born in 1954, Sandra Cisneros must have been in her early teens, or about the same age that Esperanza Cordero is in the novel. At the time, I remember being struck by the immensity of the area, by the sheer size of the Latino community in Chicago. Until to that time, I had lived all of my life in south Texas, where I was born, about an hour north of the Mexican border. As some readers know, south Texas is considered an out-of-the-way place, visited mainly by re-tired people from the northern states who vacation there during the winter months in the semi-tropical weather of the Rio Grande Valley. Although about 85 percent of the people in south Texas are Mexican Americans, there, too, as in almost all communities where there are large concentrations of Hispanics in the United States, education is not tailored to make a difference in the lives of Latinos.

It was not until I lived and worked for two consecutive summers in Chicago in 1967 and 1968 that I saw firsthand a large, concentrated population of urban Hispanics. I remember driving through block after block, mile after mile of crowded Latino neighborhoods and densely populated business areas, consisting of grocery stores, hardware and auto parts businesses, pharmacies, printing supply shops, and, of course, cantinas or bars and dance halls where touring musicians stopped for weekend fiestas, weddings, *quinceañeras* (fifteenth-birthday celebrations for young women), and dances. Most of the commercial establishments were older, two-story, turn-of-the-century dilapidated Victorian houses and buildings, the paint peeling and in obvious disrepair The crowded neighborhood apartments and low-income people that Cis-neros captures in her book were certainly in evidence. The owners or managers of these establishments often resided near the premises, or in upper-level flats above the businesses that sometimes also rented rooms and apartments, as *Mango Street* shows in the cases of Alicia, Aunt Lupe, Elenita, Geraldo, Edna and Ruthie, The Earl of Tennessee, "Ma-macita," Rafaela, Sally, Minerva, Gil the African American furniture man, Esperanza's neighbors, and her own parents. Everywhere I went I heard Spanish spoken among the parents and older citizens, and a type of urban Chicago English among the younger Latinos, most of whom were Mexican Americans, though there were also sizeable numbers of Puerto Ricans, Salvadorans, and people from other Latin American countries, as I have said. Most of the younger people, I learned, could speak some Spanish but not enough to carry on extended conversations like their parents. The parents, on the other hand, did not tend to speak English, since in this part of Chicago there really was no need for English, everything being available and accessible in Spanish. Indeed, sometimes I felt I was in the Hispanic section of Los Angeles or Miami or in the large barrios of Houston, Dallas, El Paso, or Tucson.

This is the barrio environment that Cisneros memorably renders in *Mango Street*. The U.S. Census notes that in 1990 Chicago had a population of 2,783,726 people, consisting of 1,074,471 blacks, 1,056,048 whites, and 545,852 Hispanics, or 40 percent black, 40 percent white, and 20 percent Hispanic population. In 1970, Chicago had a larger population of 3,369,000 inhabitants. We do not know how many Hispanics lived in Chicago in the late 1960s because census takers apparently did not separate out Hispanics from the larger white population at that time. Latinos, in other words, did not factor in as a voting group then, so likely we were not accurately counted either, since how those of us who cared to vote cast our ballots did not really matter to the people and the parties who shape the laws and the policies.

Sandra Cisneros's Chicago makes Esperanza feel that she is "a tiny thing against so many bricks" (75). That, indeed, is why, in the trees in the chapter called "Four Skinny Trees" appeal so much to the urban Esperanza. Outside of her own mother, father, brothers, and sisters, Esperanza finds little nurturing and warmth in the rest of her environment. Her world is not as threatening a place as Dickens's London, but it is a difficult, unpredictable arena, especially for young Latinas. Hispanic girls like Esperanza, who are about to become women, are represented as available prey, as desirable sex objects waiting to be claimed, appropriated, and then possessed and imprisoned by the Latino males, who are represented as watching and waiting for the women in the neighborhood.

In the chapter titled "The Family of Little Feet," Esperanza and her friends Lucy and Rachel—who also figure in "Velorio," the lead poem in Cisneros's 1987 collection *My Wicked Wicked Ways*—learn that there is a certain "magic" in walking down the streets in their mothers' high-heeled shoes. Not liking what he thinks he sees, Mr. Benny, the neighborhood grocer, stops the girls to ask:

> [Does] Your mother know you got shoes like that? Them are dangerous, he says. You girls too young to be wearing shoes like that. Take them shoes off before I call the cops. (41)

This is the tough street language of Chicago's Latino people, and calling "the cops," of course, is what the grocer does when he sees what appears to be either prostitution or budding prostitution in the mean streets around his store.

Esperanza and her friends, Cisneros suggests, feel giddily empowered, oddly authenticated by Mr. Benny's remarks, for his words inform the girls, even though they are too innocent to comprehend what is actually being said, that the men are beginning to notice them as women. This development unfortunately is the most important lesson in the essential education these girls receive. Conferred with this type of new appreciation, the young women saunter happily down the sidewalk, aware that they are growing more valuable with each step they take. In keeping with the commercial values of the barrio streets, they are now being looked at and will soon be desired, reflecting, in turn, the larger social preoccupation with feminine sexual attractiveness. The very excitement brought on by this increased desirability, Cisneros's narrative suggests, endangers the life of Latinas In a vignette entitled "Sire," Esperanza writes:

> I don't remember when I first noticed him looking at me—Sire. But I knew he was looking. Every time. All the time I walked past his house. Him and his friends sitting on their bikes in front of the house, pitching pennies. They didn't scare me. They did, but I wouldn't let them know. I don't cross the street like other girls. Straight ahead, straight eyes. I walked past. I knew he was looking. I had to prove to me I wasn't scared of nobody's eyes, not even his. (72)

Looking at the women with desire precedes sexual commerce, sought or not, which is to say that Mango Street becomes more threatening every time Esperanza Cordero steps out into the street after this juncture.

In the last ten pages of the book, we suddenly learn that Esperanza has been raped, not by Sire, but by an unidentified young man who calls her "Spanish girl" and disappears into the night (100). We are left to surmise that he is likely one of the guys whom Esperanza's friend Sally kisses in the get-the-car-key game that she plays with the boys behind the old blue pickup (97). In the following chapter, Sally abruptly marries a "marshmallow salesman" (101), leaving behind the other Latinas who sit by their windows through the long days, waiting for some man to somehow take them to a better life. The resourceless men who do marry them end up imprisoning their wives in nearby apartments, which are rendered bleak and nearly hopeless.

What is the relationship between the rape that Esperanza endures and the feelings she has for the different life she wishes she could have? At the start of the book Esperanza informs us that she would rather live elsewhere. But it is not until the last vignette of her narrative, in a sketch entitled "Mango Says Goodbye Sometimes," that she reveals the following sentiment: "I like to tell stories. I am going to tell you a story about a girl who didn't want to belong" (109).

"I like to tell stories" reminds us that *Mango Street* features Esperanza telling us stories in her words not too many years after the events she narrates. Her way of telling us her story tells us she is a strong woman, who, having been raped, knows that Latinas in her neighborhood have no real options, other than to follow the custom of allowing themselves to be trapped in marriages that soon turn sour. Yet despite her tough daily barrio life, and despite the unattractiveness of the male-female unions she sees and totally rejects (88–89), Esperanza still manages to live up to her name, communicating hope to readers in similar circumstances. *Mango Street* for this reason is dedicated "a las mujeres," that is, to the women whom Cisneros knows will understand the nature of oppressive life of Latina women.

The emphasis on *told* stories underscores Cisneros's desire to turn the power of the oral voice into printed words, transforming Esperanza's difficult growing-up experiences into a difficult-to-forget narrative. This strategy successfully places Esperanza on the level with Zora Neale Hurston's Janie, the African American protagonist of *Their Eyes Were Watching God* (1937), for having had the resiliency to survive, and for possessing the power and the admirable ability to articulate a similar struggle against forces that severely restrict the lives of minority women in the United States.

Esperanza's other statement, "I am going to tell you a story about a girl who didn't want to belong," reads like a buried, critically unexplored confession. The sentence is important because it is followed by a paragraph that serves as the book's opening and closing refrain: "We didn't always live on Mango Street. Before that we lived on Loomis on the third floor, and before that we lived on Keeler. Before Keeler it was Paulina, and before that I can't remember" (109–10).

It is not that Esperanza cannot remember where she lived before Paulina, but rather that all of the apartments rented by the Cordero family have been as unattractive as their house on Mango. For Cisneros and Esperanza, all the streets in Hispanic Chicago are as disregarded as this forgotten community where all the women and men live hopelessly surrounded by fear, desperation, and a common desire to escape elsewhere. Cisneros amply suggests the dead-endedness of the many lives, though she also emphasizes the sunnier moments Esperanza's life to maintain reader interest.

Despite the grim reality that leads to Esperanza's sexual assault, many readers do not pay sufficient attention to Esperanza's rape because it occurs so close to the end of the book. The rape is abruptly and powerfully rendered, and then immediately dropped. Cisneros does not dwell on the recovery, not only because the pain and hurt of such an attack have been so ably described by other ethnic texts, but also because Esperanza has no real recourse. By not reporting her sexual victimization to anyone, Esperanza articulates the silent or muted experience of sexual and psychological violence against Latinas that is now finding expression through literature.

The passage in which Esperanza addresses her rape is brief, but movingly captured in an apostrophe to Sally:

> Sally Sally a hundred times. Why didn't you hear me when I called? Why didn't you tell them to leave me alone? The one who grabbed me by the arm, he wouldn't let me go. He said I love you, Spanish girl, I love you, and pressed his sour mouth to mine.
>
> Sally, make him stop. I couldn't make them go away. I couldn't do anything but cry. I don't remember. Please don't make me tell it all. (100)

Many serious issues should be discussed further, especially when the novel is read in a classroom setting. Why, for example, does Esperanza keep quiet, instead of being outraged enough to seek some kind of vindication or satisfaction? Has the Latina woman been so victimized that one response to rape is to block out or to proceed with life as if an assault has not occurred? The text remains silent on these important ethical and social issues, but the implications are disturbing, particularly in light of cases like the Kennedy-Smith rape trial in Florida, the Mike Tyson case in Indiana, and other high-visibility media cases that raise questions about justice, fairness, and violence between the sexes.

The text implicitly encourages us to remember the fun that Esperanza, Lucy, and Rachel had walking in their mothers high-heeled shoes, and, like the girls, to dismiss Mr. Benny's warning. Unlike the mature, ironic voice employed by Morrison's Claudia in *The Bluest Eye*, Cisneros's Esperanza innocently recalls their youthful laughter (17). She humorously describes how a young woman's hips seem to sprout overnight: "One day you wake up and they are there," she says, "Ready and waiting like a new Buick with the keys in the ignition" (49). But, she adds, significantly: "Ready to take you where?" Her hips *are* her new Buick, and they are ready, but to go where? Can a young Latina from the barrio go where she can truly live a different kind of life instead of imitating the lives she sees all around her?

Why does Esperanza end with the statement: "I am going to tell you a story about a girl who didn't want to belong"? The sentence expresses exactly the opposite view that almost all ethnic fictions underscore. The standard formulation of the ethnic position is usually: "I am going to tell you a story about a girl [or a boy] who didn't belong" in the larger American society, not of one who "didn't *want to* belong." What these characters are concerned with, of course, is their place in the larger culture, the one that also made a Richard Wright or a James Baldwin feel excluded. Cisneros, however, tells us that Esperanza "didn't *want to* belong" either to her Latino community or to American society. Why? What young person would willfully choose Esperanza's life? To live among the disheartening squalor and unattractive surroundings of the forgotten and dangerous streets that the United States offers Latinas who live on Mango, Loomis, Keeler, and Paulina is no special treat.

At one point, Esperanza provides us with a poem that allows us to see the nature of her desire to escape:

> I want to be
> like the waves on the sea,
> like the clouds in the wind,
> but I'm me.
> One day I'll jump
> out of my skin.
> I'll shake the sky
> like a hundred violins. (60–61)

This is a poem about being someone else, of jumping out of her skin, much like the young chimney sweep who is washed clean of his soot in Charles Kingsley's *The Water-Babies* (1863). Esperanza's dream is to do something grandiose that will take her and all Latino girls like her past the limitations of their world. What are her real prospects? Her Aunt Lupe, the dying woman whom she describes as "Dark. Good to look at.

In her Joan Crawford dress and swimmer's legs," encourages Esperanza to "keep writing," for writing will "keep you free" (61). Writing allows Esperanza to "tell stories," to create a fictive reality that makes the harshness of her Mango Street world palatable enough so that she can capture the moments and scenes that engage readers.

At different junctures in the text, three neighborhood women who lead frustrated lives move Esperanza toward her future. The women are her Aunt Lupe, who dies; Alicia, who lives in Guadalajara, Mexico; and especially the "cat-eyed" sister, who emerges out of nowhere, for a *velorio*, a wake, for the baby sister of Lucy and Rachel. Along with her two other sisters, "las comadres" or co-mothers, the "cat-eyed" *comadre*— who appropriately remains unidentified, like other supporting Hispanic women who occasionally appear in literary works or in the media, and who are not otherwise made to matter—finally brings Esperanza face to face with her essential self: "When you leave you must remember to come back for the others. A circle, understand? You will always be Esperanza. You will always be Mango Street. You can't erase what you know. You can't forget who you are" (105).

Esperanza would have willingly left the world of Mango Street and likely endeavored to forget her past, like Gualinto or, unsuccessfully, like Anthony Quinn in real life. But the "cat-eyed" *comadre*, apparently aware of others who have not returned or remembered "to come back for the others," is determined to make her understand that belonging is not a matter of *wanting* to belong or not. "You can't erase what you know. You can't forget who you are," she says, hoping to convince Esperanza that she cannot create a better future by seeking to escape her unattractive past.

Esperanza desires a house of her own, a quiet place for the future that she will write:

> A house all my own. With my porch and my pillow, my pretty purple
> petunias. My books and my stories. My two shoes waiting beside the bed.
> Nobody to shake a stick at. Nobody's garbage to pick up after.
>   Only a house quiet as snow, a space for myself to go, clean as paper before
> the poem. (108)

Her dream house is a combination of Virginia Woolf's idea that a woman writer requires at least one room of her own, and Gaston Bachelard's sense of the phenomenological space that a writer needs and will occupy, as Julian Olivares has brought out.[2]

The last pages of *Mango Street* describe a complex leave-taking in-

volving love, hate, nostalgia, lament, desire, and the accompanying
emotions that complicate lives when people are uncertain or ambivalent
about the future. In a 1991 interview featured in *Publishers Weekly*, Cisneros located her awakening as a writer to the moment when she realized she was different:

> It was not until this moment when I separated myself, when I considered
> myself truly distinct, that my writing acquired a voice. I knew I was a
> Mexican woman, but I didn't think it had anything to do with why I felt so
> much imbalance in my life, whereas it had everything to do with it! My race,
> my gender, my class! That's when I decided I would write about something
> my classmates couldn't write about.[3]

For Cisneros and her fictive Esperanza, the sentiments in printed words
on a page provide the relief, the "clean as paper" arena, the necessary
space that she as a writer requires in order to address "so much imbalance in my life."

Such a realization would not have occurred for Esperanza if the "cat-
eyed" *comadre* had not provided her with a good reason for leaving
Mango Street. Telling her, point-blank, to "remember to come back.
For the ones who cannot leave as easily as you," the *comadre*'s words direct Esperanza toward her calling as a writer.

The directive appears to stun Esperanza, because, from the start of
her narrative, her sole objective has been to leave Mango Street. Her
rape, we would surmise, should further fuel that desire, even though the
two events are left unconnected. But the barrio *comadres* who know that
Esperanza writes understand that her own true freedom can only be secured through writing. They know that she cannot and should not forget who she is, because in effect Esperanza represents all the women she
leaves behind who "cannot leave as easily as" she can.

In the closing pages of the book, what would have been Esperanza's
beeline out of her Mango Street world is psychologically turned, as the
comadre says, into "a circle." Persuaded now to turn her journey out of
the barrio into a large arc that leaves Mango Street but eventually leads
back into it, Esperanza's book becomes the metaphoric representation
of her effort to reconcile the distensible forces that Cisneros has succinctly compressed. By contemplating the numerous pressures har-
nessed to create *The House on Mango Street*, I believe readers can appreciate the liberating spirit that motivated Cisneros to create Esperanza
and her *mundo* to guide young women and to edify all Americans and
readers throughout the world.

10

Ana Castillo's *Massacre of the Dreamers:* Communicating the Chicana Experience

The title of Ana Castillo's *Massacre of the Dreamers: Essays on Xicanisma* (1995) is meant to inform readers that when Hernando Cortés arrived on the eastern shores of Montezuma's kingdom in 1519, Montezuma ordered that thousands of his dreamers, his diviners of the future, be put to death for prophesying the end of the vast Aztec empire. Because the Spanish conquerer was mistaken for Quetzalcoatl, the mythic god of the Aztecs who was expected to return from the east, Cortés was able to conquer the Aztecs in Tenochtitlan, Mexico's central valley, two years later. Castillo contends that the massacre of the prophets, who dreamed of a better life for the Mexica Empire, "is happening again throughout the globe" and that the responsibility of "silenced dreamers rendered harmless" by the world's larger forces is stoutly to articulate the connection between the tragedy that is happening to today's Latinas and that forgotten event.[1]

The ten essays comprising this collection were initially written to fulfill the requirements for a doctoral degree in American Studies at the University of Bremen in Germany in 1991. Her aim "in offering my interpretation and analyses has been to have my view serve as a springboard for further intellectual discussion" of matters that affect Latinas, issues that have seldom, if ever, been discussed at length in

American culture. As in the case of the 1992 Nobel Peace Prize winner Rigoberta Menchu, whom she cites with admiration for speaking out for third world women (7–8), in *Massacre of the Dreamers* Castillo rhetorically advances some of the passionate prose exhibited in her novels.[2] Readers who have little or no sense of how insignificant and unappreciated Chicanas and other Latinas who live in the United States can be made to feel may be astonished by the uninhibited ardor of Castillo's candid essays.

Massacre of the Dreamers is a hard-hitting book that spiritually seeks to connect the lives of today's Latinas as rendered by Sandra Cisneros, Gloria Anzaldúa, Cherrie Moraga, María Elena Viramontes, Carmen Tafolla, Angela de Hoyos, Evangelina Vigil, and other Chicana writers to the lives of ethnic Amerindian women throughout the world. Her objective is to create gender solidarity in the face of little appreciation and considerable abuse. Castillo argues that social systems designed by men to advance civilizations often make progress at the expense of socially and economically disenfranchising women. Latina women, in particular, Castillo claims, are used without being properly paid or credited. Since few Amerindian Latinas have recourse to justice or other established ways to seek redress, especially from the people for whom they work, they often remain mistreated.

Castillo's compassion, ironically, is quite Christian, but she does not credit or attribute her defense of women to the Catholic Church or any other established religion. Religion and the established Church, indeed, receive harsh criticism for their disregard of indigenous women. The nature of that criticism is a measure of her anger, of Castillo's sense that religion has not eased the pain and suffering of women who have been burdened with caring for civilizations throughout history.[3]

Focusing on the widespread plight of the mestiza/Mexican-Amerindian woman, Castillo employs language that some readers see as unnecessarily abrasive in explaining "our five-hundred-year status as countryless residents on land that is now the United States." She does not mark the beginning of Mexican American subjugation from the 1848 Treaty of Guadalupe Hidalgo, but from the 1521 overthrow of Montezuma by Cortés. Her need to throw off the constraints and impositions of the European colonizing efforts that Octavio Paz trenchantly discusses in *The Labyrinth of Solitude*, as well as those of American society, sometimes overrides her accompanying counterdesire to invite encouragement and support for her views. Castillo, however, clearly places more importance on speaking forthrightly to a world that her past experience tells her is not likely to pay her much attention— that, indeed, would not likely mind seeing pugnacious Chicanas like her silenced, much as Montezuma silenced the dreamers of a message he did not like.

Massacre of the Dreamers articulates philosophical views that are more invitingly expressed in books such as Sandra Cisneros's *The House on Mango Street* and *Woman Hollering Creek*, and in Castillo's own novels, *The Mixquiahuala Letters* and *So Far from God*. These fictive works offer different rhetorics on the lives of Latinas that cannot be easily generalized. Books like the evocative *Canícula: Snapshots of a Girlhood en la Frontera* by Norma Elia Cantú, an autobiography of growing up female in Laredo, Texas, and Gloria Anzaldúa's *Haciendo Caras/Making Face* and *Borderlands*, for example, highlight a pervasive, though little-known, disregard for Latina women that creates exasperation among Latinas. The latter books underscore the fact that Mexican American women constantly struggle with a wide variety of psychological and sexual realities prompted by unnecessarily protective or abusive males who restrict and shape many of the unsavory experiences that Chicana women endure.

In the early days of the Chicano literature, the complaint was often heard that women were not provided with enough literary space and attention, and this omission is what Chicana writers have more recently taken to center stage in Chicano literature. Helena María Viramontes's 1986 collection *The Moths and Other Stories*, for instance, dramatizes loss of innocence, abortion, female guilt, budding sexuality, and abrasive male-female relationships, issues that individually and collectively have unfolded a series of emphases in Chicano literature that the earlier male-authored texts seldom mentioned. These newer publications are driven by what Maria Herrera-Sobek and Helena Maria Viramontes see as "the love of Chicanas for themselves and each other [that] is at the heart of Chicana writing. For without this love, they could never make the courageous move to place Chicana subjectivity in the center of literary representation, or depict pivotal relationships among women past and present, or even obey the first audacious impulse to put pen to paper."[4]

Besides educating readers about the real-world psychological conditions of Latinas, Castillo's *Massacre* very ambitiously attempts to explain the historical and the social forces that have kept many Latinas and most third-world women tied to their domestic duties, allowing them few opportunities to educate themselves and improve their living conditions:

Men and women who are not parents do not always comprehend fully the extent to which women raising children are stretched. My own baby did not sleep through the night until he was about fifteen months old. When he was turning two and being weaned and potty-trained, we moved from Chicago to California where he soon became very sick with pneumonia. I did not have health insurance and nursed him at home. In California, he developed allergies and asthma and for several years we had many difficult days and nights that went into weeks when he suffered from this condition. Caring for healthy children is demanding, but caring for sick children—and all children get sick—is particularly stressful for their primary caretakers. (202)

The abrasiveness that some readers find objectionable in Castillo's *Massacre of the Dreamers* in large part emanates from these anxieties and from the desire to have a normal life that is often not available.

Brown mothers (especially but not limited to low-income), deal everyday with antagonism against them that is pervasive in society—from the police officer who stops her on the pretext of charging her with a traffic violation but questions whether or not she is a citizen, to employment where she may have worked her way up to management but is harassed by resentful co-workers as if her position is owed solely to Equal Opportunity Employment policies, to shabby treatment by salesclerks and snubbing from neighbors in her new neighborhood. In addition to her own experiences, negative attitudes also affect her children, such as through school desegregation programs, gang rivalries, neighbors and their children who pick up on their parents' disapproval of people of color living nearby. Therefore, as brown mothers, we are not only dealing with education, health, and economic burdens, but with ongoing experiences that degrade us and our children. (202)

Regarding education, Castillo both explains the realities that Hispanic parents face and provides sensible advice:

We must not only be vigilant about the education that our children receive once they are on their way to learning the three Rs in elementary school, but the kind of education they receive in many schools primarily still run by white-dominated administrators and faculty. Today, gross stereotypical assumptions continue about our children by those who presume to be educators. We may not have the time to join PTAs but we must make the time to let teachers and administrators know we care about our children's curriculum. There is a current attitude among school officials that parents must also be held accountable for their child's education. I concur wholeheartedly; but by the same token, we, of a marginalized culture must hold our schools accountable for the kind of education they are giving our children. Examine your children's textbooks, talk to your children as often as possible about their day at school, keep attentive to what is going on. When and if you feel something should be questioned, question it. (203)

American scholarship, the media, and schools, Castillo contends, have not informed people of how a young American Latina woman who is "a mestiza born to the lower strata" is made to feel as she goes about her daily life in America or wherever she may be throughout the rest of the world.

Since her German dissertation committee was apparently receptive to listening to an articulate Chicana, Castillo capitalized on an occasion seldom, if ever, previously extended to a Chicana woman to speak about her life and the lives of the other Latinas she represents. Speaking as if she were using a microphone that historically has not been provided to Latinas in the United States, Castillo voices truths that Chicanas have seldom asserted so forcefully. The central message that emerges from all of Castillo's heart-felt presentation is: "I am treated at best, as a second-class citizen, at worst, as a non-entity" (21).

Readers used to the conventions of the printed word may object to or be repelled by her tone, by her assumptions, or by what in other places may read as an unnecessarily belligerent message. Castillo, however, feels that she is revealing the extent to which she has felt repressed, oppressed, mistreated, imposed upon, and passed over most of her life (209–10). She believes that her words should be listened to and not deflected or dismissed as the views of an angry woman. She is angry in certain places, but she holds that her anger is justified, given what Latinas daily endure. As such, she feels she speaks for many other women who simply do not have an opportunity to express their complaints and grief against a society that pays Latinas virtually no attention. Throughout her work, the emphasis is more on what she has felt in her life and on her need to express the nature of her experiences, rather than on the form in which she delivers her views. She is sufficiently aware that the media are likely to label her and the persona that she constructs for relaying the book's message as feisty and outspoken. However, she hopes that her readers will understand the anxieties under which a Latina mother labors, since she represents herself as lacking the comforts and the self-assurance of a Virginia Woolf, "an Anglo woman born to economic means" (21).

As a member of a "marginalized culture" excluded by America's mainstream thinking, socially accepted behavior patterns, and mores, her life and views speak for many other Chicanas and Latinas who would never consider communicating their sentiments about what life for Chicanas is like, since the social divisions are felt to be so wide:

At an early age we learn that our race is undesirable. Because of possible rejection, some of us may go to any length to deny our background. But one cannot cruelly judge such women who have resorted to negation of their own heritage; constant rejection has accosted us since childhood. Certain women indeed had contact early on in their lives with Mexico and acquired enough identification with its diverse culture and traditions to battle against the attempts of white, middle class society to usurp all its citizens into an abstract culture obsessed with material gain. (38)

Castillo is not concerned with glossing over with polite or acceptable niceties some of the harsh realities that she and women like Esperanza in Cisneros's *Mango Street* have endured and include in their books.

In the United States, she straightforwardly asserts, the brown-skinned Latino "race is undesirable," and because "constant rejection has accosted us since childhood," she does not hesitate to reveal social and psychological truths that we have heard expressed in different ways by Paredes, Quinn, Cisneros, and other Mexican American writers. The difference is that Castillo is more direct because her message is more urgent in 1995. These realities, she maintains, explain some of the ways that Latina women tend to be perceived, represented, and treated, not specifically and only by the American media, but by many people in the course of everyday life throughout the United States. Such treatment angers and frustrates the Latinas whom Castillo speaks for—women Castillo urges readers to understand and to see in a new light as we enter the twenty-first century.

Given her life experiences and what fellow Latinas and other women have told her, Castillo believes that she needs to educate all Americans about the plight of Mexican American women and to challenge Chicanas and other third-world women to recognize themselves in the mirror of her message:

I know you. You are Mexican (like me). You are brown-skinned (like me). You are poor (like me). You probably live in the same neighborhood as I do. You don't have anything, own anything. (Neither do I.) You're no one (here). At this moment I don't want to be reminded of this, in the midst of such luxury, such wealth, this disorienting language; it makes me ashamed of the food I eat, the flat I live in, the only clothes I can afford to wear, the alcoholism and defeat I live with. You remind me of all of it.

You remind me that I am not beautiful—because I am short, round bellied and black-eyed. You remind me that I will never ride in that limousine that just passed us because we are going to board the same bus back to the neighborhood where we both live. You remind me of why the foreman doesn't move me out of that tedious job I do day after day, or why I

got feverish and too tongue-tied to go to the main office to ask for that
Saturday off when my child made her First Holy Communion.
    When I see you, I see myself. (25–26)

By addressing other Chicanas and general readers in this direct manner,
Castillo makes it difficult to deflect or refuse to acknowledge the racial
bonds, class structures, and other divisions that separate Americans.
Such issues, as I have suggested throughout this study, are rarely addressed in American culture, because as a society we are very uncomfortable when we force ourselves to discuss racial realities we do not
know how to address or improve. What is admirable and poignant about
Castillo's straightforward language is her sensitivity to women who,
much like Gualinto in Paredes's *George Washington Gomez*, develop an
inclination to deny realities in American culture and heritage due to the
difficulty of having to deal constantly with the ubiquitous pressures of
racism and discrimination

    Since Castillo's prime objective is to educate Latinas and the rest of
the world so that women will stand up instead of allowing themselves to
be imposed upon by men, the media, and other forces that constrain and
defeat them, her views cast an altogether different light on Latinas. In
chapter 3 of *Massacre*, for example, Castillo argues, as did Sandra Cisneros in *Mango Street*, that males throughout the world have historically
used and abused women, and that Latino men perfunctorily mistreat
women. In chapter 4, she discusses how the church and other established social forces collectively militate to keep Latina women from expressing their true feelings and views.

    Because the psychological pain and rejection that Latinas experience
have not previously been revealed so starkly, Castillo's language startles
readers, challenging society vicariously to experience how Latinas feel
about macho, chauvinist cultures that promote and engender many of
the miseries that poorer women endure in silence because no relief is
available. Castillo's goal is to encourage readers to understand that the
cultural coordinates that quietly continue to promote unfair gender
practices need to be discussed and examined carefully, if societies are to
stop treating Latinas and women in general as worthless human beings.
Indeed, the analysis that Castillo provides, if employed pedagogically,
could be used to help develop more respectful and better relations between men and women.

    Central to Castillo's thesis is her view that men tend to commodify
women, to use women as they see fit. She expresses this in Marxist lan-

guage: "as capitalism intensifies so has the oppression of women, who come to be seen as property, producers of goods and reproducers" (64). The Arab, Spanish, and Mexican civilizations are all implicated for downplaying the importance of women: "we continue to be purposely rendered invisible by society" (41). By selecting traits commonly associated with Latinas, and by referring to a number of social science studies, Castillo advances theories to explain sexuality, women's spirituality, and what Castillo calls the "the mother-bond principle" that could usher in what she desires, "a truly nurturing society." Pursuing such an objective, Castillo believes, would bring about more nourishing relationships between mothers and daughters and fathers, producing "motherguides," her term for a new type of community that would consciously work to educate and prepare the next generation of young people (194).

Castillo states that she is "inclined to object to the claim that we [Latinas] are simply in search of identity." Rather, she is concerned with "asserting" what she desires to see, for the nature of the dialogue and "the polemic as I see it, has to do with terminology and semantics not with the facts of our existence" (12). For Castillo, "spirituality and institutionalized religion are not the same thing. Spirituality is an acutely personalized experience inherent in our on-going existence. Throughout history, the further man moved away from his connection with woman as creatix [sic], the more spirituality was also disconnected from the human body" (12–13).

Castillo proposes that studying women's roles is central to the benefit of civilization. This leads her directly to address her relationship to feminism in various parts of her book:

> Feminists of color in the United States (and around the world) are currently arduously re-examining the very particular ways our non-Western cultures use us and how they view us. We have been considered opinionless and the invariable targets of every kind of abusive manipulation and experimentation. As a mestiza, a resident of a declining world power, a countryless woman, I have the same hope as [Adrienne] Rich who, on behalf of her country aims to be accountable, flexible, and learn new ways to gather together earnest peoples of the world without the defenses of nationalism. (24)[5]

Too many women throughout the world feel "countryless," argues Castillo, because male chauvinistic ideas about nationalism fail to consider seriously the views and needs of women. Castillo would cast aside institutions and entities that repeatedly overlook women and have shown no particular interest in listening to or helping Latinas.

This desire to express herself as unshackled as possible is the salient characteristic of Castillo's passionate essays. *Massacre of the Dreamers* tells readers that brown-skinned Latinas have never really been heard as people with views and ideas, as intellectuals who can examine history and find ways to improve our relationships with people who are different. Latinas, Castillo believes, need to retrieve what can serve them from the past to alter the daily unattractive realities under which they live. The educational challenge is formidable, but Castillo encourages women not to be afraid to counter the destructive ideas of machismo. In her examinations of Islam, the Spanish civilization, and the practices of the New World, for instance, she underscores what women historians have argued: that standard, written histories emphasize the achievements of the cultures that men have created, leaving out the high costs paid by women in virtually all societies.

Castillo is aware that her views will invite criticism, especially from scholars who will question the connections and conclusions she draws, as well as the manner and tone in which she makes her points. She knows that her premises, arguments, and conclusions may be called into question, but the risks do not discourage her from asserting herself, from articulating thoughts seldom revealed by other U.S. Latinas from whom society has never heard. Her sense of the role of women in the history of civilization empowers Castillo to forge ahead, encouraging Latinas to clear the obstacles by calling attention to historical connections that have seldom been noticed, let alone appreciated and championed:

> DREAMERS AND MAGICIANS, BRUJAS Y CURANDERAS: As descendants of the Mexic Amerindians, ours is a formidable and undeniable legacy. Among our most ancient ancestors are the Olmecs, whose origins in the Americas predate 1000 B.C. and who "we might possibly call Magicians," as Frederick Peterson refers to them in his book *Ancient Mexico: An Introduction to the Pre-Hispanic Cultures.* etc. (15)

I cite this particular passage to show one of the several ways in which Castillo directly addresses disenfranchised Latina women. Her hope is to draw strength and power from a lost, difficult-to-access, quiescent legacy in order to awaken people of both sexes to a new sense of themselves. Seeking to alert current-day Latinas and Latinos to the existence of ancient connections, Castillo suggests that this history, even if unaccessible through books, should help us in our efforts to improve our communal thinking and daily behavior. In places her injunctions are not sufficiently clear, yet her spirit is courageous and irrepressible. Castillo is concerned with establishing a different type of reality, one that will change the psychological coordinates by which most Hispanics live in a world that has silenced us and made so many of us give up trying to provide a better place for ourselves in the United States.

Castillo is "actively devoted to real social change" (38), which requires real change in how Latina women are perceived by both themselves and others, and in how they are represented in the media and throughout American culture. Such grand and desirable goals, of course, are directly shaped by how we educate Americans and the world. *Massacre of the Dreamers* is Castillo's aggressively assertive manifesto calling for a new realization of the potential that society wastes in Latinas because they are undervalued, underappreciated, and denied opportunities to express and to actualize themselves differently. Although Latinas have not enjoyed the privilege or pleasure of shaping themselves in the eyes of American society, Ana Castillo demonstrates a newfound leonine freedom of expression that clearly benefits all women.

11

Chicano Writing versus
Chicano Life

f some readers remain skeptical about my contentions and interpretations regarding the psychologically unhealthy connections between the educations dispensed in the schools and the nature of the relations between the American media and Latinos, the two postscripts that close this study should illustrate how Latino citizens are routinely excluded from American life. Even though Latinos have shown an interest over the years in participating in the American experience, sociopolitical, economic, class, and race forces at a number of levels both within and outside of America's pluralistic society constantly resist our full inclusion in American civilization.

Aside from reiterating how the same message can be extracted from the history of Chicano literature, the closing postscripts show how white majority society refuses to enter into a more productive relationship with a Hispanic population that generally seeks to be more cooperative. I hope the inclusion of these incidents will allow readers to see for themselves why some Latinos are not interested in interacting more with mainstream American culture. This is not to say that most interactions are negative, but only that requests that seek to alter the status quo to improve the situation of Latinos and our relations with other Americans are often turned down or ignored. Most Latinos, unfortunately, are used to being rejected, and most of us have learned, since we have been effectively taught, to keep quiet when disillusioned. When Latinos choose to reveal that our requests have been disregarded or turned away, generally some mainstream, influential citizens remonstrate, suggesting that if Latinos know what is good for the community, we would remain low-key and agreeable to the way things are.

Before proceeding to such evidence, however, I briefly wish to extend several observations that I earlier made about how Chicano literature can be enhanced. I do so, again, to promote interest in the ways that Chicano and Latino life, in all its multiplicity, can better interact with American culture. By doing so, I hope to increase the number of readers, researchers, and supporters who follow developments in a field of study that can only grow as the Latino population increases, and as mainstream America finds that it cannot long continue to ignore a population whose fortunes affect all of American society.

My closing observation is that, despite the type of progress particularized by this and other studies intended to further connect Latinos to American society, I believe the lives of Mexican Americans and other Latinos are not being adequately dramatized and represented even in our own literature. This reality, however, can be corrected, and I think that when our writers are ready for a more inclusive literature, they will enlarge the scope of our thinking, especially since Chicano writing is at the point where it has to engage more readers in the future.

These observations are not meant to cause angst, anger, umbrage, or resentment, since I believe Chicano literature has slowly been coming of age. The purpose, rather, is to open up a discourse so that all Americans can participate in studying the evolution and the clear direction of the literature that Mexican American, Puerto Rican, Cuban American, and other American Latino authors have been creating. I mention creating an ongoing conversation because, as previously stated, Chicano life and culture are seldom talked about in positive ways in media circles and in the education arena. The media are increasingly turning to tabloid news about mainstream American personalities, and K–12 educators unfortunately tend to deny the proven fact that poorer educations continue to be meted out to Latinos and other minorities year after year, generation after generation. The issue is not only that all kinds of tests consistently tell us that Latinos receive considerably less quality attention in the classrooms of America, but that not enough educational resources are provided for the improvement of America's ethnic students.

Observations and remarks usually made off the record in private conversations by critics and writers need to be made increasingly public by Latino writers. If more readers are to be attracted to Chicano literature, I think it behooves us to study attentively the kinds of lives that Mexican Americans and other Latinos from all socioeconomic classes are actually living today in light of the literature that has been and continues to be published. Only by talking openly about the needs and desires of our people and of the larger American culture in which we live can Latinos continue to create stories and poetry that will engage readers. Such interactions should then promote the kind of commerce that ought to be happening in the United States between people of different cultural and social backgrounds. For I think that American society, as we have it today, has amply shown that different cultures and literatures can create ways of looking at life that keep people apart. We now need to agree to work to connect cultures that badly require melding, nourishment, and adjustment.

Chicano literature is now at a mature enough juncture to stand the kind of internal scrutiny that I suggest, for we should be able to examine what our writers have wrought without being overly sensitive. Like a young college student who has recently graduated, Chicano literature has been raised by the caring, nurturing hands of writers, critics, and *raza* supporters in Texas, New Mexico, Arizona, California, Illinois, New York, and in other states and abroad. As the previous chapters have shown, we are immensely indebted to the writers and publishers who have constructed Chicano literature, and we need to express appreciation for the multifaceted efforts to create a literature where little existed before.

Shortly after the Civil Rights Act of 1964, critics such as Edward Simmen, Philip Ortego, and Luis Leal began to raise Mexican American consciousness. These scholars published essays and anthologies about how Mexican Americans had been portrayed in American literature. The one-sided, negative caricatures of Hispanics in a legacy promoted by the nineteenth-century Francis Parkmans and the twentieth-century Walter Prescott Webbs of the United States ironically prompted Chicanos to see that we direly needed a literature, one that could provide us with stories and poetry that would present a better picture of our people, writings capable of making us feel good about ourselves, proud of our trials and successes.

Thirty years later, I think we can say that Chicano literature still needs to include considerably more aspects of the Latino experience, if we are to engage the type of interests that Mexican Americans and other Americans need to explore. Chicano literature has so far addressed a good number of the negative school, work, and media experiences that being an American of Mexican extraction entails. But our stories still leave out too much of Chicano life as we have known it and, more importantly, as we want it to be in the coming century. The experiences of growing up, the lives of migrant workers, the quotidian everyday Chicano existences, and how we Chicanos have endured and continue to suffer and tolerate all sorts of inequities, indignities, and difficulties— these are the mainstay subjects of the Chicano literature we have produced so far. These are the subjects mainly emphasized by Chicano writers, the fictive and poetic arenas that define Chicano literature. But, as most Mexican Americans well know, Chicano life and culture is considerably more varied, complex and enormously richer than the literature that our writers have wrought so far.

We know, for example, little about the mental life of Chicanos and Chicanas, less about the life of the Mexican American or Latino professional, or the student who is daily opening up new paths for himself or herself as well as for *nuestra gente*. We know virtually nothing about the psychological and spiritual struggles of our young, middle-aged, and older citizens. Yet most Mexican Americans know and can tell engaging stories about *raza* people whom we have known or heard about, people whose lives are not even suggested, much less dramatized, in the literature that Chicano writers have published.

I make an issue of the need to recognize the rather narrow focus of Chicano literature primarily to note that our Chicano experiences are so much more than our published stories display. Chicano and Latino cultures, indeed, are richer and more complicated than currently represented in literature, since we live and breathe in at least two cultures and often in more, including the ties of our people to other Americans and to Spain, Africa, Europe, Latin America, and the Muslim and Jewish cultures, among others. Negotiating all of the different worlds Latinos inhabit requires considerable knowledge, talents, and skills, and our authors have yet to find ways to articulate not only how we survive, but, indeed, how we actually flourish, given the nature of the unappreciated and unvoiced difficulties we clearly face, negotiate, and defeat. Having provided readers with what might be called the basic impoverishments that have kept our people shackled, our writers now need to free their perspectives and scopes and offer readers new vistas. Not to envision new realities is to fail to provide for the needs of a larger emerging population, reducing and misrepresenting the fullness of the Chicano and Latino experience in American society. To risk curtailing the cultural complexity of our lives to a few already known themes, concerns, and tried or pat writing formulas is to limit both how we depict ourselves and how others see Latinos in the United States.

Whole worlds are daily experienced throughout America and the rest of the world that Chicano writers have not even begun to tap, to taste or savor, and to imagine. Our writers seem to write out of a commonly held restrictive belief that only certain types of experiences can and ought to be material for Chicano literature. Editors and publishers, to be sure, have much to do with what is accepted for publication and what is not, which is to say that the presses who publish Chicano literature also have to encourage and promote other kinds of stories and not only what are now widely recognized as Chicano stories. What we need is writing that will break the current Chicano story molds with rendering different experiences and richer, more variegated worlds that can, when properly conceived, usher in new horizons. Such a new direction would bring into our literature other Chicanos, Chicanas, and Latinos, encouraging publishers and readers to recognize other versions of the Spanish-speaking experience in the United States. The reality, it seems to me, is that the lives experienced by most Chicanos these days far outshine and belie our best fiction.

Wherever a Mexican American exists, there potentially is a great or engaging story awaiting an author's imagination. The writer's task, of course, is to arrive at the right perspective, to define the best angle of vision, the appropriate narrative voice or stance, and to erect the necessary fictive structures that capture and communicate a larger, more nourishing menu of Chicano experiences for readers. Good stories, I am persuaded, are as basic as the bringing together of different mixes of ingredients, providing readers with other realities for thought and consumption. By inventing and offering better options and vistas about our people's ken and lifestyles, by imagining new possibilities, rather than feeling and writing as if we are restricted only to what we have experienced in certain quarters of life, our writers can help readers visualize Chicanos and other Latinos leading the kinds of lives that our people need to live, if our generation is going to make a difference for American society in the next century.

So, again, after nearly thirty years, what is our best fiction?

Critics will nominate different books. The test, of course, is not only to ask critics and sympathetic readers, but also the general public. How, for instance, would the public answer these questions: What is the best Chicano literature text? How many Chicano books have you read? How many Mexican American or American Latino publications have you enjoyed and would read again? What Chicano book do you recognize? Can you name a Chicano author?

I suspect that part of the reason readers might have difficulty with these questions centers around the fact that our books do not yet sufficiently inspire readers to search for them. Most readers who buy Chicano books do so because we have vaguely heard of the authors and, once in a bookstore and with money in our pocket, we suddenly decide buy and read one of their books. But what do we look for in a Chicano book? Inspiration? Perhaps, some readers will say, but when Chicanos have suffered and endured the type of discrimination, rejections, and defeats dramatized, for instance, in the works analyzed in this study, we are not especially going to be expecting books that approach inspiration. Such a commodity would be difficult to broach, much less sustain, particularly in a postmodern society, especially given the realities that Mexican Americans face.

Chicano literature is hardly a household word at this point. Nonetheless, I am confident that someday, somewhere, Mexican American and other Latino writers will arise whose works will equal the works of the best writers. Writers may take issue with my suggestion that consideration be given more specifically to the needs of readers. But writers need readers, and readers, we know, want and seek stories that engage the imagination. Writing therefore has to attract the type of attention that opens new possibilities for the future of our people *and* all Americans. Scenes and events should please and be winsome enough to draw and to maintain the interest of readers. Critics who prescribe for writers, of course, can always be disregarded, but nonetheless writers must realize that readers will walk away from stories that either fail to engage or fail to provide for the needs of a population. Chicano literature is both a discipline and a vehicle for social change that we cannot afford to lose simply because our writers have not sufficiently developed imaginative roads for readers, or because we are insufficiently attuned to the types of good reading experiences that will engage more readers. Our literature is often prosaic and inclines too much toward the matter-of-fact, ignoring what is commonly called "a good read," that is, a book that tells an engaging story, one that people would choose to read again and again.

I am not suggesting that the only aim of our writers should be to popularize Chicano writing, though that prospect and direction can only raise the literature's visibility. The objective should not be to cater to the popular market only, as I know some writers would immediately retort. What our authors should consider is writing more with a mind toward seeing what makes a good book work, toward opening up new ways of thinking about and being Latino. Such scenarios could be patterned after the real life stories some our people have experienced, or they could be dreamed up by imaginative writers. Are we, in short, working to produce a literature, or do we seek to write literary sociologies that mainly illustrate and explain why we live as we do?

Literature, we know, eschews demonstrative exercises that are too clearly designed to communicate certain messages about certain people. The social and economic realities Mexican Americans have been forced to live with are a necessary and important part of our communal lives, but they should not be the central or the sole reason for our stories. Literature can and should also include more Esperanzas, that is, more Chicanos or Chicanas who break out of the barrio, who learn how to construct other worlds not yet normally achieved by most Mexican Americans. If such possible lives include changes in class, economic livelihood, and so on, then that is where our writing ought to consider going. America is about constant change. America is about moving away, about moving up, about moving into positions where Chicanos, too, can begin to shape not only our own futures but the futures of other people. It is time for our writers to assume these challenges, instead of avoiding them for a variety of complicated reasons that have to do with the constricting expectations that are now normally associated with Chicano literature. Chicano and other Latino authors need to open themselves up to different dialogues with the world, to other rich experiences. They need to construct well-told stories from encounters that engage the souls, imaginations, and hearts of readers. Too many of our writers write or appear to write as if hemmed in by the dire realities that Chicanos know all too well. We have well established our migrant and field worker past, and this part of our culture will continue to be significant. How can it not be? But that should not be what Chicano literature is all about.

All too often, we oddly and sadly end up celebrating Chicano experiences that do not do much for the characters, for the readers, and certainly not for our young people who are looking for better futures. Latino students are pleased to see that our struggles for a livelihood are receiving attention, but many also observe that few *viable* options, avenues, and solutions are offered or suggested by a literature that focuses too much on commonly shared problems. Many of our writers understandably ride problem-oriented theses too hard, even for those of us interested in seeing a better tomorrow. As a consequence, our books are less about the lives of Chicano characters who might capture the imaginations of readers, and more like tracts highlighting problems that Chicanos constantly encounter without sufficiently engaging the hearts and souls of readers.

Despite the modern and postmodern creative writing fashions of the day, our writers need to understand that Chicano characters have to matter; they cannot mainly be no-name, inconsequential representatives of social problems. Our writers need to have the courage to buck the fashions of the day and to shape and create new words, perhaps even new languages, as did, say, Anthony Burgess in *A Clockwork Orange*. Chicano authors may want to be as innovative and creative as Joyce or Faulkner were in their day, but they also have to know that if readers are not lured, if interest is not secured and maintained from start to finish, readers will close the pages on stories that do not challenge them to read the next page.

We need to think more conscientiously about the payoff for the reader. Authors need to invent, regardless of whether the writing of the day admits or requires it, characters for whom readers will care, not characters who do not matter—even if we are living in an impersonal, postmodern world where people feel disconnected from each other. For, if we uncritically accept fashionable, market-driven views of reality, Latinos are likely to be disregarded even more in American culture, on the grounds, I suppose, that everybody today is equally being treated indifferently and inconsequentially. My sense is that our literature should be very careful about promoting or condoning neglect, since we have so much of that already. Over the years my students have amply shown me that when readers fail to develop emotional and intellectual ties with the characters in our literature, we may as well forget the stories.

Today we need a Chicano literature that increasingly speaks to the futures of the growing number of young Mexican Americans, whom readers hardly know. For if our literature does not represent us as a people whose future needs to be taken into account, what means that employ our creative imaginations will awaken the world to the problems that we face in the United States? Chicano writers, critics, and readers have created certain expectations to which most of our writers appear to feel tied and obligated. These established patterns of writing have shaped and reshaped the past and the present. Are they to shape the future, too? Such expectations, in effect, insidiously decree that our authors continue to reproduce stories mainly along the lines that Chicano literature has already clearly developed. Dramatic departures are not encouraged; and if we are not consciously working for dramatic departures, we are not going to see them. The expectation that we will move in other directions has to be articulated; we need to create an anticipation that will somehow be fulfilled by the enterprising writers who will provide America with new kinds of Chicano books.

If a different type of book dealing with the Chicano experience should arise, it is likely that some will question whether such a book is "Chicano" enough. Yet it is exactly this kind of dramatic novel or poem that will make readers notice that Chicano literature has taken a new turn and continues to evolve. I am not trying to be harsh or inconsiderate. My purpose is to underscore some realities that I think Chicano writers seriously need to consider. Taking into account all the publications, the words of advice, injunctions, commentaries, research, achievements, dashed dreams, criticisms, and encomiums, we should now realize that Chicano literature has been experiencing the unavoidable growth spurts that accompany the creation of something new. Chicano literature, to be sure, is one of the newest branches of American literature. If only the people invested in both fields understood that fact.

The Chicano literature of the 1970s, we can generalize, was decidedly masculine and male-centered; that of the 1980s, on the other hand, was feminine, showcasing Chicanas. The 1990s have been a period of mulling over the path taken, of looking back to before 1970 and quietly taking stock of how Chicano literature has influenced and, in turn, been influenced by American culture. But to take our bearings, we need to figure out where Chicano literature should go aesthetically and practically to help both *raza* people and American civilization.

Clearly we have explored the difficulties and frustrations of being a Chicano in America, but we have not yet sufficiently begun to tap the joys, challenges, or actual advantages of living life as Chicanos and Latinos. There may not be widespread ill-will toward Latinos, but one wonders why so many of us everywhere in the United States still experience negative incidents. The future ought to be better, once we have told people what we think and how we feel.

We cannot blame only the American media or the schools for our present condition. We Hispanics can also be faulted for our inability, perhaps even our reluctance, to connect more successfully with American society. But we ought also to realize that the cultural situation of Latinos in the United States has not been successfully articulated before, and that so long as the ties between the media, education, and Chicano literature and aspirations remain unaddressed, little is likely to happen that will improve the lives of American Latinos and our relationships with other Americans.

What exactly, some readers will ask, would such a new Chicano literature look like? I don't know; I am not a fiction writer. I am a reader and a critic who is looking ahead at the foggy road before us. In doing so, I think I see more of the same. But I can also see something else that, of course, I cannot articulate, because those stories have not yet been written. Perhaps our literature should develop hypertext techniques in the cyberspace where many of us will increasingly live. Perhaps we ought to write shorter, more succinct stories, the type that can be read in fifteen or twenty minutes while waiting for a bus or a plane. I don't know. What I do know is that our writers will tell us by writing what will appeal to our tastes and fancy. I will say, however, that the stories I have lately been reading are beginning to repeat themselves, and I confess that I am not enjoying reading some of the newer works that rehash old Chicano ground.

I do know that when I pick up a Chicano story that excites and maintains my interest, I know it. When that happens, I have found out, I will also hear about that excitement from the mouths of students and other readers everywhere.

12

Postscripts

I. Media Responses to Two Public Services Requests from Latinos

everal winters ago, the streets of the central Texas area were frozen over by a cold arctic blast that usually does not sweep as far south as Austin and Bryan–College Station where we live. My wife, who was teaching fourth-grade bilingual education classes at the time, called the local television station to ask the manager to place a public service announcement for the parents of the school district's Spanish-speaking students. The request was to announce, in Spanish, that the schools would be closed due to the icy road conditions. The manager informed her that those announcements are made by the local Spanish-language radio station, which, the owner of that station had told us several months before, serves about 75,000 to 85,000 Spanish speakers in the area surrounding Bryan–College Station, the site of Texas A&M University's main campus. My wife informed the television station manager that we understood the practice, and that the Spanish radio station La Fabulosa had already agreed to make the announcement, too. By making several calls to her students, though, she had learned that many of them were watching the English-language television station to learn for their parents if the schools would be opened. The parents, of course, were interested in knowing whether they should dress their children and send them to wait at their regular bus stops.

The manager of the English-speaking station at that point flatly said that they could not place a message in Spanish because they had never done that. They did not have the facilities or the personnel for Spanish. My wife then offered to write a short announcement that could be shown on the screen after the English-language announcements about which schools were closing and which were not. The manager, however, would not be persuaded. My wife tried to reason with him, but the station manager held to his stand that the Spanish-language radio station took care of Spanish speakers, and that the English-language television station could not make announcements in Spanish because they did not have a broadcast person who spoke Spanish and because it was not their practice. We never heard another word about the issue and were not told if the matter was even considered in meetings that entertain policy changes.

On a different occasion, another bilingual teacher and my wife approached the local newspaper to ask if the editors would publish some of the writing that their bilingual fourth-graders were doing in order to encourage and support the students' endeavors. The newspaper had been running a weekly one-page series showing some of the activities and pictures of children in the local schools, and my wife and her colleague felt that it would help the teachers and the students, both in class and with the community, to promote the efforts of the Spanish-speaking children by highlighting some samples of their work. As in the case of the television station, the response was that the newspaper had not printed Spanish before and, further, that their sponsors, the people and businesses who bought advertising space in the paper, "would not like that." Latinos know when something does not please people in positions of power and authority, but, frankly, we were surprised to hear the sentiment expressed so baldly. The teachers responded by saying that they were teaching the children how to make the transition from Spanish into English so that the students could function creditably in both languages. The editor held to his position. The bilingual teachers were not helped, and the work of the Hispanic students was not published in the community's newspaper.

These two instances are provided here to show the extent to which the Latino community works to help itself, and to record the type of responses that the community's sensible requests and efforts tend to encounter from unsympathetic people who make decisions concerning the American media. These are not isolated events that occurred in the sixties, seventies, or even the eighties, as some people may suppose. These particular events occurred in 1994 and 1995, and, unfortunately, similar incidents still occur all over Texas and throughout the Southwest, as almost any Mexican American or other Latino citizen will testify.

Despite the fact that many Latinos attempt to function well both in our Spanish-speaking world and in mainstream American culture, where many endeavor to learn and to teach our children how to be better American citizens, the old infrastructure that is quietly kept in place almost everywhere in the United States does not promote change, nor do the people who control society allow space for a growing Latino population.

For the most part, Latinos today have not been upset enough to march in the streets, as Chicanos occasionally did in the sixties and seventies in California, following leaders like Cesar Chavez and Dolores Huerta. Instead, Latinos in Texas and the Southwest have tirelessly tried to create better futures by utilizing opportunities for ourselves and our children—by working within the ways and the means constitutionally available to the American citizenry.

Americans who know or remember Hispanics mainly as migrant field workers and service workers think they are seeing enormous progress when they encounter a Latino lawyer, teacher, or computer salesman. But such advances are less common than supposed. In metropolitan areas with larger concentrations of Latinos, such as Houston, San Antonio, Dallas, El Paso, Albuquerque, Tucson, San Diego, and Los Angeles, middle-class Chicanos are now more visible than in previous years. But in the middle-sized cities and smaller towns of the Southwest, after nearly thirty years of Chicano literature and activism, Mexican Americans are not much better off than we were before the 1964 Civil Rights Act. We are more visible because Hispanics comprise the fastest growing population in the United States, but this does not appear to matter where it should make the most significant difference, that is, in the schools, in the media, and in the general American way of life. Instead of providing opportunities to encourage Hispanics and bring us into the American fold, the infrastructures that sustain America's systems and institutions continue to make life difficult for Latinos, as the two requests for assistance by Hispanic educators show.

Instead of helping Spanish-speakers become more Americanized, policies and practices throughout the United States continue to keep Latinos separate and apart from the rest of America. Efforts by Hispanics are seldom highlighted by the media, seldom brought to the attention of the American public, except to show how we celebrate different holidays. Why? Because Hispanics, like African Americans and other minorities, are still being treated differently, despite so-called "color-blind" and "race-neutral" policies. Consistently undervalued, Latinos are not allowed the kind of opportunities provided white Americans, although the great majority of Hispanics also pay taxes and are as law-abiding as the neighbors next door.

Because many of our efforts continue to be defeated by old habits and public practices that give preferential treatment to mainstream white Americans from birth to death, Latinos are still being steered, subtly and blatantly, to spend our lives in America's forgotten barrios. Too many Americans still deny and ignore the fact that Hispanics are a vibrant, growing part of the American population. This is a new reality that needs to be recognized as a priority by officials and public policymakers, for if no social and educational room is made for Latinos in America, our nation faces harder times in the twenty-first century.

Americans need to realize that Latinos are the fastest-growing resource of the United States. If we do not provide for the current and future Hispanics of the country at this point in our history, we can only blame ourselves later. Providing for the future needs of Latinos requires us to realize that tomorrow is being shaped today, that the world we create today is the one in which the future will take place. If Americans cannot adjust to changing demographics, we are likely to decline as a nation. The remedy is to educate and to equip Hispanics so that we can help maintain the quality of life that Americans hope to enjoy.

If we empower all of our citizens, and not just select groups, to be responsible for themselves and their families, all Americans will benefit, especially our older citizens who will soon need increasing care and attention. At this stage in our history, Latinos in the United States are hurting, as most minority people in the United States are, largely because the attitudes, public policies, and practices of the past have not adequately provided comfortable psychological spaces for all Americans. In the next few years, we will learn whether the promises of the Constitution will materialize for all Americans; or if our high ideals apply mainly to a dominant class of Americans who do not much care for the welfare of this country's minority populations—to everyone's detriment tomorrow.

II. Race and Education Politics in Texas

This section was initially prepared in 1997 and revised in 1999 by Roberto Garcia, senior Spanish and psychology major at Texas A&M University and son of former superintendent Roberto E. Garcia of Banquete, Texas.

The following true story has been occurring in a small south Texas town thirty-five years after the Civil Rights Act of 1964 prohibited discrimination on the basis of race, color, or national origin.

According to Kathleen and Clifton St. Clair's *Little Towns of Texas* (1982), Banquete, Texas, was founded in 1830 by Irish settlers. But Mexican inhabitants reportedly welcomed the Irish and, in 1832, prepared a large banquet for them on a creek bank, four years before the famous fight at the Alamo in San Antonio. The Irish newcomers were pleased with the reception and that is why people say the town is called Banquete, which is the Spanish spelling for "banquet." The town's legend, however, also says that Banquete was named in 1836 when General Urrea, who was heading north to meet General Santa Anna at the Alamo, stopped at this location to let his soldiers rest. The first European to pass through the Banquete area is believed to have been Alvar Nuñez Cabeza de Vaca, when he wandered far and wide for nearly nine years, lost in the Texas wilderness between 1527 and 1536.

Banquete is located in Nueces County, twenty-five miles west of Corpus Christi, and about halfway between the small towns of Alice and Robstown on U.S. Highway 44. Currently, the population of Banquete is approximately 3,500, of which 75 percent are Hispanic, almost all Mexican Americans, and the other 25 percent Anglo American. Very few of the Latino citizens are professionals; most are of low socioeconomic status, working for the minimum wage in the surrounding community. Until recently, most Mexican Americans worked for Banquete's Anglo ranchers and farmers. The widespread "*patrón* system," left over from the area's earlier cattle-ranching period, lasted as late as the 1980s. Anglos, for the most part, are the land and business owners, and, as in most parts of Texas, Hispanics have worked for them for a number generations, since the nineteenth century, as sharecroppers and domestics.

Banquete is not an incorporated community, and, despite the larger Mexican American population, the school board has been dominated by the town's minority Anglo population. Since the school district was developed in the early 1900s, only three Hispanics have served on the school board. Only two Hispanics have ever served on the board at any one time. The board members are usually approved and elected largely by the Anglo population. Although in the minority, Anglos turn out to vote, unlike Hispanics, who, in the days of the $1.75 poll tax in Texas, were kept away by that fee, and have consequently never taken voting seriously. It was not until 1996 that the members of the school board reflected Banquete's Mexican American population.

In March 1993, Roberto E. Garcia was selected to serve a two-year term as superintendent of the Banquete Independent School District. Garcia was born in neighboring Alice, Texas, on February 23, 1947, son of Porfirio Laurel-Garcia and Maria Salinas-Garcia. He graduated from Texas A&I University in Kingsville in 1972 with a B.S. in elementary education and a minor in Spanish. In 1978, he received his M.A. in educational administration with a minor in history, also from Texas A&I.[1] Currently, Superintendent Garcia is working on a doctoral degree in educational administration leadership at Texas A&M University, Corpus Christi. He holds certificates in mid-management, English as a Second Language, bilingual education, elementary education, and reading. Garcia was chosen superintendent from a field of forty-five applicants, and his contract went into effect in May 1993. His twenty-five years in public school education and four years in the U.S. Navy impressed the search committee. As the first Hispanic superintendent in the history of the school district, he knew he had a sizeable challenge before him.

On assuming the position of superintendent, Garcia learned that his professional staff was approximately 85 percent Anglo and 15 percent Hispanic, while his nonprofessional staff (e.g., custodians and cafeteria workers) was 98 percent Hispanic and 2 percent Anglo. The district has three campuses—a high school, a junior high, and an elementary school. In 1997, the district had 890 students, of which 75 percent were Hispanic and 25 percent Anglo.

Garcia found that the district still operated in a traditional Texas manner, that is, according to the "good old boy system" in which professional staff assignments are made based on preference or friendship with the administration. Banquete is considered a "poor" school district when compared to other better-financed schools in the state, and it has a very small budget with barely enough resources to pay the teachers and other employees. However, it has enjoyed the reputation of being a "good" school district, in part because Banquete's schools have been educating Anglo students involved in "white flight" from neighboring school districts since the 1970s when La Raza Unida Party, led by José Angel Gutiérrez, made a failed bid for more Hispanic political power in Texas and the southwest.[2]

Garcia was also aware that 100 percent of the students who dropped out before finishing high school were Hispanic. Hispanic parents and students informed Garcia they are not made to feel welcome in the district's schools. Garcia also found that the district was behind in using technology, and that its students score low on state and national tests. The school facilities are in a state of deterioration and generally the district is in debt, even though the tax rate in Nueces County was already among the highest in Texas. If drastic steps were not taken, the Banquete Independent School District would have had a very difficult time meeting the salaries of its employees and the educational needs of the district's children.

Shortly after assuming his position, Garcia decided to reassign teachers and not to replace positions at all levels. These actions were not well received by the teachers, who basically were used to being left to do what they wanted in the classrooms. In response, many teachers left the school district. These developments ushered in feelings of resentment toward Garcia from the Anglos of Banquete, even though his goal had been to help the district survive and keep it from possibly losing its accreditation.

Garcia is also a community-involved leader, and his growing influence has drawn the attention of the farmers and ranchers who have traditionally controlled Banquete's development. When Garcia saw how things were moving, he made it known that he was not the puppet that the education board hoped he would be. Garcia believes that his involvement with the community threatened the established power structure. Their solution was to attempt to oust the Hispanic superintendent, who was perceived as starting to organize people in the community who have generally followed Anglo leadership.

As suggested earlier, Hispanic people in Banquete have not been politically involved and have traditionally accepted Anglo direction because they have not been able to win elections. Anglos, people in Banquete know, invariably vote for their candidates, regardless of qualifications. Hispanics, on the other hand, have usually been divided, splitting their votes between Anglo and Hispanic candidates. Anglos, for example, have traditionally won school board elections by approximately 250 votes, while Hispanics who have run for the school board tend to receive around 50 votes. These results have been especially disheartening to the Hispanic population, who know that there are over a thousand registered voters, most of whom are Mexican Americans. The factor that brought the Hispanic population together, however, was the Anglo attempt to terminate Superintendent Garcia.

The turmoil in Banquete began with Garcia's termination of an administrator. Almost immediately, matters came to a head during the school board election held in May 1993, a few short weeks after Garcia's contract began. The experienced female board president, who cared for the education of all children, was not re-elected after the school board decided to reorganize itself. A newly elected member was chosen as the new president. The new male board president was aligned to the Anglo farmers and ranchers, some of whom were relatives of the terminated administrator. The board at this time consisted of seven members, all Anglo. The Anglo community also began gathering signatures on a petition calling for the removal of Superintendent Garcia that only Anglos were asked to sign.

The new school board president was aware of the petition but did not inform Garcia. Soon after, the board president made known the allegations against Garcia in a private conference with the superintendent. The board president then conducted an illegal investigation, gathering information used to intimidate Garcia to resign. In gathering the information, the board president met with other board members, in violation of the Texas Open Meetings Act, and with other Anglo staff members and the school attorney. The board president also conducted investigations in the central office when Superintendent Garcia was out, and, along with a private investigator, questioned central office staff without the knowledge or permission of the superintendent.

The Superintendent had heard rumors about the Anglo petition, but he did not learn of its existence until confronted by the new school board president. When the Hispanic citizens of Banquete found out about the petition, which had 350 names, and the illegal investigations, they in turn organized and started a petition of their own. In three days, Hispanics gathered approximately six hundred signatures in support of

Garcia. The Anglo citizens had been working on their petition, in secret, for three months. Rumors began to circulate that the Anglos' petition was racist because it had only non-Hispanic surnames on it. So, in an attempt to acquire Hispanic surnames on their petition, Anglo employers threatened Hispanic employees to sign against Garcia or be fired. Hispanic employees refused. One man said, "Fire me if you want, but I will not sign the petition against a man who has not done anything wrong, only helped the community." Some Hispanic women told Garcia that for a time they were not called to do domestic work for the Anglos who had employed them for many years.

The Anglos' allegations were that Garcia was proselytizing, promoting the Catholic Church at school; that he had his secretary type his dissertation, which does not even exist; that he misused public funds when he purchased a freon recovery unit for a part-time school employee; and that he was responsible for making teachers leave the school district. Garcia met privately with the board president in early December 1995 and was told that these accusations would be made public if he did not resign. Garcia said, "You do what you have to, and I'll do what I have to, but I will not resign."

What followed was five months of community turmoil and numerous board meetings. The meetings had to be moved to the high school to accommodate the large crowds, which included Hispanic citizens, teachers, students, state-level politicians, members of the League of United Latin American Citizens (LULAC), local news media, and other Garcia friends and supporters from neighboring towns. Anglos appeared at the meetings only in very small numbers.

Anonymous threats against the superintendent and Hispanic teachers who supported him followed. One female Hispanic teacher received the following typed note:

> You ass-kissing bitch. Just who do you think you are _____'s pet? You
> deserve nothing but all the shit in the world. And you will get worse than shit
> when our new superintendent and principle [sic] take over. You Mexicans are
> so low life your [sic] not worth vomiting on. You ain't seen nothin yet until
> _____ comes back. Watch your back, your sides, your front we are coming
> after you.

This racist threat and many other forms of intimidation were received by Garcia and other Hispanics. Garcia filed complaints with the F.B.I., the Texas Rangers, and the Nueces County Sheriff's office. These reports antagonized the board members further, because their threats and pressure were not bringing about Superintendent Garcia's resignation. Anglo actions, however, succeeded only in uniting the Hispanic community, a few Anglo supporters of Garcia, and the Catholic Church. There were many special board meetings called by the school board president attempting, as indicated in the written school board agendas, specifically "to take action on the superintendent's contract."

The superintendent, however, never wavered in his belief that justice would win. He was defending, not just his own civil rights, but also his struggle to enfranchise Banquete's Hispanic people, who have traditionally been politically powerless. Garcia's struggle became, not one for his survival as superintendent, but one to uphold the dreams and hopes of fair representation and equality for the Mexican American community, which has rallied around him. He is fighting for Latinos because he knows that his actions will benefit all students and the entire community. Garcia feels that he cannot abandon the people at any cost, even at the cost, he has said, of losing his job and career.

As Garcia narrates events, they seem like something out of a 1960s civil rights movie. Anglos drive around town announcing that the Mexicans should give up and quit supporting Garcia. Some even go around tearing down signs and fliers that express support for Garcia. Banquete remains a bifurcated community, despite Garcia's efforts to serve the educational interests of both Hispanics and Anglos.

After months of meetings and attempts to terminate the Superintendent, the Hispanic community has prevailed. The superintendent's contract was renewed, and he was even given a raise, after all the allegations against him were proven false. The school board president resigned, and another male Anglo board member refused to run for reelection. A third board member, an Anglo woman, ran in the May 1996 election on a platform to "finish the job of terminating the Superintendent." She was defeated by a three-to-one margin, however, as the Hispanic community turned out in record numbers to elect three Hispanic board members.

This is the first time in fifty years that such unity been seen in the Hispanic community. Garcia has even been stopped in Corpus Christi on two occasions by Hispanic strangers who have followed the events in the Corpus Christi media, the only outlets in Texas and the nation that have followed this remarkable civil rights story, to praise him for standing up for Hispanics and for his beliefs.

Battles like the one occurring in Banquete have happened many times in the past in Texas, and they continue to occur in cities and towns throughout the Southwest, where the Hispanic presence is seen not as a resource but as a threat. The larger American population, however, rarely hears about such events, which are either downplayed or ignored in the media, largely because of the anxiety and concern they are likely to raise. Because of fears of bad relations between people of different cultures, such news information is given little or not attention. Nonetheless, struggles like these between various groups within the American community are exactly the kind of issues that we will increasingly confront as we move into the twenty-first century. These problems will not just go away—they need to be addressed productively.

Notes

Chapter 1

1. Although I use the terms *Mexican Americans* and *Chicanos* interchangeably throughout this study, the ways in which different Spanish-speaking Americans identify themselves can be the source of considerable disagreement. In California, where the largest number of Hispanics in the United States live, *Latinos* is the most comprehensive term used for all Spanish-speaking people. The term *Chicano* is preferred there, whereas Tejanos, or the great majority of Spanish-speaking people in Texas, feel more comfortable with being called Mexican Americans than Chicanos, since the latter term suggests a political activism that in the sixties and seventies was connected with a smaller number of Mexican Americans who actively sought social change. The term *Spanish American* is used more in New Mexico, whereas *Chicano* appears more common in Arizona. The term *Latino*, which also encompasses Chicanos or Mexican Americans, is used more specifically to refer to Spanish-speaking descendants of people not only from Mexico but from other countries where Spanish is the common language. People from Spain were mainly, though not exclusively, a mixture of Christians, Jews, and Moslems. The *mestizos* or Spanish-speaking Chicanos and Latinos—the subjects of this study—emerged when the Spaniards came to the New World and mixed with the indigenous people of the Americas.

2. A few Latino communities in the United States have successfully developed areas that are increasingly attracting tourists and visitors from the rest of the United States and abroad. San Antonio, Texas, and Miami, Florida, are the two best known examples, though other metropolitan centers with vision appear to be emulating that success. Dallas, Los Angeles, San Diego, Albuquerque, Denver, San Francisco, Tucson, Phoenix, and other cities, mostly in the newly emerging sunbelt Southwest, are seeing considerable benefits in advertising and featuring the Latino sections of their cities. Otherwise, Hispanic areas are likely to remain downplayed, bypassed, and economically blighted areas instead of revenue-producing cultural centers.

3. The literature about seeking success in America is extensive, varied, and consists of many novels, histories, poems, and other narratives. Here I particularly have in mind Jewish stories of success and failure, such as Michael Gold's *Jews Without Money* (1930) and Abraham Cahan's *The Rise of David Levinsky* (1917), along with

Anglo-American autobiographies such as *The Education of Henry Adams* (1907) and Willie Morris's *North toward Home* (1967). Since Chicano literature is a product of writers and of a people who struggle in many different ways to achieve success, our writings are also part of this established literary tradition.

4. I have always believed that relationships between the young and the old can either help a society or not, as I sought to show in *Youth and Age in American Literature: The Rhetoric of Old Men* (New York: Peter Lang, 1989).

5. The book that I particularly have in mind is Carey McWilliams's 1948 classic, *North from Mexico: The Spanish-Speaking People of the United States*, which is still being mined for general information by many scholars. *North from Mexico* was reissued in 1968 with a new introduction by McWilliams, and updated as a new edition in 1990 by Matt S. Meier. McWilliams's book owed much to Paul S. Taylor's monographs on Mexican labor in the United States, including *An American-Mexican Frontier* (1934), which McWilliams called "the finest single volume on Anglo-Hispano relations in print today." Constructive discourses between Latinos and African, Native, and Asian Americans would also create a less insular and healthier pluralistic American society.

6. The difference between accommodation and assimilation is that the former requires the help and support of mainstream Americans, while the latter simply requires ethnic Americans to leave their cultures and mores and to conform to the ways of the established majority population.

7. I am currently working on a manuscript entitled *Repairing Educational Systems*, which discusses how the K–12 grades can better prepare Hispanic and non-Hispanic students to be academically more competitive for higher education.

8. Leading Chicano critics Juan Bruce-Novoa and Ramon Saldívar, in particular, have invited such a dialogue with the rest of America. See Juan Bruce-Novoa, *Retrospace: Collected Essays on Chicano Literature, Theory and History* (Houston: Arte Publico Press, 1990); and Ramon Saldívar, *Chicano Narrative: The Dialectics of Difference* (Madison: University of Wisconsin Press, 1990). In *Retrospace*, Bruce-Novoa wrote: "An early reading of Mircea Eliade was a revelation: the history of peoples could be seen as the *repeated attempt* to create a livable order in the midst of imminent chaos, to instill values in a world which denied them, and to provide meaningful patterns of behavior in the face of the one overriding fact of life—death" (161, my emphasis). Saldívar is even more direct, inviting critical study of the Mexican Americans issues discussed in his book.

9. This study is not concerned with Chicano poetry, which has also been disregarded by the American literary establishment. Interested readers are referred to Cordelia Candelaria's *Chicano Poetry: A Critical Introduction* (Westport, Conn.: Greenwood Press, 1986); and Alfred Arteaga's *Chicano Poetics: Heterotexts and Hybridities* (New York: Cambridge University Press, 1997). The latter suggestively connects contemporary Chicano poetry, in both scholarly and more subjective ways, to parts of Mexico's indigenous myths and writings.

10. See my essay, "College Admission Policies, the Courts, Institutional Rankings, and Eligible Hispanic and African American Students," in *Education of Hispanics in the U.S.: Politics, Policies and Outcomes*, ed. Abbas Tashakkori and Hector Salvador Ochoa (New York: AMS Press, forthcoming).

11. See "Why Ending Open Enrollment at CUNY Is Not the Answer," *New Republic*, May 11, 1998. See also Michael Olivas's *Latino College Students* (New York: Teachers College Press, 1986), which showed, over a dozen years ago, that more than two-thirds of the Hispanic students attending college take classes at community colleges.

12. "Hispanics at Community Colleges: Graduation Statistics," *Hispanic Outlook in Higher Education*, vol. 8, no. 16 (April 10, 1998): 14–16.

13. Octavio Paz refers to Arnold Toynbee's "Universal Empire," which I have not located in Toynbee's voluminous writings. Paz's chapter on "The Conquest and Colonialism" in *The Labyrinth of Solitude: Life and Thought in Mexico* (1950; English translation by Lysander Kemp, New York: Grove Press, 1961) especially upset Mexican intellectuals when it first came out, because, like the paintings of Diego Rivera, it forced Mexican society to accept its indigenous past. In this chapter, Paz writes, "By determining the salient features of colonial religion, whether in its popular manifestations or in those of its most representative spirits, we can discover the meaning of our culture and the origins of many of our later conflicts" (100). See also Charles Gibson's *The Aztecs under Spanish Rule: A History of the Indians of the Valley of Mexico, 1519–1810* (Stanford: Stanford University Press, 1964).

14. The names and dates for these civilizations are taken from a beautifully prepared pamphlet entitled *The Mesoamericans: Great People of the Past*, published by the National Geographic Society in 1997. John M. D. Pohl, Arnoldo González Cruz, Mary Ellen Miller, and Merle Green Robertson are the consultants credited.

15. See Luis Valdez, "Introduction: 'La Plebe,' " in *Aztlan: An Anthology of Mexican American Literature*, ed. Luis Valdez and Stan Steiner (New York: Alfred A. Knopf, 1972), for an ample discussion of Aztlan.

16. Peter Matthiessen excellently captured the promise that Chavez represented for Chicanos in *Sal Si Puedes: Cesar Chavez and the New American Revolution* (New York: Dell, 1969). In the mid-1990s, similarly compassionless forces, under the leadership of California governor Pete Wilson and University of California regent Ward Connerly, joined forces to eliminate race as the only objectionable factor among others considered by the University of California's admissions office. Proposition 209 also eliminated affirmative action in California in 1996.

17. Americo Paredes, ed., *Humanidad: Essays in Honor of George I. Sanchez* (Los Angeles: Chicano Studies Center Publications, University of California, 1977) tried to remedy that neglect. During his lifetime, George I. Sanchez published numerous educational works, including: *A Guide for Teachers of Spanish-Speaking Children in the Primary Grades* (Austin, Texas: State Department of Education, 1946); *Materials Relating to the Education of the Spanish-Speaking People in the U.S.: An Annotated Bibliography* (1959; reprint, Westport, Conn.: Greenwood Press, 1971); *Arithmetic in Maya* (1961); and *Forgotten People: A Study of New Mexicans* (1940; reprint, Albuquerque: C. Horn, 1967). Regarding bilingual education, the scholarship is so voluminous that no summary will suffice. I will say that bilingual education has always been hamstrung by what politicians have done in responding to the views of a largely uninformed general public.

18. For further discussion, see my forthcoming essay, *"Hopwood,* Race, *Bakke* and the Constitution," *Texas Hispanic Journal of Law and Policy.*

19. "Hispanic Americans," a bibliographic chapter in Allen L. Woll and Randall M. Miller's *Ethnic and Racial Images in American Film and Television: Historical Essays and Bibliography* (New York: Garland, 1987), and the postscripts in this book show examples of discrimination in the media and in the general culture.

20. One of the most recent and successful efforts to communicate the wide variety of American Hispanics of all races, in 230 beautifully taken color and black-and-white photographs, is Edward J. Olmos and Yea Ybarra's bilingual *Americanos: Latino Life in the United States/La Vida Latina en los Estados Unidos* (Boston: Little, Brown, 1999). This enormously attractive pictorial feast carries a spirited but gentle introduction by the great novelist Carlos Fuentes. The pictures show, among many meditations that the individual photographs prompt, the extent to which Latinos "are both an accomplished and an unfinished people," as David Carrasco, one of the contributors, observes.

21. Michael Awkward's *Negotiating Difference: Race, Gender and the Politics of Positionality* (Chicago: University of Chicago Press, 1995) offers a wonderful testimony regarding the difficult choices that beset not only African Americans, but also Latinos interested in coming to terms with the politics of self and communal representation. The works of Asian American writers like Frank Chin in *Donald Duk,* Garrett Hongo, and others also dramatize that challenge, as do Native American writers such as Louise Erdrich, N. Scott Momaday, and Leslie Silko.

22. Historian Rodolfo Acuña expresses the frustrations of many Mexican Americans and Latinos in *Anything But Mexican: Chicanos in Contemporary Los Angeles* (London: Verso, 1996).

23. For a succinct discussion of Chicano literature since 1848, see Raymund Paredes's "The Evolution of Chicano Literature," in *Three American Literatures,* ed. Houston Baker, Jr. (New York: Modern Language Association, 1982).

Notes to Chapter 2

1. *MELUS,* the journal of the Society for the Study of the Multi-Ethnic Literature of the United States, and other scholarly journals have consistently tied American literature to our ethnic literatures. For other scholarly studies that have successfully connected the two fields, see Eric J. Sundquist's *To Wake the Nations: Race in the Making of American Literature* (Cambridge, Mass.: The Belknap Press of Harvard University Press, 1993); Thomas J. Ferraro's *Ethnic Passages: Literary Immigrants in Twentieth-Century America* (Chicago: University of Chicago Press, 1993); and Werner Sollors's *The Invention of Ethnicity* (New York: Oxford University Press, 1989). The great majority of Americanists, however, still appear hesitant to fully integrate the two fields.

2. José E. Limón's *Mexican Ballads, Chicano Poems: History and Influence in Mexican-American Social Poetry* (Berkeley: University of California Press, 1992) is the best treatment of the *corridos,* so named in Spanish because they record events in musical ballads, which the Chicano community remembers, and which, like life, inevitably *corren,* that is, run on through time.

3. The questions asked and the answers provided by writers in Juan Bruce-Novoa's in *Chicano Authors: Inquiry by Interview* (Austin: University of Texas Press, 1980) demonstrate the highly uncertain nature of their writing, as Chicano authors saw it in the 1970s.

4. Both Kanellos and Keller are extremely enterprising publishers and editors who also hold distinguished teaching appointments at, respectively, the University of Houston and Arizona State University. Besides producing most of the more recent Hispanic American texts, as managing editor Kanellos has also orchestrated and prepared the comprehensive, three-volume *Reference Library of Hispanic America*, which successfully pinpoints and discusses many of the most notable social accomplishments of American Latinos.

5. Anthropologist José R. Reyna captured a great variety of Chicano jokes in *Raza Humor: Chicano Joke Tradition in Texas* (San Antonio: Penca Books, 1980). The *chiste* or joke practices have not received much scholarly attention, but are an important component of Mexican American culture.

Notes to Chapter 3

1. In literature, the standard, almost lone work of scholarship for many years was Stanley Thomas Williams's two-volume *The Spanish Background of American Literature* (New Haven: Yale University Press, 1955). This comprehensive study was followed by Cecil Robinson's trenchant *With the Ears of Strangers: The Mexican in American Literature* (Tucson: University of Arizona Press, 1963), which was revised as *Mexico and the Hispanic Southwest in American Literature* (Tucson: University of Arizona Press, 1977. In the social sciences, one of the best attempts at describing the Mexican American experience in the United States was Joan W. Moore with Harry Pachon, *Mexican Americans* (Englewood Cliffs, N.J.: Prentice-Hall, 1970).

In his 1968 introduction to the reissue of his 1948 book *North from Mexico: The Spanish-Speaking People of the United States* (New York: Greenwood Press, 1968), however, Carey McWilliams painted a more exciting picture than was actually the case: "Since *North from Mexico* was first published in 1950 [*sic*], there has been a new burst of interest in Mexican-Americans, which, in large part, has come about as a result of activities and developments for which they themselves are responsible. Historically, the Spanish-speaking have often complained that little is know about them (which is true) and that their problems have received little attention by the larger American public (which is also true). Dr. George Sanchez, a distinguished spokesman for the Spanish-speaking, once referred to them as 'an orphan group, the least known, the least sponsored, and the least vocal large minority group in the nation.' In the same vein, Representative Edward R. Roybal of California, himself of Mexican-American descent, has said that 'the Mexican population of the Southwest . . . is little known on the East Coast and not much better understood in the Southwest itself.' A Mexican-American was quoted in *Newsweek* as saying, 'We're the best kept secret in America.' But this is certainly no longer the case. Suddenly the nation has discovered Mexican-Americans. Witness the feature stories about them in *The Wall Street Journal* (May 3, 1966), *Newsweek* (May 23, 1966), *Time* (April 28, 1967), *U.S. News and World Report* (June 6, 1966), and other publications.

In this introduction to the reprint edition, I have sought to summarize certain important developments since 1950 which account for the new burst of interest and concern."

2. See "Population Change and Income: Implications for Business Activity and Fiscal Resources," in Steve H. Murdock et al., *The Texas Challenge: Population Change and the Future of Texas* (College Station: Texas A&M University Press, 1997). Hispanics in other states face comparably bleak economic scenarios.

3. Alfredo J. Estrada, "Which Companies Are Providing the Most Opportunities for Hispanics?" *Hispanic*, January/February (1997): 58–78. "The Hispanic Voter," a survey of 755 voting-age Hispanics in Dallas, Houston, San Antonio, Miami, New York, Chicago, Los Angeles, and San Francisco, discovered that 86 percent are teaching their children Spanish, and that 80 percent appreciate political candidates who speak to them in Spanish. Mark Penn, one of the pollsters conducting the survey, which was sponsored by Univision, the country's largest Spanish-language television network, told reporters that "Hispanics provide the crucial swing vote in some of the nation's largest states." The survey also discovered that 70 percent of Hispanics support bilingual education, and that as a group Hispanics tend to vote "overwhelmingly Democratic." See *Politico, the Forum for Latino Politics*, politicol@aol.com, vol. 1, no. 34, April 27, 1998. Univision/Latinolink.com/Cox Newspapers.

4. Richard Natale, "The Latin Factor: Hollywood Plugs into a Burgeoning and Profitable Ethnic Market," *Entertainment Weekly*, May 12, 1995, 14; Alyssa Glass, "The Push for Professional Growth," *Hispanic Business*, vol. 19, no. 2 (February 1997): 14.

5. It is useful to compare the following statistics, provided over thirty years ago by Carey McWilliams in his 1968 introduction to *North from Mexico*, to the professional membership numbers I earlier provided. Of course, not all professionals are members of associations, but a comparison is nonetheless instructive. McWilliams wrote, "This growing political influence of the Spanish-speaking reflects new educational and economic gains and the rise of a new middle class. Among Mexican [American] males in the Southwest today, some 29,229 are engaged in professional, technical, and similar work, either as employees or as self-employed persons: 3,761 as teachers in elementary and secondary schools, 404 in colleges and universities, 3,044 as engineers, 2,357 as designers and draftsmen, 2,130 as auditors and accounts, 1,866 as technicians, 1,291 as clergymen, 1,405 as musicians and music teachers, and, of course, quite a number as doctors, lawyers, and social workers. Not many Mexicans [Americans] have yet achieved recognition as writers and artists, but there is a wealth of talent in the group that will some day—and fairly soon—burst forth on the national scene." One can study and draw a variety of conclusions from these statistics, but I will settle here for asking: How many Chicano writers today are known "on the national scene"?

6. Being an affirmative action beneficiary, my position is that no better idea has surfaced in over thirty-three years of debate and discord. See my "Affirmative Action: Best Idea, So Far," in *Hispanonotícias: The Hispanic Caucus of the American Association for Higher Education*, June 1995.

7. In his classic *North from Mexico*, McWilliams wrote: "Above all it is important

to remember that Mexicans are a 'conquered' people in the Southwest, a people whose culture has been under incessant attack for many years and whose character and achievements as a people have been consistently disparaged. Apart from physical violence, conquered and conqueror have continued to be competitors for land and jobs and power, parties to a constant economic conflict which has found expression in litigation, dispossessions, hotly contested elections, and the mutual disparagement which inevitably accompanies a situation of this kind. Throughout this struggle, the Anglo-Americans have possessed every advantage: in numbers and wealth, arms and machines. Having been subjected, first to a brutal physical attack, and then to a long process of economic attrition, it is not surprising that so many Mexicans should show evidence of the spiritual defeatism which so often arises when a cultural minority is annexed to an alien culture and way of life. More is involved, in situations of this kind, than the defeat of individual ambitions, for the victims also suffer from the defeat of their culture and of the society of which they are a part" (132).

8. Victor Landa, "Hispanics Turn Up the Volume with Business Boom," *Austin American-Statesman*, July 16, 1996, A9.

9. S. H. Murdock, *An America Challenged: Population Change and the Future of the United States* (Boulder, Colo.: Westview Press, 1995), 51–52.

10. Ibid., 113.

11. Harriet D. Romo and Toni Falbo's *Latino High School Graduation: Defying the Odds* (Austin: University of Texas Press, 1996) documents how Hispanic students move and are moved through the educational pipeline. The subtitles to the chapters in their book succinctly capture what Latino students tend to hear, based on the attitudes that shape practices and policies. The instructive subtitles are: "You're Not College Material"; "Well, She's Mexican. She's Going to Drop Out"; "I Didn't Want to Be 20 When I Graduated"; "I Guess No One Wants Me"; "Don't Be Like Me—Stay in School"; "What Would I Change? Everything."

12. See S. Robert Lichter and Daniel Amundson, "Distorted Reality: Hispanic Characters in TV Entertainment" (Washington, D.C.: Center for Media and Public Affairs, September 1, 1994).

13. Selena's tragic murder was so unexpected and dramatic that her death was especially mourned throughout the Latino world. The major media outlets of the United States also took note. Shortly after her death, *Time* magazine placed her picture on the front cover, I think a first for a Mexican American woman. Throughout the rest of 1994, both Latino and mainstream publications continued to carry stories and photographs of Selena; one in *Newsweek* as late as October 23, 1995, said that "Selena's music, Tejano, is the rollicking soundtrack to the border country, fusing Hispanic culture to Anglo pop, connecting the present to the past." Indeed, it is through Selena that the Mexican Americans and mainstream Americans have momentarily taken public media notice of each other, an instance which shows that such a relationship is possible and healthy for members of American society.

14. This particular dialogue wonderfully captures some of the psychological and cultural difficulties that have not been so crisply and succinctly expressed in Chicano literature.

15. In "Turning Public Schools Around" (*San Antonio Express-News*, May 26,

1998, 5B), newspaper columnist Molly Ivins writes: "Moaning about the public schools in this country is now a major national pastime. Indeed, a loud claque has concluded that they're all hopeless and the best thing we can do is dismantle the whole system by providing vouchers for private schools. In fact, our metaphorical glass here is half-full. We have good public schools; indeed, we have some excellent ones. But we also have some awful ones and a whole lot of mediocre ones" The *Hopwood* opinion discussed earlier continued to highlight the fact that most minority students, African Americans and Hispanic students in particular, tend to attend the "awful" and "mediocre ones."

16. The 1997 Warner Brothers film *Selena*, produced by Gregory Nava and featuring Jennifer Lopez in the title role and Edward James Olmos as Selena's father, marks the first time that the lives of Chicanos from south Texas have been portrayed realistically by Hollywood. The film has been immensely popular because Selena was widely loved. Many Hispanics have seen it more than five times—telling anyone who pays attention the extent to which Latinos want to see more films about Hispanics in the United States.

17. Latino youngsters thus lighten their hair and buy green- or blue-shaded contact lenses, continuing the preference for lighter-skinned people.

18. Raymund Paredes traced dislike for Mexicans in "The Origins of Anti-Mexican Sentiment in the United States," in *New Directions in Chicano Scholarship*, ed. Ricardo Romo and Raymund Paredes (San Diego: University of California Chicano Studies Program, 1978). For a thorough discussion of similar sentiments in Texas, see historian Arnoldo De León's *The Tejano Community, 1836–1900* (Albuquerque: University of New Mexico Press, 1982). De León writes: "The immigrants, then, did not arrive [between 1821 and 1836] in Texas with open minds concerning the native Tejanos: their two-hundred year experience with 'different' peoples had so shaped their psyche that their immediate reaction was negative rather than positive. Most of the immigrants into Coahuila and Tejas, despite their honest, industrious habits, were racists. They had retained impressions acquired before their arrival in the state then reapplied and transposed those racial attitudes upon the native castes. White men had an inherent distaste for miscegenation, were acutely mindful of the significance of color, and assumed an aura of superiority and condescension toward the natives. Racial and ethnocentric feeling were evident from the very start" (11).

19. See David R. McDonald and Timothy M. Matovina, *Defending Mexican Valor in Texas: Jose Antonio Navarro's Historical Writings, 1858–1857* (Austin, Texas: State House Press, 1995), p. 29. In their introduction, McDonald and Matovina write: "Despite the efforts of Navarro and other Tejano leaders to defend their people's interests, Tejanos' economic and political influence diminished significantly in San Antonio after the U.S. annexation in 1845. They increasingly became a working underclass after statehood and, as previously mentioned, lost most of their land holdings. In the political realm, Tejano electees to the San Antonio city council decreased threefold in the first fifteen years after U.S. annexation. Five of the eight members of the city council were Tejanos in 1845, but in 1860 not a single Tejano served in that capacity." Although Jose Antonio Navarro, in particular, valiantly fought the scornful perspectives of the Anglo Americans who crowded out the Mex-

ican people who became American citizens after the 1848 Treaty of Guadalupe Hidalgo, Hispanic Americans in Texas and throughout much of the Southwest—like the Native Americans, African Americans, and the Chinese Americans along the Pacific coast—have never since been legally protected or given the same educational opportunities or considerations that the Constitution guarantees to all Americans.

José Antonio Navarro (1795–1871) deserves special attention because as a native Tejano and San Antonian, he sought the independence of Texas from Mexico, from Spain, and from foreign influences. After Texas became a state in 1845, Navarro served on the first Texas legislature. At the 1845 Texas Constitutional Convention, he successfully secured voting and citizen rights for the Texans of Mexican and Spanish descent, when some of the delegates, notably Francis Moore, Jr., of Harris County, would not have allowed Tejanos to vote. Moore argued: "Strike out the term 'white' and what will be the result? Hordes of Mexican Indians may come in here from the West, and may be more formidable than the enemy you have vanquished. Silently they will come moving in; they will come back in thousands to Béxar, in thousands to Goliad, perhaps to Nacogdoches, and what will be the consequence? Ten, twenty, thirty, forty, fifty thousand may come in here, and vanquish you at the ballot box." McDonald and Matovina go on to say that "Navarro contended that including the word 'white' in the electoral legislation was 'odious' and ridiculous.' In the end, the position of Navarro and others held sway, as Tejanos were not denied voting rights in the Constitution of the State of Texas" (20).

20. In an article in the San Antonio–based *Western Texan*, published October 14, 1852, Tejanos or Mexican Americans were patronizingly characterized as "victims of a morally and intellectually impoverished heritage" that has continued to dominate Anglo perception of Hispanics. The article continues: "It is lamentably true that our Mexican population, generally, do not occupy as high a position in the scale of morality and intelligence as is desirable; yet every one knows their former condition, and will take into consideration their former mode of life, as well as the demoralizing effect of the Government under which they lived previous to the establishment of the Texas Republic, must admit that they are reforming as rapidly as could have been expected, under the circumstances by which they have been surrounded." The morally righteous idea was "that Anglo-American influence offered [the Mexican population of Texas] a means to redeem that heritage," a culture that has always been debased and degraded in the media by the very people who were invited to immigrate to Texas by Stephen F. Austin and who then colonized the state for the United States. Quoted in McDonald and Matovina, *Defending Mexican Valor in Texas*, 23.

Most of the equal educational advances made by Mexican Americans and other Latinos in the United States have been achieved through successful legal challenges. MALDEF and other individuals and groups have reluctantly had to resort to the courts to secure equal rights and opportunities. See the chapters "Compelled to Litigate" and "A Sustained Legal Attack" in Guadalupe San Miguel, Jr.'s excellent study, *"Let All of Them Take Heed": Mexican Americans and the Campaign for Educational Equality in Texas, 1910–1981* (Austin: University of Texas Press, 1987).

Notes to Chapter 4

1. Jorge A. Banales, "Hispanics Protest Television Portrayal," United Press International, Washington News, September 7, 1994.

2. "Minority Participation in the Media": Hearings before the Subcommittee on Telecommunications, Consumer Protection, and Finance of the Committee on Energy and Commerce, House of Representatives, Ninety-Eighth Congress, First Session, September 19 and 23, 1983, 20–21.

3. Our American histories also do not sufficiently remind us that two hundred years earlier, between 1540 and 1542, Francisco de Coronado explored New Mexico at about the same time Álvar Núñez Cabeza de Vaca was wandering through Texas and Juan Rodriguez Cabrillo was exploring southern California.

4. James Ernest Crisp, in his 1976 Yale University Ph.D. dissertation, "Anglo-Texan Attitudes toward the Mexican, 1821–1845," concluded: "The evidence adduced in this study shows that before, during, and after the Texas Revolution [1836], Anglo-Texas attitudes were extremely complex, sometimes contradictory, and usually in a state of flux." Crisp argued that "the Mexican served as a 'negative image' for Americans, and that the American self-image largely defined the categories within which the Mexican was viewed. The image which Americans had of themselves was undergoing a crucial transformation precisely during these years of Anglo-American settlement in Texas—there was an increasing emphasis on *race* as opposed to a devotion to republican principles as an explanation for the development of a peculiar American character and identity." This historical perspective, in light of today's *Hopwood* case, should lead us to ask how the education of the citizenry, during the last 175 years, has made a difference in Texas, or in the rest of the nation, for that matter. My position is that more needs to be done for Latinos, because clearly what we have in place is not yet effective, regardless of what defenders of the status quo say.

5. Chicanos became more active after 1964 Civil Rights Act of 1964, which is usually seen as a watershed event. We also have to remember, however, that Mexican Americans had been seeking recognition long before the 1960s. In his 1976 University of Texas dissertation, titled "The American G.I. Forum: A History of a Mexican American Organization," Vernon Carl Allsup wrote: "The Mexican American people did not suddenly become aware of the problems confronting them in the turbulent decades of the sixties. Nor did an 'awakened minority' flounder among an Anglo manipulated society until rescued by proponents of La Raza. Americans of Mexican origin have fought for their place in American society throughout the twentieth century. One of the most important periods of this struggle began in the immediate years after World War II. Returning veterans did not accept the subordinate status that Anglo America felt was a proper and traditional 'place' for these people. The cutting edge of this movement was the American G.I. Forum. Beginning in Texas and spreading throughout the United States, Mexican American Forumeers established the 'identity' of Mexicanos, pursued policies and programs beneficial to all minorities, and represented *la gente* [the people] most ably. As the more militant and young Chicanos of the 1960's demanded the rights of American, the G.I. Forum continued its opposition to prejudice, and its advice

for Mexican Americans. Indeed, I contend that the Chicano movement was a natural transition of the 1950's; the groundwork was laid by people like the members of the American G.I. Forum."

6. It is instructive to read what Arnoldo De León wrote about Texas in *The Tejano Community, 1836–1900* (Albuquerque: University of New Mexico Press, 1982): "In 1850, foreign born Anglo males twenty-one and over made up about 47 percent of the Anglo males of voting age and older, while in 1900 the percentage of foreign born Anglo males twenty-one and over amounted to about 27 percent. However, Tejano illiteracy did prove a serious disability. Minimal education not only restricted their familiarity with state and national issues but inhibited their grasp of political operations. Their educational handicap gave the Anglo majority a vast edge for it left a minority of more literate and knowledgeable Tejanos to work and speak in behalf of the Tejano community. As can be seen in the census schedules, Tejano males twenty-one years and over collectively outnumbered their Anglo counterparts in South, Central and West Texas by at least 1,420 in 1900. However, in the same year, only 2,248 (12.9 percent) of the Tejano males of voting age were literate and either American born, naturalized, or filed. About 14,005 (88.2 percent) of the Anglo males of voting age were literate, American born, naturalized or filed. The Tejano community, therefore, was weakened even before whites employed external mechanisms that made Tejanos a powerless constituency.

"Diverse tactics were employed to minimize Tejano involvement. Race relations were characterized by the refusal of Anglos to accept Mexicanos organizing along ethnic lines with intentions of electing an 'all Mexican' ticket aiming for self-determination. Texas Rangers could be, and on occasion were, swiftly dispatched to abort such a plan. Further, the news media could mobilize public opinion against any attempts at self-improvement; for example, newspapers branded the followers of Juan Cortina and Catarino Garza, the Tejano activist who pronounced against Mexican President Porfirio Diaz in 1891, as ignorant greasers and *pelados* easily led into misadventure and crime. Also, Anglos might have tolerated the Mexican vote when it could be controlled, but attempts at disfranchisement to insure white supremacy abounded" (24–25).

Notes to Chapter 5

1. Aside from the work of education scholars like Harriet Romo and Toni Falbo, very few useful studies are available on Mexican American teenagers. Nicolás Carrasco's "The Relationship between Parental Support and Control and Adolescent Self-Esteem in Mexican, Mexican American and Anglo American Families" (Ph.D. dissertation, University of Texas, 1990) is helpful in this regard. About twenty years ago, I encountered the first "Mexican American psychology" classroom textbook. Though psychologists have remained engaged, mainly by case studies of Mexican Americans, I have not found any psychology textbooks on how Mexican Americans grow, develop, and mature.

2. Luis Valdez's *Actos* (San Juan Bautista, Calif.: Menyah Publications, 1971) were the wonderfully engaging, impromptu plays that Valdez composed and directed for the well-known traveling Teatro Campesino. Valdez's performances en-

tertained *raza* workers out in the agricultural fields during the days when Cesar Chavez was organizing the grape growers in the California in the 1960s.

3. Charles Ramirez Berg's *Poster Art from the Golden Age of the Mexican Cinema* (Austin: University of Texas Press, 1997) features 840 film posters that were commercially produced during the 1940s, 1950s, and 1960s. These posters were used to promote the films produced by the Mexican movie stars that I mention and other less well known Mexican actors. When I was growing up, as I have said, our parents took my brother and I to see these popular films that were shown weekly in McAllen, Texas. This collection of poster art is part of the Agrasánchez Film Archive of Mexican Cinema in Harlingen, Texas, and it opens up a whole world of American culture that has not been recognized or acknowledged by students of American Studies.

4. The history of picking cotton in the nineteenth century has been documented in a study chosen by the Organization of American Historians as the best first book published by a scholar in the field of American history for 1997. Neil Foley's *The White Scourge: Mexicans, Blacks and Poor Whites in Texas Cotton Culture* (Berkeley: University of California Press, 1997) discusses how the cotton economy, race, class, and gender mixed in Texas from the Civil War period to the New Deal programs of the 1930s.

5. See, for example, Félix F. Gutiérrez and Jorge Reina Schement, *Spanish-Language Radio in the Southwestern United States* (Austin: University of Texas Press, Center for Mexican American Studies, 1979), for a sense of this Hispanic media culture, which provides one of the mainstays that help keep Mexican Americans connected to Spanish-language events and customs.

6. Manuel Peña discusses this music in *The Texas-Mexican Conjunto: History of a Working Class Music* (Austin: University of Texas Press, Center for Mexican American Studies, 1985).

7. The best book of the period to capture this life from a cultural anthropology perspective was William Madsen's *The Mexican Americans of South Texas* (1964; reprint, New York: Holt, Rinehart and Winston, 1973). As far as literary works, we had at most little-known memoirs like Carroll Norquest's *Rio Grande Wetbacks: Mexican Migrant Workers* (Albuquerque: University of New Mexico Press, 1972), an interesting book whose title suggests one of the main ways that Hispanic and Anglo relationships were seen in south Texas. In the 1920s, Norquest's father traded his Kansas farm for several acres of Rio Grande Valley land, and Norquest's own five acres in time grew to one hundred and twenty. Most of what used to be his farm land is now the site of the University of Texas–Pan American in my hometown of Edinburg. The student population of the University is over 13,000, more than 80 percent of whom are Hispanics who graduate from the Rio Grande Valley high schools in Hidalgo, Cameron, Starr, and Zapata counties. It would be instructive to compare this book to Jovita Gonzalez's unpublished 1930 University of Texas dissertation entitled "Social Life in Cameron, Starr, and Zapata Counties." Jovita Gonzalez Mireles also wrote *Caballero*, published posthumously in 1996.

8. In Sandra Cisneros's *The House on Mango Street* (Houston: Arte Publico Press, 1984), the narrator, Esperanza, says, "It is the Mexican records my father plays on Sunday mornings when he is shaving, songs like sobbing" (10).

9. Guadalupe San Miguel, *"Let All of Them Take Heed": Mexican Americans and the Campaign for Educational Equality in Texas, 1910–1981* (Austin: University of Texas Press, 1987), x.

10. The one recent exception is the Carlos H. Cantu Hispanic Education and Opportunity Endowment, established in February 1999 at Texas A&M University. President and CEO of the ServiceMaster Company, Cantu has personally committed $1 million "to seek solutions to the nation's serious Hispanic drop-out problem," states the announcement establishing the endowment from the University Relations office. "Cantu says several disturbing statistics led him to fund the endowment: Hispanic students are nearly four times more likely than Anglos and more than twice as likely as African-Americans to drop out before earning their high school diplomas. Approximately 500,000 eighth- to twelfth-grade Hispanic students drop out of school annually. 'We are losing leaders of the future, and it is our responsibility to address this problem before it is beyond repair' says Cantu, a 1955 graduate of Texas A&M. 'My hope is that this endowment will help us determine the root cause and hopefully come up with some answers.'"

Notes to Chapter 6

1. See, for example, Martha Menchaca's excellent ethnographic history of the Mexican-origin people of Santa Paula, California, in *The Mexican Outsiders: A Community History of Marginalization and Discrimination in California* (Austin: University of Texas Press, 1995).

Notes to Chapter 7

1. From the time of Francis Parkman's *The Oregon Trail* (1847) through the first six decades of the twentieth century, most Americans did not see anything wrong with excluding minority people from being part of the American experience. In *The Southwest in American Literature and Art: The Rise of a Desert Aesthetic* (Tucson: University of Arizona Press, 1997), David W. Teague shows how the mainstream magazines at the turn of the century encouraged a racism that we have now forgotten, but which continues to shape many of the prevailing views about which we are not educating people. In the *Century* magazine in 1902, for example, Teague locates one such passage written by Ray Stannard Baker: "It will be seen therefore, that the Southwest is peopled with the very best Americans, segregated by the eternal law of evolutionary selection, with almost no substratum of the low-caste European foreigner to lower the level of civilization. Of course there is no danger from the Indians, Negroes, Mexican, or Chinese, because there is rarely any mixing with them by marriage, as formerly. With such a start, and such a commingling of Americans from all parts of the Union, the man from Boston rubbing elbows with the Atlanta man, and Kansas working side by side with Mississippi, it would seem that the region may one day produce the standard American type" (103). Theodore Roosevelt's theory of Anglo-Saxon progress in his *Winning of the West* (New York: Putnam, 1889) helped fuel this kind of rhetoric, which has never been successfully countered by education in the schools.

2. Readers of Tomas Rivera's . . . *y no se lo tragó la tierra/ . . . and the earth did not part* (Berkeley: Quinto Sol Publications, 1971) are left to surmise that the home of the anonymous youth in Rivera's work is Crystal City, Texas, Rivera's own hometown and the political home of La Raza Unida Party.

3. In *Otros Dias: Memories of "Other Days". . . from Mexico in Revolution to a Life of Medicine in Texas* (Westford, Mass.: Grey Home Press, 1984), Octavio Garcia, M.D., discusses the racial discrimination that existed in south Texas during the 1930s. Speaking about the education of his son, Garcia wrote: "Wishing to advance his religious training, and also to avoid the rampant discrimination that was prevalent in the public schools to children bearing a Latin name, we enrolled him in the local parochial school, where he learned his ABCs. I was not entirely pleased but felt this was the best I could do until he was old enough to be sent away to a larger school to broaden his education" (241).

4. See Guadalupe San Miguel, *"Let All of Them Take Heed": Mexican Americans and the Campaign for Educational Equality in Texas, 1910–1981* (Austin: University of Texas Press, 1987).

5. All parenthetical page references in the text to this chapter refer to Americo Paredes's *George Washington Gomez* (Houston: Arte Publico Press, 1990). I quote extensively from the work because Paredes's text is not generally known and deserves wider recognition. At this point, the following dialogue ensues:
"They walked in silence for a while, then Gumersindo said, 'After all, it's their country.'
" 'Their country!' Feliciano half-shouted. 'Their country! There you are. Their filthy lies are all over you already. I was born here. My father was born here and so was my grandfather and his father before him. And then they come, they come and take it, steal it and call it theirs.' He dropped his voice. 'But it won't be theirs much longer now, not much longer, I can tell you. We'll get it back, all of it' " (20).

6. See, for example, Leon F. Bouvier and Dudley L. Poston, Jr., *Thirty Million Texans?* (Freeman, S.D.: Pine Hill Press, 1993). The 1990 U.S. Census makes similar projections of large population increases of Hispanics for other parts of the country.

7. See chapters 6, 7, and 8 of Lawrence Levine's *The Opening of the American Mind: Canons, Culture, and History* (Boston: Beacon Press, 1996) for the best discussion I have seen of how Americans have traditionally seen immigrants and how education has served and ought to continue to serve to unify Americans.

8. For a highly laudatory portrait of the Rangers, see Walter Prescott Webb's *The Texas Rangers* (Cambridge, Mass.: Houghton Mifflin, 1935).

9. The slang term *rinches* rhymes with another Chicano slang word, *pinche*, which means stingy. Mexican Americans use both terms pejoratively.

10. For scholarship on the *corridos*, see José Eduardo Limón's *Dancing with the Devil: Society and Cultural Poetics in Mexican-American South Texas* (Madison: University of Wisconsin Press, 1994); Limón's *Mexican Ballads, Chicano Poems: History and Influence in Mexican-American Social Poetry* (Berkeley: University of California Press, 1992); and Americo Paredes's *With His Pistol in His Hand: A Border Ballad and Its Hero* (Austin: University of Texas Press, 1958).

11. See David Montejano's influential *Anglos and Mexicans in the Making of Texas, 1836–1986* (Austin: University of Texas Press, 1987).

12. Students of American Studies simply are not familiar enough with the complex nature of the relations between the Spanish-speaking settlers already living in Texas, California, and the Southwest and the Anglo settlers who began moving in after the Lewis and Clark expedition opened up the West. Following the war with Mexico in 1848, the United States agreed to honor the language, customs, and the property rights of the Spanish-speaking American citizens, as Richard Griswold del Castillo has brought out in *The Treaty of Guadalupe Hidalgo: A Legacy of Conflict* (Norman: University of Oklahoma Press, 1990).

In *"It's Your Misfortune and None of My Own": A History of the American West* (Norman: University of Oklahoma Press, 1991), Richard White offers a paradigm-changing perspective on "Manifest Destiny." Instead of seeing the story of the American West as one of inevitable progress and expansion, White emphasizes conflict and conquest and reluctant cultural accommodation. This is closer to the type of relationship that existed between Hispanic settlers and Anglo newcomers in California following the 1848 Treaty of Guadalupe Hidalgo. See, for example, Genaro Padilla's archival research regarding Mariano Vallejo, Hubert Howe Bancroft, and others in *My History, Not Yours: The Formation of Mexican American Autobiography* (Madison: University of Wisconsin Press, 1993). Padilla writes: "Whereas slave narratives were published and often widely distributed to promote the abolitionist cause, Mexican American personal narratives—for example, the scores of personal narratives collected from Mexican Californians in the 1870s [by Bancroft]—were meant to function only as supplemental material for American historians and were, therefore, as we shall see, quite intentionally not published" (9).

13. F. Arturo Rosales documents Mexican American efforts for justice and equality in *Chicano! The History of the Mexican American Civil Rights Movement* (Houston: Arte Publico Press, 1997), a book that shows how Chicanos have asserted our civil rights and cultural heritage. Although his conclusions are historically accurate, I am less sanguine about the longevity of the changes Rosales lists, because, even though Chicano life has improved, long-lasting changes have not, in my opinion, significantly affected or informed larger American society much.

14. On pages 9–49 of *George Washington Gomez*, Paredes attempts to capture a sense of the animosity that existed in the border area of the Rio Grande Valley between the English-speaking and Spanish-speaking inhabitants. It is very clear that the events of the novel are played against the historical backdrop of the Carranzistas (13–14), and against an even more distant, now rather irrecoverable period, which Paredes sketches in passing: "Early in the eighteenth century, before there was a United States and when Philadelphia was a little colonial town, Morelos was founded on the south bank of the river. During the century that followed it grew into a large and prosperous city. Its outer limits extended north across the river into what was then part of the same province, a vast expanse of territory teeming with the half-wild cattle and horses that were a prime resource for the people of Morelos. Then came the Comanches and the *yanquis*. And so it came to pass that one day in 1846 an army of the United States was encamped on the north bank of the river which different Hispanic explorers had given different names: Rio de las Palmas, Rio Grande del Norte, Rio Bravo. The army was preparing to push southward toward the heart of Mexico" (35).

15. See Ricardo Romo's "Mexican Workers in the City: Los Angeles, 1915–1930" (Ph.D. dissertation, University of California at Los Angeles, 1975); Rodolfo Acuña's *Occupied America: A History of Chicanos*, 2d ed. (New York: Harper and Row, 1981); José Eduardo Limón's "El Primer Congreso Mexicanista de 1911: A Precursor to Contemporary Chicanismo," *Aztlan*, Spring/Fall 1974): 84–117. Acuña details an enormous amount of internecine violence along the following lines: "The brown scare was most intense in Texas and the number of Chicanos killed by rangers, local authorities, and vigilantes climbed into the thousands. There local groups, individuals, and the *mutualistas* began to express their protests against such outrages more actively. For example, when Gregorio Cortez was finally captured and convicted in 1901, 'Free Cortez' committees were established. On June 19, 1911, Antonio Gomez, 14, was asked to leave a place of business in Thorndale, Texas. He refused and had a fight with a Texas-German who died from a wound inflicted by Gomez's knife. Gomez was taken from jail by a mob and beaten and his body dragged around town tied to the back of a buggy. The *Orden Caballeros de Honor* protested the Thorndale assassination" (306).

16. Gualinto's father-in-law, who used to be a Texas Ranger and had moved to Colorado, says on meeting Gualinto: "George Washington Go-maize. . . . They sure screwed you up, didn't they, boy?" The dialogue continues:

"Frank," his wife said gently. "Don't use such language, please."

"You look white but you're a goddam Meskin. And what does your mother do but give you a nigger name. George Washington Go-maize" (284).

At this point, Gualinto decides to change his name legally to George G. Gomez, the middle G. standing for his mother's maiden name, Garcia. Mexican Americans used to be subjected to this type of psychological abuse inflicted by former Texas Rangers more than they are today. Nonetheless, such sentiments still persist in the general population, as the postscript at the end of this study suggests.

17. Even in the late 1930s, Paredes had to explain the political correctness involved in properly referring to Mexican Americans: "Latin American (or simply Latin) was a polite term Anglotexans used when they meant Greaser. Or Mexican, for that matter. The word Mexican had for so long been a symbol of hatred and loathing that to most Anglotexans it had become a hateful and loathsome word. A kindly Anglo hesitated to call a friendly Mexican a Mexican for fear of offending him. Even the Mexicotexan stumbled on the word when he said it in English. In Spanish *mexicano* has a full and prideful sound. The mouth opens on the full vowels and the voice acquires a certain dignity in saying *mexicano*. But in English it is much different. The lower lip pushes up and the upper lip curls contemptuously. The pursed lips go "m-m-m." Then they part with a smacking, barking sound, "M-m-mex-sican!" Who doesn't understand will think he's being cursed at. It is also a word that can be pronounced without opening your mouth at all, through clenched teeth. So the kindly Angloamerican uses Latin American to avoid giving offense" (118).

18. Paredes continues analyzing Gualinto in this vein: "And then there was that gnawing feeling of doubt, of insecurity. Gualinto had learned a lot in school. He could speak, read, and write English very well. He knew a great deal about history, literature, and other subjects. But he did not know what he wanted to study in col-

lege, or what he wanted to be once he really was an educated man. And how he was supposed to help his people, as his mother and his uncle expected him to do" (158).

19. See Ramon Saldívar, "The Borderlands of Culture: Americo Paredes's *George Washington Gomez* and Chicano Literature at the End of the Twentieth Century," *American Literary History* 5, no. 2 (Summer 1993): 272–93.

20. In his preface to "*Let All of Them Take Heed*," San Miguel writes: "At another level, there are the individual Mexican Americans who have attended segregated public schools over the years. Their story is also complex and diverse. For some, there are fond memories of school activities gone by—for example, the joy of participating in extracurricular activities with their close friends or the excitement of winning a cheerleading contest. For others, the school years have been negative in general; they have been victims of humiliating and depressing incidents of racial discrimination and social ostracism. Generally speaking, the ambitions of these students, their perceptions of that schooling experience, and the impact of the public schools on their lives have been neglected by historians. The political battles of the Mexican American activists—their successes and failures—likewise have not received much historical attention" (ix).

21. In the novel, a good number of the students who make it out of the junior high school are filtered out during the high school years: "The Jonesville-on the-Grande Public School Auditorium was packed tight with sweating bodies that graduation night. The weather had changed definitely toward summer, and it was oppressively hot. As usual, two different classes graduated simultaneously that night, the junior and the senior high school graduates. The junior high class was large, *almost a hundred pupils of which some eighty percent were Mexican*. The high school seniors were *less than twenty* and there were *only four Mexicans among them*, one of them being Gualinto Gomez" (272, my emphasis). Although the majority of high school graduates today in Hispanic areas are Latinos, most do not enter higher education for a variety of reasons, including poor academic preparation, lack of financial support, and the need to earn a living for themselves and their families. Scholarships and grants, as we know, are available only to the best students, largely weeding out Hispanics and African Americans who do not usually receive long-term care and attention.

22. About Gaulinto's internal cultural conflict, Paredes writes: "Consciously he considered himself a Mexican. He was ashamed of the name his dead father had given him, George Washington Gomez. He was grateful to his Uncle Feliciano for having registered him in school as 'Gualinto' and having said that it was an Indian name. He spoke Spanish, literally as his mother tongue; it was the only language his mother would allow him to use when he spoke to her. The Mexican flag made him feel sentimental, and a rousing Mexican song would make him feel like yelling. The Mexican national hymn brought tears to his eyes, and when he said 'we' he meant the Mexican people. 'La Capital' did not mean Washington, D.C. for him but Mexico City. Of such matter were made the basic cells in the honeycomb that made up his personality.

"But there was also George Washington Gomez, the American. He was secretly proud of the name his more conscious twin, Gualinto, was ashamed to avow publicly. George Washington Gomez secretly desired to be a full-fledged, complete

American without the shameful encumberment of his Mexican race. He was the product of his Anglo teachers and the books he read in school, which were all in English" (147–48).

23. I have in mind *The Wings of the Dove* and *The Ambassadors*, where readers do not learn what the main characters will do with their lives until the closing sentences of the novels. While teaching at the University of Texas at Austin, where he was a professor of English and Anthropology for many years, Raymund Paredes informed me that Americo Paredes, who passed away on May 5, 1999, taught the novels of Henry James during the 1960s.

24. In *Race Matters* (New York: Vintage Books, 1994), Cornel West describes the same self-loathing and self-hatred response in African Americans. Using Michael Jackson as an example, West points out how the world-famous singer and performer has so internalized white standards that many of his attempts to improve his physical appearance and features show the extent to which some minority people are willing to go to appeal to the larger culture's standards of beauty and attractiveness, rejecting some African American and Latino features and looks. West writes: "For example, Michael Jackson may rightly wish to be viewed as a person, not a color (neither black nor white), but his facial revisions reveal a self-measurement based on a white yardstick. Hence, despite the fact that he is one of greatest entertainers who has ever lived, he still views himself, at least in part, through white aesthetic lenses that devalue some of his African characteristics. Needless to say, Michael Jackson's example is but the more honest and visible instance of a rather pervasive self-loathing among many of the black professional class" (137).

25. In his final conversation with Feliciano, Gaulinto has changed so dramatically that he holds out no hope for Mexican Americans to the unfazed Feliciano. "Then you see no future for us," says Feliciano. Gaulinto answers, "I'm afraid not. Mexicans will always be Mexicans. A few of them, like some of those would-be politicos, could make something of themselves if they would just do like I did. Get out of this filthy Delta, as far away as they can, and get rid of their Mexican Greaser attitudes." Looking out toward the Rio Grande River, Gualinto espies a neighbor: "There's Juan out there. . . . Perhaps if we send him to Minnesota or Alaska his skin will turn white and he can get rid of his Mexican Greaser attitudes" (300).

26. See Walter Benn Michaels, "Autobiography of an Ex-White Man: Why Race Is Not a Social Construction," *Transition*, vol. 7, no. 1 (Summer 1998): 122–43.

Notes to Chapter 8

1. All quotations cited in the text of this chapter, unless otherwise noted, are taken from *The Original Sin: A Self-Portrait by Anthony Quinn* (Boston: Little, Brown, 1972).

2. For a incisive interpretation of this affair, see Mauricio Mazón's *The Zoot Suit Riots: The Psychology of Symbolic Annihilation* (Austin: University of Texas Press, Center for Mexican American Studies, 1984). Luis Valdez's play and the Universal Pictures film *Zoot Suit* (1991) were also based on the Los Angeles Sleepy Lagoon Trial

(1942–1943), which Quinn sought to avoid, despite the fact that his mother knew the parents of some of the youngsters involved in the incident.

3. Quinn, of course, has provided Hollywood gossip columnists with much to talk about since the 1930s. According to Scott Siegel and Barbara Siegel's *The Encyclopedia of Hollywood* (New York: Facts on File, 1990), 332–33, in 1965, at fifty years of age, following twenty-eight years of marriage, Quinn divorced his first wife, Katherine De Mille, adopted daughter of Cecil B. De Mille, who was known for directing the film *The Ten Commandments*. Although he underwent quadruple bypass surgery in 1990, two years later Quinn "revealed the birth of his 12th child, Patricia—his fourth to be conceived out of wedlock." Quinn is currently eighty-five years old and was married for twenty-nine years to his second wife, Iolanda, with whom the actor had three sons. See also "Embarrassment of Riches" in *People Weekly*, September 6, 1993, p. 80.

4. Alvin H. Marill, *The Films of Anthony Quinn* (Secaucus, N.J.: Citadel Press, 1975), p. 14. This wonderful book of photographs follows Quinn's cinematic career from his earliest acting roles. Marill writes: "Anthony Quinn did not speak English until he was twelve—he really hadn't needed to until he went to Belvedere Junior High and later to Polytechnic High School in Los Angeles—and when he did, he discovered that he had a speech defect. 'I was tongue-tied. Anyway, I had an operation on my tongue and paid for it on the installment plan. I was about eighteen, I guess, and worked in a drama school as a janitor. The teacher, Mrs. Katherine Hamill, gave me speech lessons. Then I was in a couple of plays while I was at the school. Once I did Noel Coward's *Hay Fever*. I got the part because the leading man took sick, and I was so nervous, I played the whole scene with my fly open' " (15). For a useful and concise summary of Quinn's accomplishments, see Luis Reyes and Peter Rubie, *Hispanics in Hollywood: An Encyclopedia of Film and Television* (New York: Garland Publishing, 1994), 470–73.

5. Most Latinos who have been successful in life know that they are achievers because they have worked hard to overcome discouraging obstacles to which they can testify. For this reason, successful Latinos often mistakenly believe that if other Latinos worked hard, they, too, would succeed. No doubt some would. But successful Latinos usually overlook the fact that they themselves are exceptions. Latinos who succeed in the United States tend to be exceptional people who are committed to succeeding. As a group, they are not easily daunted by obstacles that stop or discourage the great majority of other Hispanics who are not encouraged by anything in American society to become more than they are.

6. Quinn, indeed, represents himself as the macho type that many Chicana writers lambaste and excoriate. In Sandra Cisneros's story "Never Marry a Mexican," which was published in *Woman Hollering Creek and Other Stories* (New York: Vintage, 1991), her narrator says, "So, no. I have never married and never will. Not because I couldn't, but because I'm too romantic for marriage. Marriage has failed me, you could say. Not a man exists who hasn't disappointed me, whom I could trust to love the way I've loved. It's because I believe too much in marriage that I don't. Better to not marry than live a lie" (69).

7. "Autobiographical Disclosures: Tino Villanueva Interviews Anthony Quinn," *Americas Review* 16, nos. 3–4 (Fall/Winter 1988): 110–43.

8. Ibid, 133.

9. I think this is very much Feliciano Garcia's intention, too, when he tells George Washington Gomez's first-grade teacher, the Mexican American Miss Cornelia, that George's name is "Gualinto . . . an Indian name" (110).

Notes to Chapter 9

1. All page citations in the text of this chapter refer to Sandra Cisneros's *The House on Mango Street* (New York: Vintage Books, 1991). This novel was first published in 1984 by Arte Publico Press. Vintage Books reissued the novel, making it one of the most successful Chicano works to "cross over" into mainstream American literature.

2. See Julian Olivares, "Sandra Cisneros's *The House on Mango Street* and *The Poetics of Space*," in *Chicana Creativity and Criticism: Charting New Frontiers in American Literature*, ed. María Herrera-Sobek and Helena María Viramontes, special issue of *Americas Review*, vol. 15, nos. 3–4, (Houston: Arte Publico Press, 1988), and Herrera-Sobek's "The Politics of Rape: Sexual Transgression in Chicana Fiction," in the same issue, deals with rape in Chicana short stories and plays, contextualizing and amplifying my discussion here.

3. Jim Sagel, "Sandra Cisneros: Interview," *Publisher's Weekly*, March 29, 1991, 74–75.

Notes to Chapter 10

1. Ana Castillo, *Massacre of the Dreamers: Essays in Xicanisma* (New York: Penguin Books, 1995), 16. All page numbers cited in the text of this chapter refer to this edition. In transliterations of Nahuatl, the language of the Aztecs, the *Ch* sound is represented by an *X*, explaining why Castillo uses "Xicanisma" rather than the relatively more recognizable "Chicanisma."

2. Robin Wilson, "A Challenge to the Veracity of a Multicultural Icon," *Chronicle of Higher Education*, January 15, 1999, reports that anthropology professor David Stoll has published a book "based on more than 120 interviews" where he contends that Menchú's famous book "cannot be the eyewitness account it purports to be." See Stoll, *I, Rigoberta Menchú and the Story of All Poor Guatemalans* (Boulder, Colo.: Westview Press, 1999).

3. Castillo's views on Chicanas and religion should be compared to the case elaborated in Jay P. Dolan and Gilberto Hinojosa, eds., *Mexican Americans and the Catholic Church, 1900–1965* (Notre Dame: University of Notre Dame Press, 1994).

4. Yvonne Yarbro-Bejarano, "Chicana Literature from a Chicana Feminist Perspective," in *Chicana Creativity and Criticism: Starting New Frontiers in American Literature*, ed. Maria Herrera-Sobek and Helena Maria Viramontes (Houston: Arte Publico Press, 1988), 139–45.

5. The reference is to Adrienne Rich's "Toward a Woman-Centered University, 1973–1974," in *Lies, Secrets, and Silence: Selected Prose 1966–1978* (New York: W. W. Norton, 1980). Castillo read widely in preparing her essays on Xicanisma, both among known mainstream books and articles and less-known materials.

Notes to Chapter 12

1. The name of Garcia's alma mater was changed in the early 1990s to Texas A&M University–Kingsville, as part of a south Texas lawsuit settlement filed by the Mexican American Legal Defense Education Fund. MALDEF claimed in the late 1980s that the state of Texas had not historically provided the largely Hispanic population of south Texas with the necessary educational programs and opportunities to encourage professional pursuits and further education. Since the beginning of the 1990s, the state legislature has been working to make what amends it can, but the Texas budget is now tight due to the losses in the oil business revenue that Texas enjoyed in the years before 1985.

2. José Angel Gutiérrez, who is now a lawyer and a professor of political science at the University of Texas at Arlington, has recently published a long-awaited autobiographical, inside view of his younger years as a political activist. See *The Making of a Chicano Militant: Lessons from Cristal* (Madison: University of Wisconsin Press, 1999).

Bibliography

Acosta, Oscar Zeta. *The Autobiography of a Brown Buffalo.* San Francisco: Straight Arrow Books, 1972.

Acuña, Rodolfo. *Anything But Mexican: Chicanos in Contemporary Los Angeles.* London: Verso, 1996.

———. *Occupied America: A History of Chicanos.* 2d ed. New York: Harper and Row, 1981.

Adams, Henry. *The Education of Henry Adams: An Autobiography.* Boston: privately printed, 1907.

Allsup, Vernon Carl. "The American G.I. Forum: A History of a Mexican American Organization." Ph.D. dissertation, University of Texas, 1976.

Alonzo, Armando C. *Tejano Legacy: Rancheros and Settlers in South Texas, 1743–1900.* Albuquerque: University of New Mexico Press, 1998.

Alurista, *Floricanto en Aztlan.* Los Angeles: Chicano Studies Center, 1971.

Anaya, Rudolfo. *Bless Me, Ultima.* Berkeley: Quinto Sol Publications, 1972.

———. *Heart of Aztlan.* Berkeley: Editorial Justa Publications, 1976.

Angelou, Maya. *I Know Why the Caged Bird Sings.* New York: Random House, 1969.

Anzaldúa, Gloria. *Borderlands/La Frontera: The New Mestiza.* San Francisco: Aunt Lute Book Co., 1987.

Anzaldúa, Gloria, ed. *Haciendo Caras/Making Face[s], Making Soul: Creative and Critical Perspectives by Feminists of Color.* San Francisco: Aunt Lute Foundation, 1990.

Anzaldúa, Gloria, and Cherrie Moraga, eds. *This Bridge Called My Back: Writings by Radical Women of Color.* Watertown, Mass.: Persephone Press, 1981.

Arteaga, Alfred. *Chicano Poetics: Heterotexts and Hybridities.* New York: Cambridge University Press, 1997.

Augustine, Saint. *The Confessions of St. Augustine, Bishop of Hippo.* New York: Liveright, 1943.

Awkward, Michael. *Negotiating Difference: Race, Gender and the Politics of Positionality.* Chicago: University of Chicago Press, 1995.

Bachelard, Gaston. *The Poetics of Space.* New York: Orion Press, 1964.

Baldwin, James. *Conversations with James Baldwin.* Jackson: University Press of Mississippi, 1989.

———. *The Fire Next Time.* New York: Dial Press, 1963.

————. *Nobody Knows My Name: More Notes of a Native Son*. New York: Dial Press, 1961.

Barrio, Raymond. *The Plum Plum Pickers*. Sunnyvale, Calif.: Ventura, 1969.

Bouvier, Leon F., and Dudley L. Posten, Jr. *Thirty Million Texans?* Freeman, S.D.: Pine Hill Press, 1993.

Bradstreet, Anne. *The Tenth Muse (1650) and: from the manuscripts: Meditations divine and morall, together with letters and occasional pieces*. Gainesville, Fla.: Scholars' Facsimiles and Reprints, 1965.

Bruce-Novoa, Juan. *Chicano Authors: Inquiry by Interview*. Austin: University of Texas Press, 1980.

————. *Retrospace: Collected Essays on Chicano Literature, Theory and History*. Houston: Arte Publico Press, 1990.

Cahan, Abraham. *The Rise of David Levinsky*. New York: Harper and Brothers, 1917.

Calderón, Hector, and Jose David Saldívar, eds. *Criticism in the Borderlands: Studies in Chicano Literature, Culture, and Ideology*. Durham: Duke University Press, 1991.

Canales, José T. *Juan N. Cortina Presents His Motion for a New Trial*. San Antonio: Artes Graficas, 1951; reprint, New York: Arno Press, 1974.

Candelaria, Cordelia. *Chicano Poetry: A Critical Introduction*. Westport, Conn.: Greenwood Press, 1986.

Cantú, Norma Elia. *Canícula: Snapshots of a Girlhood en la Frontera*. Albuquerque: University of New Mexico Press, 1995.

Carrasco, Nicolás. "The Relationship between Parental Support and Control and Adolescent Self-Esteem in Mexican, Mexican American, and Anglo American Families." Ph.D. dissertation, University of Texas at Austin, 1990.

Castillo, Ana. *Massacre of the Dreamers*. New York: Penguin Books, 1995.

————. *The Mixquiahuala Letters*. New York: Doubleday Anchor Books, 1986.

————. *So Far from God*. New York: W. W. Norton, 1993.

Cervantes Saavedra, Miguel de. *El Ingenioso Hidalgo Don Quijote de la Mancha*. Madrid, 1605 and 1614.

Cisneros, Sandra. *The House on Mango Street*. Houston: Arte Publico Press, 1984.

————. *My Wicked, Wicked Ways*. Berkeley: Third Woman Press, 1987.

————. *Woman Hollering Creek and Other Stories*. New York: Vintage, 1991.

Constant, Benjamin. *Adolphe*. 1816; reprint, Philadelphia: David McKay, 1925.

Crisp, James Ernest. "Anglo-Texan Attitudes toward the Mexican, 1821–1845." Ph.D. diss., Yale University, 1976.

De León, Arnoldo. *The Tejano Community, 1836–1900*. Albuquerque: University of New Mexico Press, 1982.

Delgado, Abelardo. *Chicano: Twenty-five Pieces of a Chicano Mind*. Denver: Barrio, 1969.

Dolan, Jay P., and Gilberto Hinojosa, eds. *Mexican Americans and the Catholic Church, 1900–1965*. Notre Dame: University of Notre Dame Press, 1994.

Ellison, Ralph. *Invisible Man*. New York: New American Library, 1947.

Estrada, Alfredo J. "Which Companies Are Providing the Most Opportunities for Hispanics?" *Hispanic*, January/February, 1997, 56–78.

Fernandez, Roberta, ed. *In Other Words: Literature by Latinas of the United States*. Houston: Arte Publico Press, 1994.

Ferraro, Thomas J. *Ethnic Passages: Literary Immigrants in Twentieth-Century America*. Chicago: University of Chicago Press, 1993.

Fiedler, Leslie. *What Was Literature? Class Culture and Mass Society*. New York: Simon and Schuster, 1982.

Flanagan, Thomas. *The Year of the French*. New York: Holt, Rinehart and Winston, 1979.

Foley, Neil. *The White Scourge: Mexicans, Blacks and Poor Whites in Texas Cotton Culture*. Berkeley: University of California Press, 1997.

Foucault, Michel. *Discipline and Punish: The Birth of the Prison*. London: Allen Lane, 1977.

———. *Madness and Civilization: A History of Insanity in the Age of Reason*. New York: Vintage Books, 1965.

Four Hundred Fifty Years of Chicano History in Pictures. Albuquerque: Chicano Communications Center, 1976.

Galarza, Ernesto. *Barrio Boy*. Notre Dame, Ind.: University of Notre Dame Press, 1971.

Garcia, Ignacio M. *United We Win: The Rise and Fall of La Raza Unida Party*. Tucson: Mexican American Studies Research Center, University of Arizona, 1989.

Garcia, Lionel G. *Leaving Home*. Houston: Arte Publico Press, 1985.

Garcia, Octavio. *Otros Dias: Memories of "Other Days" . . . from Mexico in Revolution to a Life of Medicine in Texas*. Westford, Mass.: Grey Home Press, 1984.

Garza-Falcon, Leticia M. *Gente Decente: A Borderlands Response to the Rhetoric of Dominance*. Austin: University of Texas Press, 1998.

Gibson, Charles. *The Aztecs under Spanish Rule: A History of the Indians of the Valley of Mexico, 1519–1810*. Stanford.: Stanford University Press, 1964.

Glass, Alyssa. "The Push for Professional Growth." *Hispanic Business*, February, 1997.

Gold, Michael. *Jews without Money*. New York: Horace Liveright, 1930.

Goldfinch, Charles W. *Juan N. Cortina, 1824–1892: A Re-Appraisal*. New York: Arno Press, 1974.

Gonzalez, Jovita, and Eve Raleigh. *Caballero*. Edited with an Introduction by Jose Eduardo Limon. College Station: Texas A&M University Press, 1996.

Gonzalez, Rodolfo "Corky." *I Am Joaquin. Yo Soy Joaquin: An Epic Poem, with a Chronology of People and Events in Mexican and Mexican American History*. Toronto and New York: Bantam Books, 1972.

Griffin, John Howard. *Black Like Me*. Boston: Houghton Mifflin Company, 1960.

Griswold del Castillo, Richard. *The Treaty of Guadalupe Hidalgo: A Legacy of Conflict*. Norman: University of Oklahoma Press, 1990.

Gutiérrez, Félix F., and Jorge Reina Schement. *Spanish-Language Radio in the Southwestern United States*. Austin: University of Texas Press, Center for Mexican American Studies, 1979.

Gutiérrez, José Angel. *The Making of a Chicano Militant: Lessons from Cristal*. Madison: University of Wisconsin Press, 1999.

Gutiérrez-Jones, Carl. *Rethinking the Borderlands: Between Chicano Culture and Legal Discourse*. Berkeley: University of California Press, 1995.

Herrera-Sobek, Maria, and Helena Maria Viramontes, eds. *Chicana Creativity and*

Criticism: Charting New Frontiers in American Literature. Houston: Arte Publico Press, 1988.

Hinojosa, Gilberto Miguel. *A Borderlands Town in Transition: Laredo, 1755–1870.* College Station: Texas A&M University Press, 1983.

———. *Tejano Origins in Eighteenth-Century San Antonio.* Austin: University of Texas Press for the Institute of Texan Cultures at San Antonio, 1991.

Hinojosa, Gilberto Miguel, and Jay P. Dolan. *Mexican Americans and the Catholic Church, 1900–1965.* Notre Dame, Ind.: University of Notre Dame Press, 1994.

Hinojosa, Rolando. *Becky and Her Friends.* Houston: Arte Publico Press, 1990.

———. *Estampas del Valle y Otras Obras/Sketches of the Valley and Other Works.* Berkeley: Editorial Justa Publications, 1980.

———. *Klail City y Sus Alrededores.* Havana: Case de las Americas, 1976.

"The Hispanic Voter." Survey. Politicol@aol.com, vol. 1, no. 34, April 27, 1998. Univision/Latinolink.com/Cox Newspapers.

"Hispanics at Community Colleges: Graduation Statistics." *Hispanic Outlook in Higher Education,* vol. 8, no. 16 (April 10, 1998): 14–16.

Hurston, Zora Neale. *Their Eyes Were Watching God.* 1937; reprint, Urbana: University of Illinois Press, 1978.

Infante Quintanilla, Jose Ernesto. *Pedro Infante, el Maximo Idolo de Mexico: Vida, Obra, Muerte y Leyenda.* Monterrey, Mexico: Ediciones Castillo, 1992.

Ivins, Molly. "Turning Public Schools Around." *San Antonion Express-News,* May 28, 1998, 5B.

James, Henry. *The Ambassadors.* New York: Harper and Brothers, 1903

———. *The Portrait of a Lady.* Boston: Houghton Mifflin, 1881.

———. *The Wings of the Dove.* New York: Charles Scribner's Sons, 1902.

Kanellos, Nicolás, ed. *Reference Library of Hispanic America.* 3 vols. Detroit: Gale Research Inc., 1994.

Kellner, Douglas. *Media Culture: Cultural Studies, Identity and Politics between the Modern and the Postmodern.* London: Routledge, 1995.

Kernan, Alvin B. *The Death of Literature.* New Haven: Yale University Press, 1990.

La Bamba. Dir. Luis Valdez. Columbia Pictures, 1987.

Landa, Victor. "Hispanics Turn Up the Volume with Business Boom." *Austin American-Statesman,* July 16, 1996, A9.

Lauter, Paul. *The Heath Anthology of American Literature.* 2 vols. Lexington: D.C. Heath, 1990.

Leland, John. "MexAmerica: Born on the Border." *Newsweek,* October 23, 1995, 80–84.

Levine, Lawrence W. *The Opening of the American Mind: Canons, Culture and History.* Boston: Beacon Press, 1996.

Lewis, C. S. *The Allegory of Love: A Study in Medieval Tradition.* London: Oxford University Press, 1936.

Lichter, Robert S., and Daniel R. Amundson. "Distorted Reality: Hispanic Characters in TV Entertainment." Report issued September 1, 1994. Washington, D.C.: Center for Media and Public Affairs.

Limón, José Eduardo. *Dancing with the Devil: Society and Cultural Poetics in Mexican-American South Texas.* Madison: University of Wisconsin Press, 1994.

————. "El Primer Congreso Mexicanista de 1911: A Precursor to Contemporary Chicanismo." *Aztlan*, Spring/Fall 1974, 85–117.

————. *Mexican Ballads, Chicano Poems: History and Influence in Mexican-American Social Poetry.* Berkeley: University of California Press, 1992.

Madsen, William. *The Mexican-Americans of South Texas.* 1964; reprint, New York: Holt, Rinehart and Winston, 1973.

Matthiessen, Peter. *Sal Si Puedes: Cesar Chavez and the New American Revolution.* New York: Dell, 1969.

McDonald, David R., and Timothy M. Matovina. *Defending Mexican Valor in Texas: José Antonio Navarro's Historical Writings, 1853–1857.* Austin: State House Press, 1996.

McWilliams, Carey. *North from Mexico: The Spanish-Speaking People of the United States.* 1948; reprint, New York: Greenwood Press, 1968.

Menchaca, Martha. *The Mexican Outsiders: A Community History of Marginalization and Discrimination in California.* Austin: University of Texas Press, 1995.

Mendez, Miguel. "Ambrosio Ceniza," in *Tata Casehua and Other Stories.* Berkeley: Editorial Justa Publications, 1980.

————. *The Dream of Santa Maria de las Piedras.* 1986; reprint, Tempe, Ariz.: Bilingual Press/Editorial Bilingue, 1989.

————. *Entre Letras y Ladrillos.* Tempe, Ariz.: Bilingual Press/Editorial Bilingue, 1995.

The Mesoamericans: Great Peoples of the Past. National Geographic Society pictorial pamphlet, Washington, D.C., 1997.

Mi Familia or My Family. Dir. Gregory Nava. American Playhouse Theatrical Films, 1995.

Mirandé, Alfredo. *Gringo Justice.* Notre Dame: University of Notre Dame Press, 1987.

Montejano, David. *Anglos and Mexicans in the Making of Texas, 1836–1986.* Austin: University of Texas Press, 1987.

Moore, Joan W., and Harry Pachon. *Mexican Americans.* Englewood Cliffs, N.J.: Prentice-Hall, 1970.

Morill, Alvin. *The Films of Anthony Quinn.* Secaucus, N.J.: Citadel Press, 1975.

Morris, Willie. *North toward Home.* Boston: Houghton Mifflin, 1967.

Morrison, Toni. *The Bluest Eye.* New York: Holt, Rinehart and Winston, 1970.

————. *Playing in the Dark: Whiteness and the Literary Imagination.* Cambridge: Harvard University Press, 1993.

Murdock, S. H. *An America Challenged: Population Change and the Future of the United States.* Boulder, Colo.: Westview Press, 1995.

Murdock, Steve H., Md. Nazrul Hoque, Martha Michael, Steve White, and Beverly Pecotte. *The Texas Challenge: Population Change and the Future of Texas.* College Station: Texas A&M University Press, 1997.

Natale, Richard. "The Latin Factor: Hollywood Plugs into a Burgeoning and Profitable Ethnic Market." *Entertainment Weekly*, May 12, 1995. Reprinted in Shirley Biagi and Marilyn Kern-Foxworth, eds. *Facing Difference: Race, Gender, and Mass Media.* Thousand Oaks, Calif.: Pine Forge Press, 1997.

Norquest, Carrol. *Rio Grande Wetbacks: Mexican Migrant Workers.* Albuquerque: University of New Mexico Press, 1972.

Notre Dame de Paris. Dir. Jean Delannoy. Featuring Anthony Quinn. Panitalia/Paris Film Productions, 1956.

O'Faolain, Sean. *Bird Alone*. New York: Viking Press, 1936.

Olivares, Julian. "Sandra Cisneros's *The House on Mango Street* and *The Poetics of Space*." *Chicana Creativity and Critics: Charting New Frontiers in American Literature*. Special issue, *Americas Review*, vol. 15, nos. 3 and 4 (1987): 160–70.

Olivas, Michael, ed. *Latino College Students*. New York: Teachers College Press, 1986.

Olmos, Edward J., and Yea Ybarra. *Americanos: Latino Life in the United States/La Vida Latina en los Estados Unidos*. Boston: Little, Brown, 1999.

Ortego, Philip D. *We Are Chicanos: An Anthology of Mexican-American Literature*. New York: Washington Square Press, 1973.

Padilla, Genaro M. *My History, Not Yours: The Formation of Mexican American Autobiography*. Madison: University of Wisconsin Press, 1993.

Paredes, Americo. *George Washington Gomez*. Houston: Arte Publico Press, 1990.

———. *With His Pistol in His Hand: A Border Ballad and Its Hero*. Austin: University of Texas Press, 1958.

Paredes, Americo, ed. *Humanidad: Essays in Honor of George I. Sanchez* (Los Angeles: Chicano Studies Center Publications, University of California, 1977).

Paredes, Raymund. "The Evolution of Chicano Literature." In *Three American Literatures*, ed. Houston A. Baker, Jr. New York: Modern Language Association, 1982.

———. "The Origins of Anti-Mexican Sentiment in the United States." In *New Directions in Chicano Scholarship*, ed. Ricardo Romo and Raymund Paredes. San Diego: University of California Chicano Studies Program, 1978.

Parkman, Francis. *The Oregon Trail*. Boston, 1847; reprint, New York: New American Library, 1978.

Parole! Dir. Louis Friedlander. Universal Productions, 1936.

Paz, Octavio. *The Labyrinth of Solitude: Life and Thought in Mexico*. Trans. Lysander Kemp. 1950; reprint, New York: Grove Press, 1961.

Peña, Manuel. *The Texas-Mexican Conjunta: History of a Working Class Music*. Austin: University of Texas Press, Center for Mexican American Studies, 1985.

The Perez Family. Dir. Mira Nair. Samuel Goldwyn Co., 1995.

The Plainsman. Dir. Cecille B. DeMille. Paramount Pictures, 1936.

Plato. *Symposium*. New York: Oxford University Press, 1994.

Portales, Marco. "Affirmative Action: Best Idea, So Far." *Hispanonoticias: The Hispanic Caucus of the American Association for Higher Education*. June 1995, 1, 5.

———. "College Admissions Policies, the Courts, Institutional Rankings, and Eligible Hispanic and African American Students." In *Education of Hispanics in the U.S.: Politics, Policies and Outcomes*, ed. Abbas Tashakkori and Hector Salvador Ochoa. New York: AMS Press: forthcoming.

———. *Youth and Age in American Literature: The Rhetoric of Old Men*. New York: Peter Lang, 1989.

Portillo, Estella. *Rain of Scorpions and Other Stories*. Berkeley: Tonatiuh International, 1975.

Pynchon, Thomas. *Vineland*. Boston: Little, Brown, 1990.

Quinn, Anthony. *The Original Sin: A Self-Portrait.* Boston: Little, Brown, 1972.
Quinn, Anthony, with Daniel Paisner. *One Man Tango.* New York: HarperCollins Publishers, 1995.
Ramirez Berg, Charles. *Poster Art from the Golden Age of Mexican Cinema.* Austin: University of Texas Press, 1997.
Reed, Ishmael, ed. *MultiAmerica: Essays on Cultural Wars and Cultural Peace.* New York: Viking Penguin, 1997.
Reyes, Luis, and Peter Rubie. *Hispanics in Hollywood: An Encyclopedia of Film and Television.* New York: Garland Publishing, 1994.
Reyna, José R. *Raza Humor: Chicano Joke Tradition in Texas.* San Antonio: Penca Books, 1980.
Rich, Adrienne. *Lies, Secrets, and Silence: Selected Prose 1966–1978.* New York: W.W. Norton, 1980.
Rivera, Tomas. . . . *y no se lo tragó la tierra/ . . . and the earth did not part.* Berkeley: Quinto Sol Publications, 1971.
Robinson, Cecil. *With the Ears of Strangers: The Mexican in American Literature.* Tucson: University of Arizona Press, 1963. Revised and reissued as *Mexico and the Hispanic Southwest in American Literature.* Tucson: University of Arizona Press, 1977.
Rodriguez, Luis J. *Always Running: La Vida Loca; Gang Days in L.A.* Willimantic, Conn.: Curbstone Press, 1993.
Rodriguez, Richard. *Hunger of Memory: The Education of Richard Rodriguez, an Autobiography.* New York: David R. Godine, 1981.
Romo, Harriet D., and Toni Falbo. *Latino High School Graduation: Defying the Odds.* Austin: University of Texas Press, 1996.
Romo, Ricardo. "Mexican Workers in the City: Los Angeles, 1915–1930." Ph.D. dissertation, University of California at Los Angeles, 1975.
Roosevelt, Theodore. *Winning of the West.* New York: Putnam, 1889.
Rosales, F. Arturo. *Chicano! The History of the Mexican American Civil Rights Movement.* Houston: Arte Publico Press, 1997.
Rousseau, Jean Jacques. *The Confessions.* 1782; reprint, New York: Viking Penguin, 1953.
———. *Emile.* Edited by R. L. Archer. Woodbury, N.Y.: Barron's Educational Series, 1964.
Ruoff, A. LaVonne Brown, and Jerry W. Ward, eds. *Redefining American Literary History.* New York: Modern Language Association of America, 1990.
Sagel, Jim. "Sandra Cisneros: Interview." *Publisher's Weekly,* March 29, 1991, 74–75.
St. Clair, Kathleen E., and Clifton R. St. Clair. *Little Towns of South Texas.* Jacksonville, Tex.: Jayroe Graphics Cuts, 1982.
Saldívar, Jose David. *The Dialectics of Our America: Genealogy, Cultural Critique, and Literary History.* Durham: Duke University Press, 1991.
———. *Chicano Narrative: The Dialectics of Difference.* Madison: University of Wisconsin Press, 1990.
Sanchez, George I. *Forgotten People: A Study of New Mexicans.* 1940; reprint, Albuquerque, N.M.: C. Horn, 1967).

————. *Guide for Teachers of Spanish-Speaking Children in the Primary Grades.* Austin: Texas Department of Education, 1946.

————. *Materials Relating to the Education of Spanish-Speaking People in the United States: An Annotated Bibliography.* 1959; reprint, Westport, Conn.: Greenwood Press. 1971.

Sanchez, Saul. *Hay Plesha Lichens Tu Di Flac.* Berkeley: Editorial Justa Publications, 1977.

San Miguel, Guadalupe. *"Let All of Them Take Heed": Mexican Americans and the Campaign for Educational Equality in Texas, 1910–1981.* Austin: University of Texas Press, 1987.

Selena. Dir. Gregory Nava. Warner Brothers, 1997.

Siegel, Scott, and Barbara Siegel. *The Encyclopedia of Hollywood.* New York: Facts on File, 1990.

Simmen, Edward. *The Chicano: From Caricature to Self-Portrait.* New York: New American Library, 1971.

————. *North of the Rio Grande: The Mexican-American Experience in Short Fiction.* New York: Mentor, 1992.

Sollers, Werner. *The Invention of Ethnicity.* New York: Oxford University Press, 1989.

Stand and Deliver. Dir. Ramón Menéndez. Warner Brothers, 1988.

Stoll, David. *I, Rigoberta Menchú and the Story of All Poor Guatemalans.* Boulder, Colo.: Westview Press, 1999.

Sundquist, Eric J. *To Wake the Nations: Race in the Making of American Literature.* Cambridge, Mass.: The Belknap Press of Harvard University Press, 1993.

Teague, David W. *The Southwest in American Literature and Art: The Rise of a Desert Aesthetic.* Tucson: University of Arizona Press, 1997.

Thoreau, Henry David. *Walden.* Princeton: Princeton University Press, 1971.

Tocqueville, Alexis de. *Democracy in America.* 1835–1840; reprint, New York: Alfred A. Knopf, 1994.

Valdez, Luis. *Actos.* San Juan Bautista, Calif.: Menyah Publications, 1971.

Valdez, Luis, and Stan Steiner, eds. *Aztlan: An Anthology of Mexican American Literature.* New York: Alfred A. Knopf, 1972.

Villanueva, Tino. "Autobiographical Disclosures: Tino Villanueva Interviews Anthony Quinn." *Americas Review* 16, nos. 3–4 (Fall/Winter 1988): 110–43.

Villarreal, José Antonio. *Pocho.* Garden City, N.Y.: Doubleday, 1959.

Viramontes, Maria Helena. *Under the Feet of Jesus.* New York: Dutton, 1995.

Viva Zapata. Dir. Elia Kazan. Twentieth Century Fox, 1952.

The Voice of La Raza. Dir. William Greaves and José Garcia; narrated by Anthony Quinn. Produced by Video Dub, Inc., for the Equal Employment Opportunity Commission, 1971.

A Walk in the Clouds. Dir. Alfonso Arau. Twentieth Century Fox, 1995.

Walker, Alice. *The Color Purple.* New York: Harcourt Brace Jovanovich, 1982.

Webb, Walter Prescott. *The Texas Rangers.* Cambridge, Mass.: Houghton Mifflin, 1935.

Weber, David J. " 'Scarce More Than Apes': Historical Roots of Anglo Americans Stereotypes of Mexicans in the Border Region." In *New Spain's Far Northern*

Frontier: Essays on Spain in the American West, 1540–1821. Dallas: Southern Methodist University Press, 1979.

West, Cornel. *Race Matters.* New York: Vintage Books, 1994.

White, Richard. *"It's Your Misfortune and None of My Own": A History of the American West.* Norman: University of Oklahoma Press, 1991.

Williams, Stanley Thomas. *The Spanish Background of American Literature.* 2 vols. New Haven: Yale University Press, 1955.

Woll, Allen L., and Randall M. Miller, *Ethnic and Racial Images in American Film and Television: Historical Essays and Bibliography.* New York: Garland, 1987.

Woolf, Virginia. *A Room of One's Own.* New York: Harcourt, Brace, 1929.

Wright, Richard. *American Hunger.* 1944; reprint, New York: Harper and Row, 1977.

————. *Native Son.* New York: Harper and Brothers, 1940.

Yarbro-Bejarano, Yvonne. "Chicana Literature from a Feminist Perspective." In *Chicana Creativity and Criticism: Starting New Frontiers in American Literature*, ed. Maria Herrera-Sobek and Helen Maria Viramontes. Houston: Arte Publico Press, 1988.

Zoot Suit. Dir. Luis Valdez. Universal Pictures, 1991.

Index

San Miguel, Guadalupe, Jr., 10, 74
Sanchez, George I., 10
Sanchez, Saul, 71–72, 75, 76
Santa Anna, General, 159
Santayana, George, 107
Saralegui, Christina, 44
satire, 86
school accreditation, 161
school boards, 160
school dropouts, 55, 72, 74, 75, 84, 87,
    92–93, 98, 161, 178 n. 10
schools: xii, 6, 16, 22, 45, 46, 54, 55, 57,
    63, 67–76, 83, 92, 125, 155, 156, 157,
    161, 173 n. 15, 178 n. 10, 179 n. 3,
    181 n. 18, 182 nn. 20, 21; and expecta-
    tions, 7, 40, 43, 45, 52, 60, 74, 93, 124,
    127, 157; and nurturance, 84; physical
    abuse in, 85; private, 125; textbooks in,
    22, 61
Schopenhauer, Arthur, 107
Seattle, 72
second-class citizenship, 3, 51, 59, 139
segregated schools, 182 n. 20
Selena, 43, 45, 172 n. 13
self-dialogue, 111
self-esteem, 46, 54, 67, 84, 85, 94, 122
self-image, 101, 118, 119, 125, 183 n. 24
self-inventory, 108
self-sufficiency, 42
selflessness, 90
"separatist efforts," 102
sexual harassment, 63
sexuality, 123, 126, 128–29, 142
Shaw, George Bernard, 27, 30
Shears, Bob, 29
silence, 62, 86, 92, 118, 123, 136, 141, 145
Silvestre, Flor, 61
Simmen, Edward, 147
Sinatra, Frank, 44, 69
Sioux, 104
skin color, 35–38, 53, 99, 140, 159, 173 n.
    18, 183 n. 24
slapstick Mexican comedians, 69
slave narratives, 53, 61, 180 n. 12
Sleepy Lagoon Trial, 183–84
Smithsonian Institution, 53, 59, 61
smoking, 63
Smollett, Tobias, 107
So Far from God, 137
social change, 14, 78, 135–44, 180 n. 13
social classes, 25, 71, 92, 139, 140

social infrastructure, 5, 37, 51, 59, 68, 89,
    95, 140, 157, 161
social justice, 41, 56, 77, 80, 87–88, 123,
    136, 139, 158, 164, 171–72 n. 7, 173 n.
    18, 180 n. 12
social sciences, 84, 88, 124
social spaces, 1, 12, 26, 63, 139, 157, 158
socialization vehicles, 2, 5, 6, 98, 100, 157
Society for the Study of Multi-Ethnic Liter-
    ature of the United States (MELUS), 21
Society of Hispanic Professional Engineers,
    33
socioeconomic realities, 70, 74, 75, 140–41,
    147, 159
sociohistorical works, 89, 180 n. 12, 181 n. 15
sociology of Chicanos, 27, 80, 89
sociopolitical realities, 2, 10, 59, 62, 88, 97,
    147, 157, 161
Soto, Gary, 46
south Texas, xi, 61, 68, 72, 83, 85, 89, 90,
    99, 113, 127, 177 n. 7
southern California, 105, 119, 175 n. 3
Southwest, 8, 18, 53, 61, 78, 89, 92, 96, 98,
    157, 161, 165, 178 n. 1, 180 n. 12
*Southwest in American Literature and Art,
    The*, 49
Spain, 166 n.1
Spanish American, 166 n. 1
Spanish Armada, 49
Spanish civilization, 90, 142, 143
Spanish land grants, 61, 89, 174 n. 19
Spanish language, and English language, 12,
    87, 91, 128, 140, 155–58
Spanish-language radio, 70, 155
Spanish-language television, 171 n. 3
Spanish-speaking Americans, 1, 2, 3, 5, 8, 9,
    12, 19, 33, 57, 60, 77, 85, 87, 90, 96, 155,
    156, 166 n. 1. *See also* Hispanics; Latinos
Spanish-speaking people, 1, 12, 49, 83, 85,
    87, 95, 105, 166 n. 1
spiritual claims/struggles, 75, 109, 119, 148,
    172 n. 7
spirituality, 142
sports, 71
Squatter and the Don, The, 89
Stand and Deliver (film), 45
State University of New York at Buffalo, 19
Stendahl, 66
stereotypes, 43, 46–47, 48, 49, 55–57, 60,
    66, 86, 147
Stern, Howard, 49